John Farquhar

Sermons on Various Subjects

John Farquhar

Sermons on Various Subjects

ISBN/EAN: 9783337160807

Printed in Europe, USA, Canada, Australia, Japan

Cover: Foto ©Lupo / pixelio.de

More available books at **www.hansebooks.com**

ON

VARIOUS SUBJECTS.

BY THE LATE

JOHN FARQUHAR, M. A.

MINISTER AT NIGG.

CAREFULLY CORRECTED FROM THE AUTHOR'S
MANUSCRIPT, BY

GEORGE CAMPBELL, D. D.

PRINCIPAL OF MARISCHAL COLLEGE;

AND

ALEXANDER GERARD, D. D.

PROFESSOR OF DIVINITY IN KING'S COLLEGE,
ABERDEEN.

THE FIFTH EDITION.

LONDON:

PRINTED FOR T. CADELL, IN THE STRAND.

MDCCLXXXII.

ADVERTISEMENT.

IT will not be improper to acquaint the reader, that the author of the following sermons did not compose them with a view to their publication. So far from it, that the greater part of them had been so hastily written, that the copies were in many places scarce legible, and some of the best of them in the judgment of the publishers, which they could not refuse a place in this collection, either had been left unfinished at first, or have been mutilated since by accident. These however they chuse to lay before the public, in the condition in which they found them, rather than by supplying such defects, to use what they thought an undue liberty with their deceased friend, whose manner and sentiment were very much his own. The only merit they claim is the arrangement of them, and the correction of some trifling negligences in the language. Whether they have done right in publishing them, the public itself will judge. The best apology they have to offer, is their own persuasion that these discourses, with all their imperfections, have great merit, and may be of considerable use.

Mr. Farquhar's character they need not here atttempt to delineate. To the judicious and attentive reader such an attempt would be unnecessary. He will discover it in these volumes very strongly marked. Never did any performance exhibit a more genuine transcript of the disposition and sentiments of its author, than this does of the disposition and sentiments of that valuable and amiable man. It is much to be regretted, that it had not the advantage of his own correction and review. But as it is, and with all the inequality in respect of composition, that may be observed in these sermons, a good judge will not be at a loss to discern in the preacher an eminent clearness of apprehension, correctness of taste, a lively imagination, and delicate sensibility to all the finest feelings of which human nature is susceptible.

SERMON I.
1 THESS. v. 16.
Rejoice evermore. Page 1.

SERMON II.
JOHN xv. 15.
Henceforth I call you not servants, for the servant knoweth not what his Lord doth: but I have called you friends. P. 21.

SERMON III.
2 KINGS viii. 13.
And Hazael said, But what, is thy servant a dog, that he should do this great thing? P. 35.

SERMON IV.
ACTS xxiv. 25.
And as he reasoned of righteousness, temperance, and judgment to come, Felix trembled. P. 51.

SERMON V.
PSALM lxxiii. 28.
But it is good for me to draw near to God. P. 67.

SERMON VI.
MATTHEW xxii. 37, 38.
Jesus said unto him, Thou shalt love the Lord thy God with all thy heart, and with all thy soul, and with all

all thy mind. This is the first and great commandment. P. 85.

SERMON VII.
MATTHEW xxii. 39.
And the second is like unto it, Thou shalt love thy neighbour as thyself. P. 101.

SERMON VIII.
COLOSSIANS iii. 14.
And above all these things, put on charity, which is the bond of perfectness. P. 115.

SERMON IX.
PSALM li. 17.
The sacrifices of God are a broken spirit; a broken and a contrite heart, O God, thou wilt not despise.
P. 131.

SERMON X.
MATTHEW vii. 24—28.
Therefore, whosoever heareth these sayings of mine, and doth them, I will liken him unto a wise man which built his house upon a rock: And the rain descended, and the floods came; and the winds blew, and beat upon that house, and it fell not; for it was founded upon a rock. And every one that heareth these sayings of mine, and doth them not, shall be likened unto a foolish man which built his house upon the sand: And the rain descended, and the floods came, and the winds blew, and beat upon that house; and it fell; and great was the fall of it. P. 147.

CONTENTS.

SERMON XI.
PSALM xxiv. 3, 4, 5.

Who shall ascend into the hill of the Lord? and who shall stand in his holy place? He that hath clean hands, and a pure heart; who hath not lift up his soul unto vanity, nor sworn deceitfully. He shall receive the blessing from the Lord, and righteousness from the God of his salvation. P. 163.

SERMON XII.
LUKE xv. 11—24.

And he said, A certain man had two sons: and the younger of them said to his father, Father, give me the portion of good that falleth to me. And he divided unto them his living. And not many days after, the younger son gathered all together, and took his journey into a far country, &c. P. 191.

SERMON XIII.
MATTHEW xi. 29.

Take my yoke upon you, and learn of me, for I am meek and lowly in heart, and ye shall find rest unto your souls. P. 211.

SERMON XIV.
PSALM iv. 4. last part of the verse.

Commune with your own heart upon your bed, and be still. P. 227.

SERMON XV.
LUKE vii. 36—48.

And one of the pharisees desired him that he would eat with him. And he went into the pharisee's house, and

and sat down to meat. And behold, a woman in the city, which was a sinner, when she knew that Jesus sat at meat in the pharisee's house, brought an alabaster box of ointment, &c. P. 243.

SERMON XVI.
MATTHEW xxvi. 36——44.
Then cometh Jesus with them unto a place called Gethsemane, and saith unto the disciples, Sit ye here, while I go and pray yonder. And he took with him Peter and the two sons of Zebedee, &c. P. 259.

SERMON XVII.
JOHN xix. 30.
When Jesus therefore had received the Vinegar, he said, It is finished: and he bowed his head, and gave up the ghost. P. 281.

SERMON XVIII.
ISAIAH liii. 3.
He is despised and rejected of men, a man of sorrows, and acquainted with grief. P. 297.

SERMON XIX.
1 CORINTHIANS xi. 26.
For as often as ye eat this bread, and drink this cup, ye do shew forth the Lord's death till he come. P. 313.

SERMON XX.
ACTS xx. 35.
And to remember the words of the Lord Jesus, how he said, it is more blessed to give than to receive.
P. 333.

SER-

SERMON I.

1 Thess. v. 16.

Rejoice evermore.

MANY of the enemies of religion confider it as the caufe of a fevere, gloomy and unfocial difpofition. Some of the friends of religion feem to confider it in the fame light. Nothing however can be more unjuft than fuch a judgment, or productive of worfe effects. Who would choofe to dwell with fournefs and feverity? or what human creature is able to refift the fmile of chearfulnefs, and the voice of joy? If religion were fuch as it is fometimes reprefented by prejudice, or fuch as the manners of fome men who pretend to be religious, yea, I will add, who have ftrong feelings of religion, would indicate it to be, I fhould not be furprized that it had few votaries, and that men delayed to embrace it till the common feelings of humanity had left them.

Wherever a religion of this caft has been framed, I am perfuaded it is not the religion of
the

the New Testament: nor do I think, if it were, that any arguments would be sufficient for establishing it, or any further reasoning necessary for overthrowing it. But with regard to that religion, the aspersion, from whatever quarter it has arisen, is entirely groundless. Christianity, on the contrary, is the source of the best, the purest, and the most permanent joys in human life. Were there nothing more than the exhortation in the text, it would never be pretended surely that the religion of Jesus forbids all joy and chearfulness. And it may be of importance at this time to enquire into the causes of that joy which christianity encourages and promotes, and to which the apostle exhorts us in the text.

To give a particular account of the nature of that joy which the persuasion and practice of christianity excites, would be to describe the different modifications of rational pleasure and satisfaction; a description which at present I decline. I shall only observe, that when I speak of this joy, I cannot be supposed to mean a childish and laughing levity of disposition, which may brighten up the countenance, but does no more at best than play round the heart. I always understand by it that joy which becomes a man, which consists in a chearful but composed temper, which leaves a person open to every gratification that is agreeable in possession, and afterwards delightful on reflection. Let us enquire into the causes from which this joy proceeds. This enquiry, with some reflections to which it will naturally give

occasion

occasion, will be sufficient subject for our discourse at this time. *Rejoice always,* or *evermore,* saith the apostle. The grounds upon which so permanent a joy is founded must be very permanent, and must be laid deep in the human mind. Let us endeavour as plainly and as distinctly as possible to explain them.

In the first place: The joy to which a christian is called, and which may indeed be reckoned his portion, results from that virtue and integrity of life which the rules of his religion require.

It might be thought almost superfluous to shew that the Christian religion is intended to make men better or more upright. The gospel was evidently given to *teach us, that denying ungodliness and worldly lusts, we should live soberly, righteously, and godly in this present world* [a]. That this is the design of it, the tendency of its doctrines, the purity of its precepts, the nature of its motives, the example of its author, sufficiently evince. Some men may be so corrupt as to try to explain away this truth; but scarcely any man can be so audacious as barefacedly to deny it.

As christianity is thus evidently intended and calculated to make men better, I further observe, that the exhortation in the text is addressed to those upon whom it had this effect. The Thessa-

[a] TITUS ii. 12.

SERMON I.

lonians were remarkable for their *work of faith*, their *labour of love*, and their *patience of hope in the Lord Jesus Christ* [B]. They are recorded as *enfamples to all the believers in Macedonia and Achaia* [C]. Timotheus brings the apoſtle *good tidings* of their *faith* and their *charity*; and the text is immediately preceded by an exhortation ever to *follow that which is good, both among themſelves and all men*. It is manifeſt that exhortations of a general nature can only be applied to such as embrace in good earneſt the tenets of that ſyſtem where ſuch exhortations are found.

VIRTUE and integrity therefore being eſſentials to the character of a Chriſtian, whatever reſults naturally from theſe qualities belongs to him. But theſe qualities are the natural ſource of inward peace and joy of heart. Benevolence, moderation, friendſhip, ſincerity, from the very conſtitution of the human mind infuſe a pleaſing chearfulneſs and ſerenity into the ſoul. Rancour, violence, enmity, falſeneſs, diſturb its tranquillity. They occaſion ſtorms and tempeſts which are always unpleaſant, and often diſaſtrous. Juſtice, generoſity, charity, are confeſſed by an open, compoſed frankneſs of countenance and manners. Injuſtice, cruelty, ſuſpicion and ſlander, are indicated by a dark look and diſcontented manner, or by thoſe tumults of paſſion which diſtort the face and wring the heart. Temperance and ſobriety

[B] 1 THESS. i. 3.   [C] VERSE 7.

beſtow

bestow health and vigour upon their votaries. The contrary vices every one discerns in the meagre and extenuated form of that man who, after innumerable pains and sufferings, is forced, through mere old age, to relinquish life at forty. This, my brethern, is the natural and general course of things. Such are the laws impressed upon our constitution by that omnipotent Being who giveth lustre and beauty to the sun, and regulateth the wind and the waves. By his appointment, peace and joy are the offspring of virtue. In the language of scripture, *the work of righteousness is peace, and the effect of righteousness, quietness and assurance for ever* [D], whereas *the wicked are like the troubled sea when it cannot rest, whose waters cast up mire and dirt* [E].

CONSIDER with yourselves and tell me, when was it that you possessed a degree of joy which you can reflect upon at this moment with delight? was it not when you performed some action which your consciences approved of and applauded you for? When is it that you feel a conflict within your own breasts, the sensations of uneasiness and disquiet which deprive you of solid satisfaction, and unfit you for every valuable gratification? Honestly confess the truth. Is it not when any irregular passion or appetite has got the dominion over you, and hurries you precipitately to some indulgence which your heart condemns? upon

[D] ISAIAH xxxii. 17.   [E] CHAP. lvii. 20.

whom do the monsters of horror, remorse, and despondency prey? and who are they that should dread their power, and tremble lest they feel their tyranny? do not these monsters dwell in the innermost recesses of the cave of vice? and does it not require all her sorcery to prevent their appearance at the very entry of it? On the other hand; whose mind is calm and equable like the unruffled ocean; who can allay the natural thirst of his soul at the fountain of happiness? who can trace the footsteps of peace and serenity, and tread in them? Is it not the man in whose mind conscience presides as a judge, whose life it regulates as a guide, the periods of whose existence are filled up with every act of equity, meekness, charity, condescension, and compassion, which his circumstances require or permit? Does justice leave a sting behind it? or does it occasion a triumph? does the tear of sympathy, like the tear of disappointment in a vicious pursuit, rankle the soul? or does it not rather compose and soothe it? does the abstemiousness of temperance sicken the heart, like the cup of drunkenness? do the gifts of generosity produce those anxieties which ever prey upon the avaricious?

Take the matter in another light. Did you ever dwell in the house with any man who was unjust, or malicious, or envious, or debauched; and could you say of such a man, that you generally found him chearful, serene, and happy? that the day flowed on with an equal tenor, and that he saw morning, noon, and night with the same

same temper? (I speak at present merely as to this world, and a man's immediate feelings.) It is impossible in the nature of things. Who are they that most evidently display their serenity and chearfulness to their servants, their domestics, their dependants, and their connections? Is it not the virtuous and the temperate? Hail sacred Virtue, thou parent of peace and joy! let me ever bow at thy shrine, and ever venerate thy power.

I DERIVE, therefore, the first cause of that joy, which the religious possess, from their conforming to the laws of virtue and integrity, which are the laws of their nature. A machine cannot move easily if some of the principal springs are weakened or obstructed. An inferior animal cannot be happy if its appetite for food is not gratified, or if it is restrained from yielding to any of its strongest instincts. Neither can man, in whose constitution the sense and approbation of virtue are interwoven by the hand of his Maker, if he gives himself up to be the servant of sin.

I ENTER at present into no laboured or particular disquisition about the nature of virtue. Who does not perceive and feel it? who does not approve it in his neighbour? who does not admire it, in the example of Jesus? whose heart is not warmed with the inforcement and illustration of it in his precepts and parables? Alas! did we but act suitable to our knowledge and our feelings,

how

how many faints would there be among us, and how univerfally would happinefs be diffufed!

But I acknowledge that the joy which a virtuous practice infpires, if it were all that the chriftian were heir to, would, in the prefent ftate of things, be at the beft but interrupted and imperfect. The prefent fcene is various and complicated. The natural tendency of things is often obftructed. With refpect to human characters and enjoyments, effects are often obferved that are contrary to what might have been expected. It might bear a difpute whether, if there was no world after this, good fpirits, a healthy conftitution of body, with ftrong propenfities to vice, accompanied with the natural feelings of remorfe when thefe laft are indulged, were not preferable to a fickly frame, with delicate perceptions of virtue, and ardent defires to practife it, accompanied with all the difappointments which the experience of the world teacheth every man to look for. All the ferenity that virtue can of itfelf beftow may be greatly ruffled by adverfity. It may be deftroyed by misfortunes. We may affirm that joy is the firft-born of virtue, and that fhe would in the paradifaical ftate have been an infeparable attendant upon her mother, but that the ftorms and tempefts of human life, in this degenerate ftate, often difunite thofe who were defigned for perpetual affociates.

Again, other creatures feem to be totally occupied with the prefent hour, and engroffed by the

the particular pains or pleasures which they feel; but man is a being of a different kind. His hopes and fears, his wishes and apprehensions enlarge immensely the sphere of his happiness or misery. Numberless objects offer themselves to his contemplation; and the exercise of his understanding becomes a source of pleasure or pain to him. Suitable to the dignity and extent of his powers are the inlets of his joys and sorrows. It is religion alone that is able fully to supply the former, and alleviate the latter: and attention to this subject will convince us that the exhortation, *Rejoice evermore,* can only be addressed with propriety to the person who believes in religion. For I would observe in the second place, that a belief in the existence of an almighty, all-wise, benevolent being, and in his righteous government of the world, affords a genuine and rational pleasure to the human heart.

This belief is the foundation and groundwork of religion. For every one *that cometh to God must believe that he is, and that he is a rewarder of them that diligently seek him* [F]. How comfortless should we be if we knew neither whence we sprung, nor how we are supported, if we never regarded the hand that bestows our blessings, nor derived consolation under misfortunes from the reflection that every thing is regulated by unerring wisdom! If the sun did not illuminate the world, if his

[F] HEB. vi. 6.

beams did not revive and quicken both the animal and vegetable creation, how dreary a wilderness would this earth appear! But it is the observation of a heathen, that it would be less irksome and melancholy, if the sun were extinguished, than if men lived without any thought or persuasion of a supreme being and a directing providence. The consideration of these truths elevates the mind, composes the tumultuous, and restrains the disorderly passions, and fills the soul with a kind of sacred rapture. *The Lord reigneth; let the earth rejoice, and the isles thereof be glad* [g]. Because *the Lord God omnipotent reigneth, let us be glad, and rejoice, and give honor to him* [h]. Such sentiments correspond to our natural feelings. They do not force their way to the heart, but they meet with an easy and grateful reception. In the most perilous state of human life the good man adopts the language of David: *God is our refuge and strength, therefore will we not fear though the earth be removed, and though the mountains be cast into the midst of the sea, though the waters thereof roar and be troubled, though the mountains shake with the swelling thereof* [i]. Consider the joys of the wicked, and observe upon what frivolous causes they depend. Their mirth generally arises from full health, good spirits, pleasant company, thoughtless security, much liquor, prosperous affairs, and such like circumstances. An alteration happens in

[g] PSALM xcvii. 1. [h] REV. xix. 7. [i] PSALM xliii. 1, 2, 3.

these

these. Their health is disordered, their pulse becomes quick and intermitting, their spirits flag, their affairs decline, their friends desert them, their consciences are roused. Such things will often happen. Alas, what paleness seizes the ruddy cheek! with what alarms do their hearts tremble! what despondence in the down-cast eye! what tremulous agitation in the feeble joints! They have laid up no provision for this tremendous hour. They never thought that their sun would set: and he hath withdrawn his beams, and left them in an unknown, bleak and desert country. But tell me in what state of life can a good man be placed, wherein a persuasion of a supreme being, and a conviction of his righteous and wise administration, will not afford him joy and consolation? In youth and old age, in health and sickness, in prosperity and adversity, they are suitable and supporting subjects of meditation.

In the third place: the representation which religion gives us of the nature of our present state and of the immortality of our souls, infuses pleasure and hope into the mind. Amidst the struggles of human life, a good man looks forward to a better world with pleasing expectation.

We are taught by religion, that the present life is a state of trial and discipline, that we are placed here to act a certain part which will be attended with consequences of the utmost duration and highest importance. Without the knowledge

knowledge and conviction of thefe truths, what joy could we expect to poffefs? If we were of a ferious and thoughtful temper, and had only hope in this life, we fhould be of all creatures the moft miferable. On the other hand, the man who fhould run a perpetual round of diffipation and folly, whofe views were not extended beyond the fleeting term of human life, whofe imagination never foared above that fpot of ground on which he trode, though he might eat, and drink, and laugh, and dance, and be merry, I fhould have no hefitation to pronounce that he was yet a ftranger to the pleafures that are worthy of a reafonable being.

EARLY in life we are apt to look upon this world as a very pleafant theatre, upon which we may act a fhort but mirthful part. We are ready to fay, Let us rejoice in the days of our youth; but we have not proceeded far till we meet with many things to make us fober and thoughtful. We perceive an evident difproportion between the pleafures of folly and the powers of a man, and we feek about for fomething to fupport a difappointed, doubting, anxious mind. This is only to be found in religion. Religion teacheth us that our bufinefs is important; but that the proper difcharge of it will be attended with the moft beneficial confequences. It difcovers that there is a part allotted us fuitable to our faculties, and an exercife worthy of that nature which is beftowed on us. Under thefe views we cannot fold our hands in idlenefs, nor weep becaufe we have nothing

thing to do. Religion, whilſt it conſecrates a regular, decent and inoffenſive behaviour, preſcribes the worthieſt employments, as a ſuitable exertion of our immortal powers. It diſpoſeth us to receive proſperity with that ſedate and manly complacence which favourable circumſtances are calculated to promote. It inſpires a fortitude of ſpirit which enables us to ſuſtain the aſſaults of adverſity. The contemplation of immortality makes us regardleſs and almoſt forgetful of the pains that we ſuffer in our journey to it. It adminiſters the beſt conſolation under thoſe diſtreſſing circumſtances which every man, who thinks at all, muſt expect to meet with. I have in my eye at preſent the loſs of friends, of children, of connections endeared by a thouſand ties. Such loſſes are, and from the nature of things muſt be, very frequent in the world. To part for a time is tolerable. But ah! to part for ever, if this were the conſequence of death, I ſhould think of it with diſtraction.

THE perſuaſion of immortality, and the belief of a reſurrection, were topics of joy and conſolation, with the force of which the firſt chriſtians were well acquainted, and they often apply them. It is the conſideration of theſe doctrines that the apoſtle Paul, in the fourth chapter of this epiſtle, inculcates upon the Theſſalonians. After inſiſting upon them with great energy, he concludes in this manner, *Wherefore comfort one another with*
theſe

thefe words [K]. I think it impoffible for any perfon to read our Saviour's difcourfe relating to this fubject, in the beginning and latter end of the fourteenth chapter of John's gofpel, without feeling a mixture of complacence and melancholy highly delightful to the heart.

UPON the whole, I fubmit to the decifion of every ferious hearer, whether the belief of a powerful, wife and merciful governor of the world, the profpect of a happy immortality, and an uniform practice of righteoufnefs, are not juft and fufficient caufes for producing an habitual joy and fatisfaction in a man's mind; whether they are not naturally calculated for banifhing gloom and difcontent, and for promoting chearfulnefs. I fcarcely think that any man can deny that they are. There does not appear to me to be any refinement in this reafoning. I have avoided confidering any thing of a curious and fubtle nature, as the caufe of the joy which we receive from chriftianity, becaufe, though fome fuch things might be fpecified, they are only partial caufes, and do not extend to the generality of chriftians; whereas the confiderations which I have pointed out are of univerfal influence.

I MIGHT have confidered the peculiar doctrines of chriftianity, fuch for inftance as the facrifice of Chrift, the promife of the Spirit, the refurrection,

[K] VER. 18.

of the body, the appointment of our Saviour to be judge of the world, the condefcenfion, and charity, and meeknefs of his character, as juft fources of chriftian confolation and delight: but fuch a detail could not at prefent have been entered upon, and I apprehend that every perfon will be fenfible, that though thefe doctrines are different, and that the pleafure arifing from the confideration of them admits of different modifications, yet there are fome general ends which they all have in view, and fome common principles by which they augment the joy of our minds. For inftance, does not the doctrines of the fatisfaction, of the refurrection, of the appointment of Jefus as the judge of the world, and the recollection of his character, all confpire in producing thefe confequences, to afcertain us of the placability and favour of God, and to ftrengthen our faith in a happy immortality? The doctrine of the divine affiftance is certainly moft comfortable. But is it not chiefly felt, if I may fay fo, when the doctrine is realized, when the Spirit operateth upon the minds of men in engaging them to bring forth the fruits of righteoufnefs, piety, charity, and in confirming their hopes of eternal happinefs? Thus I have all along had refpect to thefe doctrines as the principal foundations of our joy. Let us now attend to fome reflections which naturally arife from what has been faid.

In the firft place: is it not plain that we ought to confider religion as our beft friend, and the fource of our trueft and moft permanent joy? If

If we are strangers to its power and influence, we must be strangers to the noblest and most substantial pleasures of human life. For I would ask any man, what pleasures he can compare with those resulting from a well-governed mind, and a right-regulated practice, from the contemplation of Him who is the fountain of all excellence, from the prospect of dwelling for ever with God and with Jesus Christ, of enjoying an eternal serenity, undisturbed by those calamities and dangers to which we are here exposed, uninterrupted by those doubts and misgivings, which here depress us, unobscured by that ignorance and darkness which we here lament? Tell me, ye who know the human heart, ye who generously feel for the woes of others, ye who exult in the happiness of your neighbour, tell me in what light you consider those who would ravish from mortals such solacing and elevating joys? are not these the men to whom the wo pronounced by our benevolent Redeemer is justly applicable, *Wo unto you Scribes and Pharisees, for you neither go into the kingdom of heaven yourselves, nor suffer them that are entering to go in* [L].

But the pleasures of the world will still allure. And by engaging our minds to entertain a just value for these that have been just now mentioned, must we sacrifice the rest? must we banish social mirth, renounce agreeable company, and

[L] MATT. xxiii. 13.

relinquish

relinquish every innocent diversion? Where, my brethern, the necessity for this? Shall men be so foolish as to suppose things to be incompatible, which, from their very nature, can never be well relished but when conjoined? For my part, I believe that no man ever existed whose mind was solely and for ever occupied with the concerns of virtue and religion, important as they are. Such a temper is incompatible with humanity. But is the person worthy the name of a man, whose life is wholly taken up with mirth, company and diversion? If the things of this world and of the next were properly tempered together, do you really think we should be losers as to our pleasures or our dignity? Do you really think that a virtuous and religious man will receive less pleasure in company, or at a feast, in any public or private amusement, because he is virtuous and religious? I know the grounds upon which such an opinion stands; mere misapprehension, weak reasoning, and partial obeservation. I will only at present appeal to fact. Do ye not know some of the very best and most pious of your acquaintance, that enter with proper relish into all the genuine and untainted pleasures that result from the various incidents of human life? they do not indeed spend all their time in these. But in this they are not true followers of pleasure? how irksome does perpetual pursuit, and reiterated enjoyment render these things! how soon do they pall upon the sense, and wear out the appetite! how shamefully do they degrade the soul, and sink the character! Give them their just room,

C and

and I acknowledge them, I feel them agreeable: Exalt them to a place they do not merit, and their littleness becomes conspicuous. Let us therefore *hold fast our integrity* [M], and *the profession of our faith without wavering* [N]; persuaded that by so doing, we adhere to our best interests.

In the second place: We may discern the impropriety of considering religion as severe, gloomy, and unfriendly to human delight. Representations of this kind are frequent; but they are unjust and pernicious. That they are unjust appears from the tenor of the present discourse: and that they are pernicious can scarcely be disputed. Truth and utility are generally supposed to be coincident: and in the present case, experience sufficiently confirms the maxim. A more effectual method could not be devised to prevent the spread and influence of religion. A very elegant writer, who, though no professed divine, has done essential service to religion, illustrates this observation very agreeably by a similitude drawn from scripture history. " Those," says he, " who represent
" religion in an unamiable light, are like the
" spies sent by Moses to make a discovery of the
" land of promise, when by their reports they dis-
" couraged the people from entering upon it.
" Those who shew us the joy, the chearfulness,
" the good humour that naturally spring up in
" this happy state, are like the spies bringing

[M] JOB xxvii. 5, 6.   [N] HEB. x. 23.

" along

SERMON I.

" along with them the clusters of grapes and de-
" licious fruits that might invite their companions
" into the country that produced them." If we
would wish to recommend religion, it is but justice to it to exhibit it in the form that is most apt
to win and engage. If we consider the character
of our Saviour, it is full of the most amiable, gentle, and engaging virtues. The strong and perpetually present impression of divine things which
was upon his mind, made it natural that he
should not enter warmly into those scenes that are
calculated for giving innocent pleasure and enjoyment to ordinary mortals. But he was sometimes
present at them. He expressed no disapprobation
of them; and the whole complexion of his life
shews a most exalted purity without any mixture
cf forbidding austerity. Blessed be God we live
in an age when the sincerity of our religion will
not be estimated by the demureness of our look,
or the sullenness of our demeanour. Let us shew
it by more substantial and less equivocal marks;
by an uniform integrity and that general good
temper which is not merely constitutional, but derived from a clear conscience and a fervent faith.

THIRDLY: Let the consideration of the joys
which true religion permits, determine us more
strongly against all unlawful pleasures. Our duty
and our interest are strongly connected together.
If we view things soberly, we have the greatest
reason to be thankful that God has allowed us so
many causes of joy and rejoicing. To desire more
discovers the highest ingratitude. We are in some
measure

measure still in the condition of our first parents. We have a great variety of enjoyments left us. Instead of the fruit of one tree that was forbidden them, there are indeed many which we are prohibited to taste. If we venture on them notwithstanding, the consequence will be the same. We shall feel compunction and remorse incomparably stronger than all the delight we can derive from them. Let us therefore resist all solicitations and enticements to that which is evil. Let a sense of duty, the feelings of gratitude, and frequent reflection upon our enjoyments, excite us to maintain an equal and uniform lustre of virtue and religion. Instead of wantonly desiring to range through the field of unlimited indulgence, let us confine ourselves within the circle of virtuous gratification. Thus, my brethren, our lives shall be happy, our deaths serene, and our immortality glorious.

SERMON II.

John xv. 15.

Henceforth I call ye not servants; for the servant knoweth not what his lord doth: but I have called you friends.

THE different circumstances of men in society, with their different connexions and views, afford just reason for their observing a different kind of conduct in relation to one another. Distance, reserve, and a partial opening of the heart are very proper on some occasions; and though we have an undoubted claim to every instance of humanity from all those who share the same nature with ourselves, it does not follow that we have the same title to require or expect their familiarity and friendship. To give these their true value, they must be a voluntary offering, and proceed from a deliberate determination of the will. If this were not the case, and if all men were to be treated in the same manner, familiarity and friendship would be terms quite unknown, and one general word would sufficiently denote that uniform affection which would equally be due

due to the whole species. But the distinction that has now been mentioned is evidently well founded; and our Saviour had it in his eye when he uttered the words of the text. *Henceforth I call you not servants; for the servant knoweth not what his lord doth; but I have called you friends.*

Our divine master, when he entered upon his public ministry, had selected a few followers to whom he gradually disclosed the design of his mission, and revealed the doctrines of salvation. In proportion as their minds were enlightened and expanded by the force of divine truth, he proceeded to open up to them the secret things of the kingdom of God, and accompanied his communications with every instance of sincere and affectionate attachment. To leave upon their hearts the most lasting impressions of his condescension and goodness, he even disdains not to submit to a servile office in their favour, and adds the most tender assurance, that he acknowledges his connexion with them, as arising not merely from authority, but from friendship. *Henceforth I call you not servants, but I have called you friends.* From this time forward I consider you not in the light of distance and subjection, but as connected with me by much nobler and more endearing ties, even those of friendship: and consequently as having a right to all the marks of the most cordial regard, and obliged to all the instances of duty and affection which this relation merits and requires. What was said immediately to the Apostles, and applied in a particular manner to them,

extends

extends in a certain degree to every good chriſtian, and is delivered for the inſtruction and comfort of all ſuch. And I have made choice of theſe words at this time, as furniſhing proper ſcope for a diſcourſe on the advantages reſulting from that intimate relation into which our Saviour thus condeſcends to receive his followers.

I HAVE no doubt but the apoſtles and firſt diſciples of our Lord, who were admitted to the freeſt and fulleſt perſonal intercourſe with him, muſt have had a ſenſe of the importance and felicity of that intercourſe ſuperior to what almoſt any chriſtian can now attain. Perhaps ſimilar feelings indulged by us in the very ſame degree to which the natural principles of the mind, and the peculiar circumſtances of the times would carry them in the caſe of the apoſtles, might in ſome reſpects be conſidered as proceeding from a ſpirit of enthuſiaſm, which, though it may be frequently amiable, is alſo frequently dangerous. But we are to remember, as a counterpoiſe to the happineſs of the apoſtles, that they were called forth to the moſt uncommon trials of their faith and patience, and that, as they had many diſtinguiſhed opportunities of cheriſhing the tender feelings of the heart, and of confirming their faith in Jeſus, ſo alſo they were under many peculiar temptations to ſuppreſs the former, and to renounce the latter.

THE deſign of theſe remarks is to introduce an obſervation with regard to the method now propoſed,

posed, namely, that in surveying the advantages resulting from that relation of friendship into which the Son of God admits his followers, I am chiefly to take notice of those which I believe might occur to a christian of a pious and sober turn of mind, who should set himself at this period deliberately to consider the subject, and who should be more careful to declare with simplicity and ingenuous feelings of the breast, than to say things which might surprize, inflame, or excite a powerful, but transient extasy.

In the first place I would remark, that the consciousness of possessing the friendship of one, who discovered such a temper and character as shone in our Saviour, must be a source of very high gratification, even abstracting from every consideration of profit with which it is attended.

There are some principles, in the truth of which good and bad men are agreed. The sole difference, and indeed it is a very essential one, consists in the application of them. For instance, That happiness ought to be the supreme pursuit of mankind, is universally acknowledged. The great question is, How it may be obtained? No one, I think, can deny that every innocent and virtuous gratification is a natural and just object of our wishes; and if the consciousness of our having the friendship of a wise and worthy person affords such a gratification, it is undoubtedly one genuine source of happiness. That a consciousness of this kind does afford an innocent and

virtuous

virtuous gratification, it will not require much attention to be convinced. People who have lived long, and been almoft wholly engroffed by the objects of ambition or avarice, are apt to eftimate every thing by its tendency to purchafe power or riches. And fuch men pafs for being wonderfully fhrewd, and for having acquired a thorough knowledge of the world. But in truth they have only viewed it in one particular light: they have confidered men merely as they appear engaged in political or commercial purfuits. But there are very many portions of human life which muft be occupied with other concerns, and other pleafures. I appeal to the experience of my hearers, if the converfation or prefence of a friend, or even the recollection of his amiable qualities, does not allay many griefs, and heighten many joys, even where he is not able to remove the caufes of the one, and has no connexion, as the world is apt to judge of connexion, with the objects of the other. Is not the fecret working of providence, which hath united men by many other ties befides that of intereft, or the power of promoting each others fecular views?

IF a good man is confined in a dungeon, the reflection that he has the approbation and fympathy of a virtuous friend under his unjuft fufferings, will have a powerful tendency to fupport him, though he fhould be debarred from enjoying his company by the clofenefs of his prifon, the feverity of his keeper, or the diftance of a thoufand miles: while the wealth of worlds could

not

not support a tyrant in the same circumstances, conscious as he must be that he merits universal detestation. It is a law in the material world, that if one body is put in motion, and strikes another, it loses so much of the force with which it was impelled, and communicates it to that other. In like manner it is a law in the moral world, that sympathy, either perceived in another, or reflected on as actually exerted, heightens our pleasures, and alleviates our pains. The very knowledge or recollection of a virtuous friendship, I do maintain it, will pour balm into the festered soul, and revive the dejected spirit, when gold, that idol of the world, cannot purchase the smallest relief or consolation. In exquisite pain, incurable disease, or the immediate prospect of death, riches lose all their lustre, and the pursuits of ambition, like objects thrown at a distance, appear altogether diminutive. Turn your views to scenes of this kind, and you will feel the difference between a splendid apartment, a soft bed, numerous attendants, skilful physicians, which the worst of men may often command, and the affection and approbation of one virtuous friend. I put the matter strongly, because men are often insensible to the plainest truths; of which class I hold this proposition to be one, that the consciousness of possessing such a virtuous friendship, abstracted from every external advantage it may bring, affords a high gratification to the mind. I need only add, that the more excellent the person is with whom we are connected by this tie, the greater will be the enjoyment

arising

SERMON II.

arising from it. But the character of Christ, considered as exhibiting every necessary qualification for the most endearing friendship, is truly striking. What meekness, what condescension, what humane and generous sentiments, what tender and affectionate feelings did he display on a thousand occasions! Recollect his lamentations over Jerusalem. Behold his tears at the tomb of Lazarus. See his beloved disciple leaning on his bosom. Accompany him while he walks with his disciples to Emmaus. Review the history of his whole life. Hear his sublime discourses. Attend to his just, yet mild rebukes. Listen to the spirit and fervour of his prayers, and say, is it possible for your hearts to be unaffected, uninterested, uninflamed? *O that I knew where I might find him, that I might come unto him, even unto his seat* º!

I BELIEVE there are very few readers of the gospel who will not allow that the peculiar attachment which our Saviour shewed to John, must have imparted a very singular satisfaction to that disciple. Consider what constitutes the real and essential felicity of human nature, and I doubt if ever any one enjoyed so large a portion of it as this happy man, though he was neither rich, nor powerful, nor flattered, nor gratified in any worldly passion, nor exempted from the severest persecutions. Consider the state of the apostles

º JOB xxiii. 3.

in general. The pleasure they had in sitting at the feet of Jesus, and hearing his instructions while he remained on earth, and their ardent wishes to be *absent from the body*, and *present with the Lord* after his ascension into heaven, are not only free from all erroneous enthusiasm, but perfectly natural, and what every one might expect in their circumstances. I do not say that the consciousness of our Saviour's friendship, which is promised to all his disciples, will affect us so powerfully as it did those with whom he conversed, who witnessed his living virtues, who saw his face, and heard the *gracious words which proceeded out of his mouth*. Faith must fall short of vision: but will it have no effect at all? Or must not every well-disposed mind be deeply sensible of its influence? But, my brethren, the pleasure resulting from a sense of the attachment of the most worthy character in the world is not the sole or chief advantage proceeding from the friendship of our Saviour. It is attended with the most beneficial effects, and exerted in the most effectual manner for procuring and conveying the greatest blessings.

FRIENDSHIP is naturally active. It exerts itself in prosecuting useful plans, and in bestowing agreeable tokens of its sincerity and ardour. And all that is revealed in the gospel of Jesus Christ, and all the great and heroic things that he did and endured, are instances of his love and attachment to his followers equally beautiful and beneficial. The doctrines which he inculcated, tending at once

once to the comfort and to the fanctification of human nature, the precepts which he enjoined for the government of our hearts and lives, the example which he exhibited of every excellence, the inftitution of his laft fupper, the aſſurances of his continual regard and affiftance ; what are they all but fo many fubftantial memorials of the pureft and nobleft friendſhip?

SURELY the leaft attention to human nature will ſhew that theſe are to be accounted bleſſings of the firſt importance. They will bear to be tried by every teſt, and viewed on every ſide. If you conſider them as productive of the moſt peaceful and ſublime enjoyments ; if you contemplate them as proper to form the minds and manners of youth, to reſtrain their impetuoſity, to exalt their aims, and to render them both lovely and honourable; as no leſs fit for adminiſtering fupport and joy to declining years; as engaging men to improve profperity to the worthieſt purpoſes, and helping them to bear affliction with a manly firmneſs ; as adding dignity to the higheſt ſtations, and rendering obfcurity itſelf illuſtrious; muſt not their value on all theſe accounts be acknowledged and admired ? Ah, my brethren, what manner of men ſhould we be, if the doctrine and example of Jeſus had their full effect upon us! Of how many fictitious wants ſhould we be cured, with what moderation ſhould we receive, and with what magnanimity reſign what are commonly called the gifts of fortune? Were the doctrines of life and immortality deeply impreſſed on our minds,

minds, the fo much dreaded forms of old age, and pain, and ficknefs, and forrow, to whom we muft pay fome tribute in our way to heaven, though their countenances may be ftern, yet would not terrify us greatly. If we live fequeftered in the vale of folitude and poverty, and read and practife the gofpel, and review the memorials of our Saviour's friendfhip, we fhall look up to the great without either admiration or envy; and enjoying green herbs and contentment, which honeft labour and virtuous exercife have prepared us for tafting with pleafure, we fhall not repine that we do not fhare in the pernicious luxury of the rich. But if the honours and poffeffions of this world fhould be beftowed upon us, the gofpel, that invaluable legacy of Chrift to his friends, will teach us to add the true luftre to thefe by untainted integrity, univerfal humanity, and a defire to feize every opportunity of doing good.

I MIGHT render the illuftration of this fubject much fuller: but what has been faid will be fufficient to evince, that the bleffings I mentioned, when I entered on this topic of my difcourfe, are of the firft importance, and that the friendfhip which gives a right to them brings along with it the moft effential advantages.

THE fpirit of the world indeed, foftered by avarice, a fpirit which they who are actuated by it do fometimes blufh to own, fuggefts an opinion, that nothing can be an adequate exertion, or infallible evidence of friendfhip, but what contributes

butes in some way or other to a man's influence or to his figure in life. As if a purple robe were a defence against pain, remorse, despair, or death! or as if riches that are said, and I believe, often thought to be able to purchase every thing, could buy the pleasures of a good conscience, an exemption from the stings of a bad one, or a happy exit out of this world, or a right to the tree of life! *Ye simple ones, how long will ye love simplicity?* ʳ Ye are wise in the esteem of the children of this world; but listen to the verdict of a more impartial jury; let reason, experience, and inspiration speak. Since the creation of the world, mere riches or power could never render a human creature truly great, or truly happy. But I could mention many who are justly considered as lights of the world, who, though destitute of every gaudy trapping, and without any one of the boasted advantages of life, will shine for ever with the lustre of commanding virtue. Think of those who had neither staff, nor scrip, nor change of raiment, and *of whom the world was not worthy.* Where indeed are the people celebrated in the annals of time who do not glory in rewarding the merit of some of their ancestors? Reflect on these and a thousand things that will occur, and be persuaded that, in renouncing the vanities and grandeurs which you are too apt to admire, in revealing the doctrines of life and immortality, in exhibiting a pattern of perfect virtue, in offering

ʳ PROV. i. 22.

to lead you by his Spirit in the paths of righteousness, and in reconciling you to God by his cross, your Master hath given you the most valuable and durable marks of his friendship and regard.

But to mention a little more particularly one of the most important advantages resulting from the friendship of Christ; I mean that security and those hopes which it gives a man in the approach of death.

A wise man prepares against many possible evils which may never befal him. But how foolishly improvident it is, not to prepare against an evil that is certain? In youth it is wise to make provision for old age, to lay up in early years the consolations which piety and active virtue can procure, to support the feeble and tottering steps of fourscore. Yet we may never arrive at that period. But death, we are sure, is an event that will inevitably take place. The charms of sorcerers, the hoards of misers, the skill of physicians, the strength of guards, can neither soothe, nor bribe, nor terrify, nor elude that awful messenger. How desirable is it then that we should be prepared to meet him with alacrity, and fortitude! Death, my brethern, is naturally a tremendous form, and we stand in need of aid when called to encounter it. It will introduce us to a new and unknown country; and we shall sigh for some friendly conductor to take us by the hand. If in this struggle and the scene that succeeds it, the father could enjoy the com-

pany

pany of his son, the husband the society of his wife, and if brothers could lend each other assistance, it might inspire some courage. But nature forbids the intercourse. Yet the christian who relies on the promises of Jesus, knows that he shall not engage in that struggle, nor enter on that scene alone or unsupported. *When he walks through the valley of the shadow of death, he will fear no evil,* for the Lord, the shepherd of souls, *is with him, his rod and his staff shall comfort him*[Q]. Recollecting the gracious declaration of Jesus, *Whosoever doth the will of my father who is in heaven, the same is mother and sister and brother*[R], his fluttering heart is inspired with courage, and elated with hope: he departs in peace to his native land, trusting to the guidance and protection of his almighty Friend. Where now are ye, ye gilded prospects, ye gay delusions, ye pleasing dreams? Where now all the boasted schemes and hopes of the covetous, the voluptuous and the vain? Lo! They are vanished, they are nothing. And a serene, a happy death is all in all. You cannot deny the doctrine: but do you doubt the power of the friendship of Jesus? Do you doubt that a consciousness of it is able to confer this composure, and this felicity? Consult the apostles: enquire at the martyrs: recollect the last moments of the best men whom you have known to die in the full exercise of their reason: Let them bear witness: to them I appeal.

[Q] PSALM xxiii. 4. [R] MATTH. xii. 50.

SERMON III.

2 KINGS viii. 13.

And Hazael said, But what, is thy servant a dog, that he should do this great thing?

IT happened that Ben-hadad king of Syria when he was sick, heard of the prophet Elisha's being at Damascus. Prompted by a curiosity about the future that seems natural to man, and anxious to know before-hand the event of his distemper, he sends Hazael, one of his ministers and favourites, to enquire of the prophet whether he should recover or not? In obedience to his master's commands, Hazael went to execute his commission, and according to the custom of those days, took along with him a present of every good thing of Damascus. In the most respectful manner he delivers his message; for he stood before the prophet and said, *Thy son Ben-hadad king of Syria hath sent me to thee, saying, Shall I recover of this disease?* The answer of Elisha was mysterious, and probably not perfectly understood by Hazael. *Go,* says the prophet, *say unto him, Thou mayest*

certainly

certainly recover, *howbeit*, *The Lord hath shewed me, that he shall surely die.* Then fixing his countenance steadily for some time, and exhibiting the most natural and striking signs of inward emotion and agitation of spirit, he began to weep. Surprized at his tears, Hazael enquired the cause, and he answered in these remarkable words, *Because I know the evil that thou wilt do to the children of Israel; their strong holds wilt thou set on fire, and their young men wilt thou slay with the sword, and wilt dash their children, and rip up their women with child.* Such barbarous and cruel deeds seemed so shocking, that in the words of the text, Hazael in the strongest manner expresses his detestation of them. *And Hazael said, But what, is thy servant a dog, that he should do this great thing?*

It does not appear that this answer of Hazael was the effect of hypocrify, or any artful design to conceal his real sentiments; it proceeded from the natural and immediate dictates of his heart. Yet from the atrocious crime he committed the very next day in murdering his master, we have no reason to doubt, that in the war which he afterwards carried on against the united armies of the kings of Israel and Judah, the prophet's prediction was fully accomplished. And indeed, when we attend to what passes in the world, we must be sensible that the case of Hazael, though it it may be uncommon in its degree, is far from being singular in its kind.

To

SERMON III.

To trace then the caufes of this aftonifhing ignorance of ourfelves, appears to be a fubject of very general ufe and importance. When the caufes of a difeafe are diftinctly known, the application of proper remedies will prove more eafy and more certain. I intend therefore in the following difcourfe, to point out fome of the principal reafons upon which the ignorance of wicked men concerning themfelves, and the ftrange partiality in their judgments as to their future conduct, are founded; and to conclude with a few practical inferences from what is delivered.

In entering upon my fubject, I would remark, that ignorance of ourfelves is of two kinds; Ignorance with regard to our paft actions, and ignorance as to the future conduct we fhall maintain in life. Of the firft kind the fcripture affords us a very remarkable inftance in the cafe of David, who, induced by the ftriking allegory of Nathan, unknowingly paffed the feverest fentence upon himfelf. But it is ignorance of the fecond kind I mentioned, of which there is fo ftrong an example exhibited to us in the text, which I now purpofe to confider. Hazael was fo blind to his own character, that he believed himfelf wholly incapable of the crimes which he afterwards committed. Whence could this proceed? or how does it happen, that the declaration of men in fimilar circumftances are fo little to be relied upon?

The firft and moft obvious caufe of this ignorance of man proceeds from the total want of attention

tention to, and reflection upon their real characters and tempers. Is it surprising that a man should be ignorant of a subject which he has never considered? Is the meanest art and employment of life to be learned without some pains and application? It is needless to give a particular instance in any one profession; for it holds true in every one of them, that before any person understands it, he must be taught by another, or bestow labour and diligence himself. Can we expect that the general rule is not to take place with respect to the knowledge of our own minds? But are not a thousand subjects of less utility and importance, more the subjects of our reflection and meditation, than our own hearts and tempers? For rendering subjects more plain and intelligible, the ingenuity of men has devised various methods, and these methods are attended to by those whose concern it is; but instead of using and applying those rules which might be proper and useful, in order to make us acquainted with ourselves, are not most men more anxious to find out a variety of expedients, by which they may fortify and confirm themselves in their ignorance? Need I point out to you that entire dissipation of thought, that unremitting pursuit of pleasure, that perpetual levity, which are considered not only as arts to obtain present gratifications, but partly prosecuted with the very view I mentioned before, to keep men strangers to themselves, their tempers, and their dispositions? Can you name an enemy that seems more to be an object of fear to great numbers than reflection? In this situation

tion it would be next to a miracle, if a man were not ignorant of himself.

I ACKNOWLEDGE that one muſt be in ſome meaſure conſcious of what paſſes in the mind. The objects he purſues muſt be perceived by him; he muſt feel the paſſions he is perpetually endeavouring to gratify. But theſe are merely facts which he remembers to-day, but forgets to-morrow. To the generality of men they are like dividing the waters of a river by your hand; it is no ſooner removed than the ſtream joins, and you can diſcern no mark where the breach was. For inſtance, what courſe of life may we ſuppoſe Hazael to have led before his interview with the prophet? Educated at the court of a powerful monarch, by whoſe favour he poſſeſſed a high place, would it be a ſingular caſe, if he had devoted his whole time to the functions of his office, and the indulgence of his deſires? It had perhaps been frequently a queſtion with him, How ſhall I preſerve and encreaſe my power? but he had probably never aſked himſelf, What have I done to diſgrace my ſtation? or, How ſhall I act to be worthy of the favour and dignity which I enjoy? Thoſe features of his former character, which might have given a man of penetration cauſe to ſuſpect, that in caſe he ſhould arrive at ſupreme power, he would act the cruel ſcenes which the prophet predicted, Hazael himſelf had probably never attended to in any other manner, than as a *man beholding his natural face in a glaſs: for he beholdeth himſelf, and goeth his way, and ſtraight-way forgetteth*

forgetteth what manner of man he was [s]. But even this supine thoughtlessness and inattention is not the only, nor perhaps the chief cause why bad men form so partial a judgment in their own favour, and believe that they are free from the vices which lurk in some secret corner of the heart, and which wait but for a proper season to unfold themselves.

To account then for this more fully, I would observe in the second place, that there is implanted in man, a natural abhorrence of that which is evil, and a natural sympathy for the sufferings of others. Tho' we are in a corrupted and depraved state, yet in these respects we bear the marks of a divine original. The soul of man, which is the workmanship of God, is at variance, in its sentiments at least, with every cruel and barbarous action. Allow the unprejudiced and genuine feelings of the heart to judge, and nature itself will not err in applauding the virtuous and the worthy part, and condemning the contrary. If we convey our thoughts back to past ages, and observe tyrants depopulating kingdoms, and innocent subjects suffering under their rod, does not an honest indignation spring up against the former, and a powerful sympathy exert itself in favour of the latter? By his cruel decree, Herod fills the streets of Bethlehem, and the coasts round about with lamentation, weeping, and great

[s] JAMES i. 23, 24.

mourning. Herod, the barbarous deed has devoted thy name to infamy thro' all ages! Ye wretched mothers, while humanity remains, the tear of pity and of virtue will never be denied as a tribute due to your sufferings!

Now this abhorrence of evil, and this sympathy and sorrow for the miseries of others, are not principles which are confined to the virtuous and religious; they naturally operate upon all. By a series of wicked actions the impious try to stifle, and to overcome them; but till they are trampled upon a thousand times they are not totally extinguished. A silent and a seared conscience, is not an easy or speedy acquisition.

When therefore cruel and barbarous actions are represented unto us, we recoil, as it were, from the thought of them. If the passions which prompt to them are asleep (and this will often be the case with the worst of men) the better principles of our nature resume a share of their native vigour, and we cannot persuade ourselves that we would really practise what we so sincerely abhor, or occasion to others those sufferings which excite our pity to those that feel them. Let us observe whether the case mentioned in the text does not confirm this reasoning. Surely to ravage a country with fire and sword, to massacre men, women, and children, not to relent at the cry of innocence, to steel the heart against the tears of a defenceless mother, and not to spare even the helpless, uncomplaining babe who had never seen

the

the light, are deeds of the utmost inhumanity. The man who could look forward, and view himself as the author of these, would be more than a monster. At this time Hazael was removed from every thing that might excite his vicious appetite. In the presence of a person whose very appearance made him the object of reverence, he could not but feel the natural risings of his soul in favour of virtue and goodness. In this situation was it any wonder, that this man, habitually unacquainted with himself, should exclaim against his being capable of those crimes, the very naming of which chill the blood, and overwhelm the soul? *But what, is thy servant a dog, that he should do this great thing?* By being capable of so atrocious deeds, I should not only renounce the principles of virtue, but the very nature of a man.

In the third place: The partiality which bad men show in judging of themselves, and their ignorance of their real characters, are partly founded in the nature of vice.

Vice when it is continued, not only corrupts the heart, but perverts the judgment. By its deceitfulness man is hardened against the sense of those crimes he has already committed, and what is stranger still, while his heart condemns them in others, he continues to commit them himself, without being sensible that he is guilty of them. Vice is the greatest, perhaps the only sorceress upon the face of the earth. Those who drink

of

of her cup, becoming intoxicated with it, do not perceive objects in their true and proper light. Like men infected with some diseases which confer the same colour upon every thing they look at, the vicious often view themselves, not as they truly are, but through a false and deceitful medium which has a power to give a semblance of health to sickness, of honesty to corruption, and of rectitude to the greatest deformity.

THE fascination of sin then engaging men to form so wrong a judgment of the present state of their temper, and leaving them by a strange delusion in possession of their natural principles, while they are counteracting their dictates; it is impossible, but they will be still more partial, as to the judgment of their future conduct. The principles that have been already taken notice of, combine with the bewitching nature of sin in this case to blind their eyes, and to increase their ignorance. But farther it is to be observed, that vice is likewise in its nature gradual and progressive. It is known even to a proverb, that no person becomes altogether wicked on a sudden. The intermediate steps must be as it were measured before one reaches the summit. The checks of natural conscience are not restrained at once. Take an Ahab, or a Jezebel, a Manasses, or a Herod, and the least reflection will convince us that they arrived at the high pitch of wickedness which have rendered them objects of detestation, only by degrees. Observe a young person at his entering upon vice. The first crimes he
commits

commits are gone about with a timid look and trembling heart. He seems to be conscious, that the eye of God is upon him, and that he is offering an indignity to his own nature. But in a little time with less remorse and apprehension than the first steps of vice occasioned, he proceeds to daring crimes which he could not have suffered himself to think of, even for a long time after he was the servant of sin. Habits of sin, like other habits, require time to form them; but when rooted, and strengthened by a frequent exercise, they totally change the nature, and render us perfectly different creatures from what we were.

The progress of vice may be therefore compared to the rolling of a stone down a declivity: at first it moves slowly and gently, but before it reaches the bottom it acquires an impetuosity and force that are irresistible. If you were to view a river at the place of its rise, you will see a small stream, whose course might be easily stopped or changed; but as you trace it, it still increases, till it cannot be restrained by the power of man. When Hazael stood before the prophet, he had travelled but a short way in the path of vice; but he neither had the resolution, nor the inclination to controul his irregular appetites. Elisha, by the spirit which dwelled in him, unveiled the future. He pointed out some of the scenes which this man was to act in the succeeding part of his journey; but they were too distant, they were too unlike the past, and they depended too
much

much upon paffions that were at prefent quiet and dormant, for the perfon himfelf to be fenfible of them. More impartiality than can be expected is requifite for a vicious man to judge fairly of his prefent ftate ; but to difcern whether keen defires, violent paffions, an unfubdued fpirit, fit opportunities, and inveterate habits may at length carry him, is almoft impoffible. To acknowledge the pitch of vice to which he may be brought, would be to fuppofe himfelf much worfe than he really is.

FINALLY, my brethern, another reafon why wicked men are apt to flatter themfelves with their being incapable of many vices which they afterwards commit, may be difcerned from the nature of temptation. There are a great many of the moft heinous crimes that man can be guilty of, to which no particular principle or paffion in his nature leads him. To delight in cruelty, is in no fenfe natural to man, and it is but feldom acquired. But this forms no fufficient fecurity againft our committing cruel actions. The feeling no propenfity towards them, but on the contrary an averfion, gives a bias to our judgment, and makes us believe that we fhall be ftained by them: but the danger lies, not from a direct defire, but from feeing fuch and fuch actions neceffary to obtain certain ends upon which our hearts are fet. The prompter to cruel and barbarous actions is not a love of cruelty ; but the temptation may arife either from unlimited ambition, uncontrouled lufts, or a thirft of revenge.

revenge. Temptation does not always intrude itself, upon us. Till objects that excite the appetites of wicked men are in some meafure within their reach, they feldom wifh for the attainment of them. In the mean time the paffions which rule them are as it were afleep: they conceal themfelves from the view even of thofe who are governed by them. But no fooner is the temptation offered, than they awake with all their fury, and while their fway prevails, plunge the man into exceffes which he could not have believed himfelf capable of committing.

The man who fuffers one unlawful paffion to obtain the empire over his heart, has really every thing to fear. He fubmits to the dominion of a tyrant who will bear no refufal, and will never fuffer a command to be difputed. Let us confider the cafe of that man whom our text reprefents to us.

He was the favourite and minifter of a powerful fovereign. To obtain this office had been at firft probably the higheft aim of his ambition. But now he was within one ftep of the throne, his mafter's ficknefs opens the profpect; being accidentally left alone with him, the whole force of temptation overwhelms his foul, and the crown appears ready to fall on his own head. The demon takes full poffeffion of his heart; and the man who never before, perhaps in any flagrant inftance, had tranfgreffed the duty of a faithful fubject, now impelled by the luft of power, murders

SERMON III.

ders his benefactor and his king. Will dominion thus acquired be folicitous about the juftice of the means by which it muft be preferved? or will revenge never actuate the heart which ambition has fo thoroughly corrupted? Believe it not. If one devil enters, there will be feven ready to follow. What are the lives of a thoufand innocent perfons to the man who has never endeavoured to reftrain his ambition, his revenge, or his pride? The fword of Hazael is unfheathed; his unlawful paffions impel him; and the miferable inhabitants of Judea feel that all his fentiments of humanity are but weak barriers againft their force.

THUS I have endeavoured to trace fome of the principal caufes why wicked men are fo ignorant of themfelves, and form fuch a partial judgment with regard to their future conduct. Let us now attend to fome of the practical inftructions which this fubject affords. In the firft place, we may obferve in general from what has been faid, how folid a foundation is laid in human nature for virtue and religion. They approve themfelves to the natural feelings of men, and whatfoever is contrary to them is naturally hated and abhorred. It is not the language of the good only, How amiable is virtue! but even the wicked give their teftimony to the fame truth. O virtue! at thy image the worft muft bow; and while they defpife thy counfel, they muft yet confefs thy authority. In this fituation how inexcufable are they who would deny the difference

ence between virtue and vice, good and evil! On the other hand, let it be ever our care to maintain the rights of the former facred and inviolable. Let that holy religion which beſt unfolds its precepts, whofe Author gave a living example of its perfection, whofe rewards, promifes and threatnings are its fureſt and its chief fupports, be ever dearer to us than life itfelf. If not only by the light of nature, but by the clearer light of revelation, we muſt be fully fenfible of the beauty of holinefs, let us follow after the practice of it. But more particularly, I would obferve, from what hath been faid concerning the progrefs of vice, the great danger, and fatal confequences of a firſt departure from the paths of integrity. The man who once fuffers himfelf to be allured by fin, knows not how far he may proceed. *If finners* therefore *entice thee*, faith the wife man, *my fon confent thou not* [T]: In this cafe *a little leaven leaveneth the whole lump.* Let no perfon give up that which is good and right, prefuming that he will ſtop when he pleafes. I prefent you with a picture at which you ſtartle; yet if you are now initiated into vice, let a few years revolve, and you yourfelves will perhaps be the original. Let me therefore with earneftnefs exhort every one, and young people in particular, in the words of Solomon, *Enter not into the path of the wicked, and go not in the way of evil men. Avoid it, pafs not by it,*

[T] PROV. i. 10.

SERMON III. 49

turn from it, and pass away [u]. Temptation, my brethren, is powerful; we know not whether we shall be able to endure it. With fervency of heart then let us offer up that petition which is enjoined by our Master, who knew the heart, its weakness and its feebleness; *Lead us not into temptation* [x].

LASTLY: from what has been said, we may see the necessity of endeavouring to conquer every irregular and unlawful appetite. The train of vices, which one evil passion may lead us into, may be vastly great. Not only are we liable to those which have that passion for their object, but to a variety of others which may appear as means necessary in order to obtain its gratification. A city may be betrayed by one secret enemy, as well as by a thousand. Besides, my brethren, the fact is, that our sins and our follies proceed more from one principal passion than from a variety of lesser ones. This ruling passion is commonly the source of most of our errors; let us endeavour thoroughly to subdue it. I conclude my discourse in the words of the apostle. *Let us therefore lay aside every weight, and the sin that doth so easily beset us, and let us run with patience the race that is set before us, looking unto Jesus, the author and the finisher of our faith* [y].

[u] PROV. iv. 14.   [x] MAT. vi. 13.   [y] HEB. xii. 1.

E   SER-

SERMON IV.

Acts xxiv. 25.

And as he reasoned of righteousness, temperance and judgment to come, Felix trembled.

FROM the preceding part of this history we learn that the Jews entertained a most violent enmity against Paul, because they apprehended that he had an intention of destroying the whole fabrick of their law and polity. As soon as they knew of his being at Jerusalem, they laid hold on him, and having obtained leave from the chief captain to scourge him, they bound him with thongs, and were preparing to execute the sentence, when the apostle claimed the privilege of a Roman citizen. By this means he was delivered from the open effects of their malice; but intent on his destruction, they entered into a secret combination against his life. Paul having been informed of this by his sister's son, desired him to go to Lysias, and to make the matter known to him. Upon being informed of the plot, Lysias sends him under a strong guard to Cesarea, to be examined by Felix the Roman governor. The character

character of Felix, from the beſt accounts we have of him, is ſhortly this. He had paved his way to his preſent power by ſeveral intrigues, and the favour of ſome retainers to the court of Rome, at that time the moſt corrupted and vicious. He had been very active in the puniſhment and ſuppreſſion of robberies, which were then very frequent in Judea; and this gave occaſion to the encomium of Tertullus in the beginning of his oration. But he had been guilty of the groſſeſt partiality, and the moſt ſcandalous violations of juſtice in many inſtances, and of a moſt inhuman murder in the caſe of Jonathan the high-prieſt. At the period to which our text refers, he alſo lived in an infamous commerce with Druſilla, whom he had ſeduced to leave her lawful huſband, and to remain with him.

Before this man Paul is brought to anſwer for himſelf, and an accuſation having been preferred againſt him by Tertullus, whom the high-prieſt and elders had employed for this purpoſe, he delivered his defence with ſuch fortitude, magnanimity and force, that though Felix could not reſolve to acquit him, yet he ordered ſeveral indulgences to be ſhewn him in his confinement, and left him with ſome curioſity to hear him again more fully concerning that cauſe which had occaſioned his impriſonment. Accordingly, a few days after, he ſends for him, that he himſelf together with Druſilla, might receive ſome information concerning the doctrine of Chriſt.

It

SERMON IV.   53

It was at this time that the apoftle, among other articles of the chriftian faith, infifted particularly on thofe, which might moft readily touch the governor's confcience and lead him to repentance and amendment; on the indifpenfible neceffity of obferving the rules of juftice and righteoufnefs; of fubmitting ourfelves to the laws of temperance and fobriety; and on the certainty of that final judgment, wherein a retribution will be awarded according to our deferts. Upon thefe fubjects he fpoke with fuch energy and power, that the governor was alarmed, and agitated by the violent emotions of fear and remorfe. *And as he reafoned of righteoufnefs, temperance, and of judgment to come, Felix trembled.*

From this portion of facred hiftory I intend to deduce fome reflections, which may, by the bleffing of God, have a tendency to reclaim us from iniquity, or eftablifh us in religion and virtue.

In the firft place, I obferve from this paffage, that God has difcovered to us, by the immediate information of our own minds, fome of the moft effential parts of our duty and obligations. Paul properly fpoke before Felix concerning righteoufnefs and temperance, and appealed to his own mind for the conviction of the indifpenfible obligation of thefe virtues. The fame apoftle tells us in another place, *God hath not left himfelf without witnefs* [A] at any time; and that *the Gentiles which*

[A] ACTS XIV. 17.

have

have not the law, immediately delivered from heaven, *thefe having not the law, are a law unto themfelves, their confcience alfo bearing witnefs, and their thoughts meanwhile accufing or elfe excufing one another* [b]. The great rules for the regulation of life and manners are not left for the fubjects of deep enquiry and abftrufe refearches, but by the finger of God himfelf they are imprinted on our minds in the moft legible characters; for when God formed man at firft, he formed him after his own image, and gave him eyes to fee, and underftanding to difcern between good and evil: a heart to approve of, and delight in the former, and to abhor and difapprove of the latter; and though the brightnefs of the divine image is fullied in the human foul, yet it is not totally deftroyed. In what region of the earth was ingratitude ever approved and rewarded? Did injuftice or cruelty, as fuch, ever meet with the fanction of the law? Or have not piety, juftice and clemency always, and in all countries approved themfelves true, lovely, and of good report?

It is acknowledged, that when we confider things in one view, we are apt to think that the particular laws of ftates, or eftablifhed cuftoms of nations, have often contradicted the general laws of nature. But were we to examine the appearances which fuggeft this thought, or even to

[b] Rom. ii. 14.

confider

consider those instances in which the contradiction was real, they might be accounted for without overturning the principle now established. The great rules of morals may have been naturally discovered; and yet when men have endeavoured to class duties, and to descend to a greater speciality than the plain suggestions of the mind dictated, or to fix the different merits of duties, where there seemed to be a competition, or to determine precisely what were the proper external marks of our internal disposition, then they may have erred, and been much misled. We must make allowances too for wrong education, violent passions, unthinking levity, or unreasonable fears. These often give rise to extravagant and absurd institutions, which were afterwards recommended by custom, and thus implicitly received and implicitly obeyed. In this manner the candle of the Lord may, by degrees, be almost extinguished; darkness may overwhelm the soul, and error be embraced as truth.

This was actually the case in a great measure, when the sun of righteousness appeared in the world, to rekindle the sacred flame in the human mind, to point out our duty, and to lead us by his Spirit in the path of righteousness. But it is not one of the great excellencies of our holy religion, that it approves itself in the strongest manner to mankind, by its conformity to their natural principles of piety, justice, charity and temperance?

THE

The commandments prefcribed by it, are not hidden from us, neither are they far off. *They are not in heaven, that thou shouldst say, Who shall go up to heaven for us and bring them to us, that we may hear them and do them? neither are they beyond the sea, that thou shouldst say, Who shall go over the sea for us, and bring them to us, that we may hear them and do them? but they are very nigh unto thee, even in thy mouth and in thy heart, that thou mayest do them* [c]. And indeed, had we not minds formed for the knowledge and fervice of God, for the love of mankind, and for the obfervance of the rules of temperance and fobriety, we could not be the objects of religion: for religion does not beftow upon us new feelings; it only applies to thofe feelings which God has given us. Even where it points out duties, of which we fhould have otherwife been ignorant, ftill the obligation to thefe may be difcerned from their being fuitable to thofe principles which the author of religion at firft impreffed upon our hearts.

SECONDLY, In the verfe now under confideration, we have a very ftriking inftance of the power with which confcience is invefted, not only to inform us of our duty, but to punifh us for the breach of it. Paul reafoned of righteoufnefs, from which Felix, as a magiftrate, as a judge, and as a private perfon, had often departed. Felix lived in a moft infamous commerce with

[c] DEUT. XXX. 11, 12, 13, 14.

Drufilla;

SERMON IV.

Drusilla; Paul therefore discoursed of temperance. Of the obligations to righteousness and temperance, Felix, though neither a Jew nor a Christian, was not ignorant: and when his transgression of these obligations was recalled to his mind, it naturally excited sensations of pain and remorse. But when the minister of Christ represented to him the awful retribution for the deeds done in the body, then his inmost soul was roused. The apostle's words coincided with his own natural apprehensions, and the vengeance of heaven seemed already to have overtaken him. His whole frame was agitated; and, unable to bear it longer, he immediately remanded the prisoner.

Thus God has conferred upon conscience a most sacred authority, which no man can violate without being self-condemned, and suffering the most terrible punishment from its reproaches. Of this we have the fullest attestations in history, both sacred and profane. In the height of prosperity indeed, a sense of guilt may be sometimes overpowered and laid asleep; but the least accident or affliction awakens it, and shews that the fire had decayed for a little, only to flame with the greater violence. Even prosperity does not always prevent the sense of guilt: remorse, like some inveterate and incurable disease, preys constantly upon the heart of those who by their deeds have given birth to it, and shews that their judgment lingereth not. We have a very striking instance of this in one of the tyrants of Sicily. After acquiring the royal authority by injustice, cruelty,

cruelty, and murder, he lived in the utmost splendor, but he was constantly harrassed by tormenting fears, proceeding from his aggravated guilt. He dreaded the just punishment of his crimes from his domestics, and his very children. One of his ministers having asked the possession of his splendid station for a day; he cloathed him in his royal robes, placed him upon his throne, set before him the most costly entertainment, and ordered the most illustrious attendance to be paid him; but as an emblem of the continual apprehension of his own mind, he suspended a naked sword from the cieling by a single hair, directly over his head; and thus he sat, constantly dreading that the day in which he attained his wish'd-for dignity would prove the last of his life. I need not make any remarks upon this history, nor multiply examples of wretches, who from awakened consciences have endured misery similar to that of this tyrant. *The wicked are like the troubled sea, when it cannot rest, whose waters cast up mire and dirt. There is no peace, saith my God, to the wicked* [D]. A respite indeed may, by want of reflection, by dissipation or some other cause, be obtained for a little from the reproaches of a guilty conscience; but this can never be called true peace.

It is a very remarkable property of this faculty, that it applies any suffering which befals a person to the crime which it condemns, tho' it be

[D] Isaiah lvii. 20, 21.

SERMON IV.

not directly inflicted as a punishment for that crime, and forces him to consider it as a token of the just vengeance of heaven. We are not informed, that any punishment immediately followed, upon the crime of Jacob's sons, in selling their brother as a slave, or that they were touched with a sense of ther iniquity; but they were no sooner imprisoned in Egypt, after an interval of many years, under a pretence of their being spies (which, if they had been as innocent in other respects, as they were in this, might have appeared an event in the ordinary course of Providence, than their consciences immediately applied the punishment as the just reward of their guilt. Therefore do *they say to one another, We are verily guilty concerning our brother; in that we saw the anguish of his soul when he besought us, and we would not hear; therefore is this distress come upon us* [E].

It is farther worthy of observation, that, even where the mind is left in uncertainty as to the import of any unusal event, a guilty conscience is immediately roused and dreads the worst. When Belshazzar sat at his feast, and the hand appeared writing on the wall, as he was ignorant of what was written, he might have imagined it to be good as readily as evil: but his guilt was his interpreter; and though he did not understand the writing, this informed him, that it betokened no good to

[E] GEN. xlii, 21.

him.

him. *Therefore was his countenance changed, and his thoughts troubled him, so that the joints of his loins were loosed, and his knees smote one against another* [F]. How natural was it for confcience to prefent the reflection to Herod, when he heard of Chrifts miraculous works, that it was John the baptift whom he had beheaded, that had arifen from the dead, and performed thofe wonderful things?

Conscience then may be lulled for a little, but the moft trivial thing imaginable may awaken it. The wicked man has to dread a dark night, a folitary fituation, an accidental expreffion, any common or uncommon incident. When Felix called for the apoftle, he intended nothing but a little entertainment; but before he arofe, how juft reafon had he to fay, as Ahab faid to Elijah, *Haft thou found me, O mine enemy* [G]? The happinefs of the wicked, my brethren, may be compared to fo many figures in the fand: The wave no fooner comes to the place where they are, than they are razed. By our Omnipotent Creator confcience is placed within our breafts, as our ruling faculty. It erects its tribunal there, and accufes, judges, acquits, or condemns. How irrefiftible its power! Who ever exalted himfelf againft it, and profpered? Or what colour of life is fo black and difmal as that, where a man is at enmity with his own mind?

[F] DAN. V. 6. [G] I KINGS xxi. 20.

SERMON IV.

In the third place, The text leads our view to two men of very oppofite characters, and in very different circumftances; in fuch a manner as tends to correct the judgment we are apt to form with regard to power and external appearances. We fee Felix a Roman governor, furrounded with the minifters of his will, attended to with all the marks of regard, fpoken of with refpect, and addreffed with that flattery which it requires an uncommon degree of virtue not to take pleafure in. Would not the ambitious who moved in an inferior fphere, judge this man to be crowned with a garland compofed of flowers which conferred an uncommon luftre and honour upon the wearer? yet liftlefs days and hours are often the lot of the great. It was probably when neither bufinefs engaged him, or a lawlefs or irregular appetite folicited a gratification, that he refolved to hear Paul by way of entertainment, or perhaps out of compliment to Drufilla, who was a Jewefs, and might be fomewhat interefted in a caufe, which had occafioned fuch an uproar in Jerufalem. Paul therefore is fent for; and appearing before one, who had both the pretext, and the power of inflicting immediate death upon him, he feems the object which calamity had fet up to pierce with her fharpeft darts. In the mind of the Romans who were prefent, did not the defire naturally fpring up, and did not ardour give it utterance? May I ever be an attendant upon the happy Felix! but from the fears which poffefs, or the fate that may overtake that wretched prifoner, may I ever be delivered!

But

But how widely does man misjudge, when he looks only at what ftrikes the external eye? For power and grandeur, though purfued with the utmoft keennefs as the companions, yea as the very parents of happinefs, are frequently deceitful phantoms, totally unconnected with that great object of all human wifhes. We have a very ftrong inftance of this before us; a very little reflection will foon engage us to reckon the prifoner the great and the happy man, and the judge the mean and the unhappy wretch. To be fenfible of this, let us draw afide the outward veil by which we may be impofed upon, and look into their hearts.

Felix, then, was the fubject of many ungovernable paffions, which like fo many harpies, continually cried for gratification; and that they might be gratified, plunged him into a thoufand exceffes, the reflection upon which filled him with difapprobation and abhorrence of himfelf. His guards furrounded him, and power employed all her artifices to make him happy; but from a fecret corner guilt often bent his bow, and pierced him with the arrows that are the moft ftrongly barbed, and the moft deeply penetrating of any that are borne in the quiver of affliction. When he looked within, he difcerned his foul to be black with guilt. Beyond the fleeting and precarious profpect of a few years, which even his paft experience could inform him, would be far from being years of unmixed joy, hope did not adminifter from her cup one cordial drop to fupport his fpirit;

SERMON IV.   63

rit; but defpair hovered round him, and tho' he avoided the fight of this monfter with the greateft care, yet fhe often intruded into his prefence, and overwhelmed his mind. For can we think, that the words of this prifoner roufed the terrors which had never been rouzed before, by any of thofe purfuits in which he had been engaged, by any of thofe injuries he had committed, or by any of that blood he had fhed? Be not deceived then. Felix, in fpite of appearances, was the prey of ungovernable, unfatiable paffions, at enmity with himfelf, haunted by the fenfe of his guilt, and often tormented with thofe diftreffing fears, which were augmented by confidering them as the prefage of future and greater punifhment.

Let us turn our view next to Paul. Tho' ftanding at the tribunal of a judge, and accufed as a criminal, yet what greatnefs, and erectnefs of mind does he difcover? Neither the evils which furrounded him, nor the evils which threatened them, could overwhelm his mind, becaufe he had forefeen them, and was willing to endure them for his Mafter's fake. The tears of his friends were ready to break his heart, before he went up to Jerufalem; but at that very time, he was ready to endure not only bonds, but death, for the name of the Lord Jefus[u]. By what avenue was it poffible for misfortune, grievous misfortune, to enter, and feize the man who could apply to him-

[u] ACTS XX. 24.

felf

self this all-powerful confolation; *Herein do I exercife myfelf, to have always a confcience void of offence toward God, and toward men?* [1] Bleſſed God! what a calmneſs and ſerenity does a clear conſcience diffuſe over the moſt diſagreeable external circumſtances; while to a guilty mind, often in the very meridian of proſperity, there appears nothing but darkneſs and deſpair!

And now, my brethren, having from this portion of ſcripture ſhewn the manner in which God has diſcovered many branches of our duty; having illuſtrated the natural power and authority of conſcience; and having endeavoured to eſtabliſh a juſt meaſure for eſtimating human happineſs; let me draw a few inferences by way of application.

We have ſeen that even the light of nature pointed out the duty of man in many inſtances, and led him to diſcern his own fault in not attending to it; but the light of nature was only as a light ſhining in a dark place. Let this therefore excite our gratitude, that we live in a period, when *the day ſpring from on high has viſited us.* Let us be thankful that the clouds and darkneſs which overſpread the world are diſpelled by the ſun of righteouſneſs, which has ariſen, as with health and healing under his wings. And whereas, when conſcience in a natural ſtate was once

[1] ACTS xxiv. 16.

awakened,

SERMON IV. 65

awakened, there could scarcely remain any hope, but a fearful looking for of judgment, (for unassisted reason could not certainly inform a man, that even an alteration of conduct could procure an interest in the favour of an once offended God) let us ever adore that Saviour, *by whom peace is proclaimed on earth, and good will to men* [K]. For be it known unto you, men and brethren, that through this man is preached unto you the forgiveness of sins ; and by him all that believe are justified from all things from which ye could not have been justified [L], not only by the informations of reason, but even *by the law of Moses.* But did Christ die that sin might abound? God forbid. No; he died, not only that the guilt of sin might be washed away, but also that the power of sin might be subdued in the hearts of his followers ; for though he is merciful to every penitent, he is a consuming fire to all the workers of iniquity.

2. IF, besides all natural advantages, God hath vouchsafed to us the superior blessings of revelation for our information and direction, what manner of men ought we to be? If Felix, a heathen and an idolater, trembled at the words of an apostle for the violations of the laws of righteousness and temperance, how much more should we, if we are guilty of the like transgressions? If the natural dread of a future judgment had so great influence upon his mind, what

[K] LUKE ii. 14.   [L] ACTS xiii. 38, 39.

F   emotions

emotions ought the clear revelations of it which we enjoy, to excite in our breasts? To us God hath given full assurance, that *he will judge the world in righteousness by that Man whom he hath ordained* [M]. Ought not then the convictions of a future retribution, supported by the force of God's authority, the express declarations of his word, as well as the admonitions of your own consciences, to excite you to forsake every sin? Let him that defrauded his neighbour, defraud him no more; let the drunkard forsake his strong drink, and live temperately. Let the licentious abandon pleasure, and follow Christ; for he that saith, that he loveth Christ, and yet doth not obey his commandments, is a liar, and the truth is not in him.

[M] ACTS xvii. 31.

SERMON V.

Psalm lxxiii. 28.

But it is good for me to draw near to God.

PARTIAL views of human life, and hasty opinions of the events which occur in it, often occasion much fluctuation of mind, and uncertainty of conduct, by giving rise to sentiments of infidelity and distrust in relation to the superintendance and rectitude of providence. The reception which those views meet with, strongly marks the character of the mind; for the views themselves, to people who are accustomed to think, are at times almost unavoidable. It appears from this psalm, that the writer of it had been deeply distressed with them, and with the dark prospects which they presented; in so much that, on some occasions, they even tempted him to regard virtue as a name, and piety as a shadow. *Verily I have cleansed my heart in vain, and washed my hands in innocency.* But to a virtuous mind, the anguish of the impression prepares for its cure. In this situation,

tuation, the venerable and complacent form of religion steps in to our aid. By her words, equally fraught with sublimity and sweetness, she elevates the dejected soul, and pours into the festered heart the balm of divine confolation. The sanctuary of God was the place where the Psalmist expected to have his doubts cleared, and his anxieties removed. Thither therefore he goes; and there religion opens to him such extensive and soothing discoveries, as entirely dispel his painful thoughts. By the meditations which she suggests, he regains his former serenity and firmness, and acquires that confidence in the administration and protection of the Almighty, which is always so highly agreeable, but which few thoughtful men of sensibility are able invariably to maintain. The tenor of these meditations we may observe from the 17th verse to the end of this psalm. The words of my text contain a calm and deliberate reflection of the Psalmist, as the result of a perfect consideration of his subject, and will afford very suitable matter for our instruction at this time.

To draw near to God, primarily denotes those approaches which the Israelites made by means of their priests, to the visible symbol of the divine presence they had in the temple, in order to ask counsel of the Lord, and to receive answers respecting the expressions of their piety, and the regulation of their conduct. Upon such occasions, they always intermingled acts of devotion: and as in these, the sense of the divine presence is

more

SERMON V.

more immediate and lively, the phrafe came naturally to fignify all religious acts, and exercifes of the mind. In this fenfe, it feems principally ufed in the text. That it denotes religious acts in general, appears alfo from the character which God gives of the Ifraelites in the 29th chapter of Ifaiah, the 13th verfe; *This people draw near me with their mouth, and with their lips do honour me:* That is, they are punctual in the obfervance of the external forms and ceremonies of worfhip. When the primary and moft proper fenfe of a phrafe is loft, it often happens, that the fecondary and more figurative acceptation remains. Accordingly in the New Teftament, when the Jewifh œconomy was wholly altered, and there was no room left for a literal application of the words in queftion, they are, both in the epiftle to the Hebrews, and the epiftle of James, adopted to fignify acts of chriftian devotion; and as they are expreffive of the operation and feelings of our minds, they fignify thefe more ftrongly than any language would do that were entirely ftripped of metaphor and figure.

The text then furnifhes a proper foundation for confidering the advantages of devotion in general; and the confideration of thefe fhall conftitute the fubject of this difcourfe.

When I fpeak of the advantages which attend the religious acts of the mind, it is perhaps fuperfluous to fay, that I underftand thefe acts to be fincere and well intended. Sincerity and good intention

tention are essentially requisite in all the duties of piety and morality. They distinguish the christian from the formalist: they recommend the timorous prayer of the humble publican, while the want of them renders the pompous declarations of the proud pharisee frivolous and vain. In these circumstances lies the difference between the zeal of Peter and the kiss of Judas; between the tearful eye and downcast heart of the beloved disciple standing at a distance, and the mock honours paid to our Saviour by a servile multitude. Is it necessary to add that religious acts and exercises can be of no consequence or utility farther than a man's temper and conduct are correspondent to them? That ceremonies should compensate for immoralities; that a transient devotion should atone for vicious habits; that he who prospers by the wages of iniquity and the gains of oppression, or who without restraint gratifies any appetite or any passion, should meet with acceptance from his maker, on the account of any rites and forms of religion whatever, are suppositions alike absurd and impious. *He that turnaway his ear from hearing the law, even his prayer shall be abomination* [N]; and the only possible aggravation of his guilt is when he offers up his prayer with a wicked heart.

Having said thus much to prevent mistakes, I proceed to consider the advantages which attend

[N] PROV. xxviii. 9.

the religious acts and exercises of the mind. *It is good for me to draw near to God.*

IN the first place, they are accompanied with a sensible pleasure and self-approbation.

ONE thing in this world is set over against another. Every thing is relative, and there must be some comparison before we can pronounce concerning pleasure or pain, good or evil. The gratifications of life arise to man from the consonance between certain powers of his mind, and certain objects that are adapted to them. Thus far hath the God of nature provided for our enjoyment. If those gratifications are perceived and relished, we pronounce the mind to be in a healthful state: if not, we reckon it diseased, and the fault lies not in man's original frame, but in his own unnatural and vicious perversion of it. Thus we feel, and thus we judge. By the pleasure, then, and self-approbation which accompany the exercises of devotion, I mean those agreeable sensations, and that delightful consciousness which they produce in well-regulated spirits, and which every man who has the least candour remaining, though he has so far perverted his own mind as not to possess them, must acknowledge to have a strong foundation in nature. That they have such foundation will appear whether we consider the faculties that are employed in the acts of devotion, the object to whom they are directed, or the emotions which accompany them.

In the exercises of devotion our highest faculties are employed. By our capacity to recognize a superior hand directing the affairs of the universe, we are distinguished from every other creature in this lower world. The sun shines upon the beasts of the field, and upon the birds of the air, as well as upon man. The general influences of heaven chear and animate them. The earth affords them shelter and sustenance. They share with us many pleasures, and are affected with many similar pains; but man alone perceives an invisible and over-ruling power, putting every thing in motion, and directing every thing to its proper end. By skill and culture, it is possible to train some other creatures to an imitation of many human actions, and greatly to improve their natural sagacity; but to transport them for an instant into the region of invisible things, transcends the utmost efforts of human ability. The conclusion most natural and most familiar to man, which, had it not been for the corruption of his heart, or the refinements of false philosophy, he had never lost sight of, is That a God exists; a conclusion impossible to be taught by art to inferior animals. In the exertion then of this prerogative shall man find no delight? Hath the Deity stamped his own image upon us, and made us able to discern his attributes; and hath he annexed no pleasure to this deduction of our reason, or to this feeling of our hearts, and the impressions connected with either? Believe not, my brethren, that God hath dealt so unequally, so partially with the creatures of his hand. It is our dignity, it is our privilege, to be susceptible of the impressions

SERMON V.

preffions of religion; and in vain fhall we purfue fubftantial joys, if we exclude this as a confiderable fource of them. The ox feels no want while he feeds in rich paftures, the bee fucks the fragrant flower impregnated with the dew of heaven, and afks for nothing more. The birds of the air gather the grain which the liberal hand of heaven fcatters, and pour forth the notes of unallayed delight. But man the mafter of the world pines for fomething more. The univerfe is too little for him, and nothing lefs than God, nothing lower than the views which religion prefents, and the affections which it infpires, can fatisfy his all-grafping mind.

WE are made for contemplating great and magnificent objects with pleafure. A mountain, a river, the fea, the heavens, attract the attention of the moft uncultivated fpirit. Heroic deeds, noble fentiments, extenfive fchemes are furveyed with pleafure, and recorded with admiration by every people upon the face of the earth; but the grandeur of every material or mental object that the univerfe can furnifh, fades and difappears when we raife our thoughts to the fource and ftandard of all greatnefs. The greatnefs of every other object is comparative and derived; the greatnefs of God abfolute and original. In his eye the earth is a fpot, the mountains atoms, the heavens a curtain, the moft exalted human excellence imperfection.

BUT further, the feelings which the acts of devotion give fcope to, are all of the nobleft and moft amiable kind, and therefore from our very constitution

constitution accompanied with the most sensible delight. In devotion we not only contemplate with admiration the ever-living cause of all perfection and felicity, but with gratitude we acknowledge his beneficence to us. All gloomy and desponding ideas disappear, and we confide in that power which raised us from the dust, and made us rational and immortal creatures. The love of our hearts is the natural tribute to the goodness that creates and sustains worlds without number, and living beings beyond calculation. The hope of immortality irradiates our minds, and we rejoice in the government of him with whom *a thousand years are but as one day*[o]. Is it possible to indulge sentiments like these, and to derive no pleasure from them? Search the world and tell me if there are any subjects so fit to employ, so calculated to please the human mind. We were made for pleasure, we feel the desire of it interwoven with our inmost frame. The man that says he despises it, is a liar. Place it only on the right object: seek it not in gold: it is not annexed to temporal power: sensual delights are but a phantom. Our true joy is not here. It is risen: it is with God. It is more precious than rubies, more valuable than hidden treasures. Let us aspire after it, and gratify our souls by giving scope to the most virtuous and most exalted feelings of our hearts. Let reverence, gratitude, love, adoration demonstrate to us that we were made

[o] 2 PET. iii. 8.

SERMON V. 75

for fomething nobler than to grovel upon this earth, and to figh after its deceitful enjoyments.

In the fecond place, The advantages which attend the religious exercifes of the mind appear from the influence they have upon the temper and conduct, both refpecting fociety and ourfelves.

I will not fay that there can be no morality where there is no piety, becaufe different parts of our frame anfwers to thefe different branches of our duty; and a perverfion of one part does not infer an annihilation of the other. But in every cafe where piety is wanting, morality has loft its fureft and beft fupport. It is alfo worthy of obfervation, that the more extenfive our theatre of action is, and the more cultivated fome of the powers of our minds are, the more we ftand in need of piety in order to preferve the purity and integrity of our hearts. A favage who fcarcely thinks of God, is not, in fuch danger of tranfgreffing the focial duties of his narrow fphere, as the civilized citizen who proves without argument that religion is an impofture, and believes without reafon that devotion is hypocrify. In the contracted fituation of the favage, to yield to the impulfes and inftincts of nature, conftitutes the moft important part of his duty and bufinefs. In the cafe of the civilized citizen, to render his focial conduct worthy of approbation, it muft be grafted upon principles that correfpond to his more enlarged

views

views and more extensive connections. Our desires, our wants, our hopes, our fears, our capacities for virtue, and our propensities to vice, increase with the improvement of our knowledge, and our advancement in all the arts of polished life. Now to restrain those propensities to vice, to cultivate those capacities for virtue, to resist temptations so multiplied, and to regulate such various impulses, the aids of religion become absolutely necessary. In fact, how few men, who have no principle of piety, are strictly observant of the duties of social and domestic life? Honour, custom, humanity, pride, natural temper, prove restraints in many instances. But such restraints are weak, partial, and confined. A man truly conscientious is ashamed to hear those encomiums which it is fashionable to lavish on the man of honour and humanity, as he is called, who is nevertheless unfaithful to his wife, or careless about his children, who triumphs in the ruin of female innocence, and esteems the tie of friendship no defence against injuries of the blackest nature. I believe there are many merchants who have no fixed principle of religion, that will not forge bills, or falsify accompts, that will be regular correspondents and just dealers, that will tell honestly the quality of their goods, and be punctual to a day in their payments. This is their duty and their interest; so far they do well; and piety, if it could be possessed in this employment without these qualities, would never compensate for the want of them. But do these qualities constitute a man of virtue and integrity

SERMON V.

integrity in all the focial relations of life? Or, if he tranfgreffes one of the duties of thofe relations, will thefe qualities give him the leaft compunction of mind on this account? Suppofe I were affured of his poffeffing all thefe, fhould I be the lefs fearful of coming within his power, if I had offended or hurt him, however innocently? To a man who is above the arts of difhonefty, how fweet very often is the morfel of revenge! He is an unexceptionably good man, as it is called upon the exchange, yet his fervants may feel the feverity of his temper, his dependants may groan under the rod of his oppreffion, and his poor neighbours may be fick or ftarve without engaging his affiftance, or exciting his compaffion. When we defcend to the lower ftations of life; if they have loft all regard for religion, what expectation can we entertain of their virtue or fobriety? Fawning to their fuperiors and employers; but almoft always tyrannical or ill-tempered at home: pilferers to encreafe their fubftance; and yet almoft for ever intemperate and debauched in the ufe of it: given to fraud in every inftance where they can gain by it; yet almoft continually plunged by their vices into poverty and wretchednefs.

On the other hand, is there not a natural tendency in the fpirit of devotion to improve the character in every good quality refpecting our private conduct? What can more powerfully enlarge and ennoble the mind, than the contemplation and adoration of God? What can more
vigoroufly

vigorously prompt to the exercise of the social affections, than the consideration that they are implanted in us by the common parent, and that a regard to them is our duty as his children? What can more effectually imprefs a sense of the dignity of temperance, and the meanness of debauchery, than a reflection on our divine original, and a view of our immortal prospects?

THESE, one should think, are the natural fruits of a pious disposition: But when it is further considered, that all the duties of morality, love, candour, forgiveness, condescension, humanity, charity, temperance, are exprefly commanded in the scripture, and particularly recommended by an example that cannot fail to have the strongest influence upon the mind of a real christian, that the same authority which enjoins us to love the Lord our God with all our heart, enjoins us also to love our neighbour as ourselves, can we be so blind as not to perceive an intimate connection between these different branches of our duty? Are we disposed to adore the perfections of God, and acknowledge the authority of God? And will sentiments of this kind seriously entertained and frequently repeated have no influence but in those moments when they are present to the mind? Or will they not give some tincture to the temper and behaviour? Will the contemplation of perfect excellence raise no desire after obtaining a portion of it? Will frequent views of the vanity of time and the importance of eternity have no effect in subduing pride, in

restraining

SERMON V.

restraining impatience, and in arming with fortitude? Will all the considerations that are mentioned in the new testament, of our being the children of God, the temples of the Holy Ghost, the brethern of Christ Jesus, the heirs of his promises, the expectants of his glory; will all these be of no use in engaging us to purify our minds, and to keep ourselves unspotted from the world?

But fact is the great decider of all disputes. If it appears from fact, that the exercises of devotion are nowise subservient to the good conduct of this life, let them be confined to those who consider them as a fit preparation for another; but if the reverse be found true, let all who are solicitous about the most valuable interests of the present life be sensible of their importance.

If a reasoner, to shew the little use of piety, should urge, as is frequently done in questions of this kind, some examples of great external appearances of devotion, where the characters which exhibit them are yet tainted with avarice, injustice, intemperance; and should exult in this as a proof that devotion hath no influence on practice, I must certainly entertain a poor opinion of his discernment. The question is not about the effects of an appearance of piety, but about the effects of piety itself. Surely experience teacheth us to distinguish between appearances and realities: and indeed a great external show of devotion, except in people of weak understand-

ings

ings and warm paffions, gives rather a prefumption of the want of that quality than of the poffeffion of it. Were we to difpute about the weight of gold, would it be fair to prefent a gilt counter to prove its lightnefs? But the univerfal fenfe and judgment of the world about the characters of the men we are here fpeaking of, evidently fhow that there is a real foundation for afferting that true devotion has a natural tendency to improve, in every refpect, the moral character. For, if it has no fuch tendency, why fhould every human creature exprefs a peculiar indignation againft the vices of fuch men? For what reafon fhould they confider thofe vices as fo highly aggravated? Why fhould the impious wretch hold up his face, and fay that he is not fo bad as the man who pretends to piety, and yet treads in the fame fteps with himfelf? Thus the mouth of fuch reafoners condemns them, and their own lips teftify againft them.

Again; if particular inftances of moral virtue fhould be taken notice of in men who have had little fenfe of devotion, and yet have appeared equal or perhaps fuperior in thofe inftances to many who have been unqueftionably actuated by that principle; neither is this any thing to the purpofe. Character does not confift in feparate and detached efforts, but in an uniform or prevailing tenor of life. Great allowances are to be made for natural difpofitions, for original differences in judgment, imagination, affection. Even the devotional fpirit does not furmount every obftacle, obstacle, and conquer every temptation. The man of piety may yield to a passion which never actuated a worse man. But stating the case fairly, and that is, supposing the force of virtuous propensities and of vicious inclination equal in any two men, which of the two would improve most in the former, and be at greatest pains to restrain the latter? The man that fears God, or the man that fears him not? Which of the two would feel most compunction upon a deviation from rectitude, or most anxiety to recover the right path? I might appeal to your own judgments: I might almost appeal to the judgments of the vicious. But experience, as I hinted before, is the great decider of all disputes. If there be, as it is certain there are, a great variety of instances in which men filled with the spirit of devotion have been found blameless in their lives, and conspicuous for the purity of their morals, while they ascribed these attainments to that very spirit of devotion, and those influences of divine grace which are inseparably connected with it, must not this be acknowledged decisive upon the point? Were we to select particular instances, I should mention the prophets and apostles, great numbers of the primitive christians, some of the first reformers. Some of the most opposite principles in other respects might be ranked with them. Even several heathens might be considered as examples of the truth of our doctrine, and in that list I should particularly distinguish a Socrates and an Antoninus.

G   In

In the third place: The advantages which attend the religious exercises of the mind will appear, when we consider them as a resource under the evils and calamities of life, and a solace under the most distressful circumstances that can befal us.

There can be no greater folly, nor any more certain source of disappointment, than inattention to the general lot of humanity. If we consider life in itself, without taking into the account the means which providence and religion furnish for rendering it more easy and agreeable, the most melancholy descriptions of it are scarcely overcharged. Helpless in infancy, thoughtless in childhood, rash in youth, headstrong in manhood, feeble in declining years, decrepid in old age; in every stage liable to accidents, to diseases, to dissolution. Thus surrounded with a thousand evils, can we expect to be happy, if we have no higher refuge than this world affords? It is not in human power to avoid the pang of sorrow sometimes; and if we have no consolation when it comes, it will perfectly overwhelm us. The pains, the distempers, the disappointments, the injuries from men, the reverses of fortune, the loss of friends, the nameless calamities to which we are daily subject, who can tell how many or how grievous they may prove? Ah think, what multitudes are this day, from events unforeseen and unavoidable, plunged in bitterness of soul, who lately thought that their mountain stood strong, and that their houses should never be moved! Mirth does well for a season, but the house of mourning is upon fome occafions appointed for all the children of men. Need I, in proof of this, recur to the inftances of Job, of the prophets, of the apoftles? Need I mention the fall of tyrants, the cataftrophe of empires, the havoc made by the peftilence, or the ravages by the fword? Indeed, my brethren, the foul of man feels that *man is born to trouble as the sparks fly upwards*, that *he confumes his days in vanity, and his years in trouble*; and if he fhould deny it with his mouth, his heart would give him the lie. But where fhall he find confolation under thefe afflictions, if he has not previoufly acquainted himfelf with God? On the contrary, what folacing reflections will break in upon his mind from the principles of piety, and the acts of devotion? How powerfully will thefe affuage the bitternefs of anguifh, and check the fentiments of defpondence! From this fource a fecret joy will fpring up in the heart, when the tears of grief are falling upon other accounts. Let not the young and the gay imagine that mournful fcenes are at a diftance. No perfon can tell how near they may be; and wifdom confifts in preparing for what fooner or later will probably happen to us all.

I SHALL conclude with two paffages of fcripture that are much to our prefent purpofe, and ferve to fhew the unconquerable power of piety amidft the greateft calamities. The former is David's triumph in the midft of public danger and diftrefs: *God is our refuge and ftrength, a very prefent help in trouble: therefore will we not fear, though the earth be removed, and though the mountains*

tains be carried into the midst of the sea; though the waters thereof roar and be troubled, though the mountains shake with the swelling thereof. There is a river, the streams whereof shall make glad the city of God, the holy place of the tabernacles of the most High. God is in the midst of her, she shall not be moved; God shall help her, and that right early. The heaven raged, the kingdoms were moved; he uttered his voice, the earth melted. The Lord of Hosts is with us, the God of Jacob is our refuge [P]. The other is the conclusion of Habakkuk's hymn: *Although the fig-tree shall not blossom, neither shall fruit be in the vine, the labour of the olive shall fail, and the field shall yield no meat, the flock shall be cut off from the fold, and there shall be no herd in the stalls; yet I will rejoice in the Lord, I will joy in the Lord of my salvation. The Lord God is my strength* [Q]. Thus *blessed is the man, O God, whom thou causest to approach unto thee* [R]. To God, therefore, *let us draw near, with a true heart, in full assurance of faith* [S].

[P] PSALM xlvi. 1—7.   [Q] HAB. iii. 17. 19.
[R] PSALM lxv. 4.   [S] HEB. X. 22.

SERMON VI.

MATTHEW xxii. 37, 38.

Jesus said unto him, Thou shalt love the Lord thy God with all thy heart, and with all thy soul, and with all thy mind. This is the first and great commandment.

IN the preceding verses we are told that a young lawyer, with a view either to inform himself of the knowledge and abilities of Jesus as an instructor, or to obtain some answer which might give occasion to traduce him to the people, asks him this question; *Master, which is the great commandment in the law?* The words which I have now read, contains our Saviour's reply, which is so agreeable to reason, and to the express doctrine recorded in the Old Testament, that, as we see from the parallel place in the evangelist Mark, this young man, who seems not to have been destitute of candour and ingenuity, freely owned its truth, and applauded Jesus for it. I need scarcely inform any of you, that these expressions of loving God *with all our heart, with all our soul, and with all our mind,* are only intended

to

to denote the warmth, the vigour, and the steadiness of the affection But though the precept be very easily understood, and though Christians are ever ready to join in this enquiry, and to say, *Master, thou hast answered well*, yet it must be acknowledged, that many of those who call themselves Christians, seldom seriously consider its high importance among the precepts of religion. They rarely feel the force of the principle which it inculcates actuating their hearts; and consequently are strangers to its powerful and extensive influence. In discoursing therefore from these words. I shall 1st. show the reasonableness, and endeavour to impress your hearts with a sense of the duty here commanded, love to God.

2dly, I shall consider some of the reasons, on account of which the precept enjoining it may be termed *the first and great commandment*.

First. I propose to show the reasonableness, and to endeavour to impress your hearts with a sense of the duty here commanded, love to God. When we consider the constitution of the human mind, we must acknowledge, that whatever is upon the whole conformable to that constitution, is reasonable. The indulgence of human desire is only then wrong and unreasonable, when the desire is perverted, or when the indulgence is forbidden by some power or faculty, which is superior or more excellent. Now love is one of the affections of the soul, one of those original principles which man has received from the hand of

SERMON VI.

of his Creator. Its natural and proper object is whatever is good, amiable, or worthy in character. The obfervation of fuch qualities neceffarily excites this affection; and when exercifed upon thefe, the moft exalted and divine powers of the mind confent in giving it their fanction.

WHEN we obferve any perfon remarkable for integrity, or any perfon whofe delight is to do good, and to fpread happinefs, is it in our power to with-hold our approbation? Is not our love a tribute, which we are obliged to pay? When Job fed the hungry, clothed the naked, and adminiftered confolation to the diftreffed; when, in his own expreffive language, *he became eyes to the blind, and feet to the lame* [A], how natural was it, that love and admiration fhould prompt the young and the old to join in bleffing him, and how readily do the fame fenfations fpring up in our breafts when we read his hiftory? The king who is willing to die, if his people be but fpared; the hero who bravely facrifices his life for his country; the patriot whofe conftant toils are employed to fave a finking land, are, even fuppofing the influence of their actions fhould not extend to us, the genuine objects of love and veneration.

BUT by the appointment of providence our affections are moft ftrongly excited by objects with which we have the moft immediate connection.

[A] JOB xxix, 15.

Where

Where goodness or worth appear to be exercised for promoting our advantage, they most quickly raise, and most firmly attach our love.

Have you the happiness of possessing one whom the world calls your friend, and whose actions correspond to that sacred name; who shares, and by sharing redoubles your joys, who advises you when doubts overwhelm you, who smooths the brow of care, and partakes in all your afflictions? Have you a friend of this character? Or if you have parents who reared you with the utmost tenderness, to whom you were dear as life, what affections do you feel arising in your breasts when you think of them? are they not those of love, and of gratitude, which is nearly allied to love? It is just as natural to expect these in every human mind in such circumstances, as to expect from a field properly cultivated, warmed by the kindest influences of heaven, and warmed by its gentlest showers, a plentiful return of that seed which is sown in it. Is it not reasonable then, nay, is it not unavoidable to love men, when they are conspicuous for good dispositions and acts of beneficence?

Suppose now that the sphere of man's influence were extended, and that the imperfection which attends him through all the steps of life were removed, would he not thus be rendered more amiable, and consequently be the object of the greater love? As God therefore is not only the most powerful and the wisest, but likewise the best

best of beings, whose goodness is infinite, and whose *tender mercies are over all his works*[e], does he not justly challenge the utmost degree of love? This truth is no sooner proposed than it is acknowledged by christians. But to make not only the understanding to perceive it, but the heart also to feel it, let us more particularly consider that perfection of the divine nature, and those exertions of it which are fit for enflaming the affection. And, O Father of mercy, while I humbly attempt to delineate a portion of thy goodness, let thy grace influence all our hearts, so as to produce that love to thee which is the ornament of man here, and in which consists his perfection and happiness hereafter.

As I speak to an assembly who profess themselves disciples of Jesus, I shall at present omit the arguments that tend to establish those facts of of which you already are sufficiently persuaded. Let us then, my brethren, stretch our imaginations to the utmost, and contemplate, as well as our narrow faculties will permit, that exalted and infinite Being who has no wants to supply. View him from eternal ages, enjoying perfect felicity, and incapable of any addition of glory. Yet behold at once an act of the most unexampled power, and of the most disinterested goodness. He commands, and numberless worlds arise, replenished with life, and stored with the means of happiness. Those worlds which his power and his

[e] PSALM cxlv. 9.

goodness

goodnefs at firft formed, his goodnefs and his power ftill preferve, and from the inexhauftible fource of his bounty, all the bleffings that are poffeffed by the various order of beings, thro' the boundlefs extent of fpace, are folely derived. Could the eye of man furvey all thefe worlds, or his underftanding comprehend them, how reafonable is it to expect that they would all confent, both in declaring the glory, and proclaiming the goodnefs of their Author! But as it is only a fmall part of his works which we can comprehend, let us, my brethren, confider that fmall part with which we are beft acquainted, and take notice of fome of the moft obvious inftances of divine goodnefs.

OBSERVE how the influences of the fun, and the rains which defcend from heaven co-operate with other means in occafioning that never-ceafing fertility of this earth, by which provifion is made for the neceffities of man, and of every creature that inhabits it. Does not reafon, as well as religion, teach us to attribute this to the continued energy of nature's fovereign? Both informs us, that *the eyes of all things wait upon God. That he openeth his liberal hand, and fatisfieth the defire of every living thing* [c]. The grateful variations of day and night, the time for action, and the time for repofe, he conftituted them. The ufeful changes of the feafons are of his appointment. The mutual connection and fubferviency

[c] PSALM cxlv. 15, 16.

of the different animals, and their general subjection to man, proceed from his contrivance. Were I able, or did time permit, what an ample fund for difcourfe is here? All the works of nature, the air which we breathe, the light which directs us, the earth which yields us food, the water fo neceffary for our refrefhment, fo ufeful for the commerce of life; all, when confidered in connection with the living creatures for whofe fupport they are intended, prefent us with fo many diftinct proofs of the goodnefs of their creator. *Marvellous are thy works, Lord God almighty*[D]. The heavens and the earth fhow forth thy praife. In their continual revolutions, their voice to him that hath underftanding is, The goodnefs of our author and preferver is unfearchable. But I haften to trace fome of the marks of it with relation to man in particular. Who then beftowed upon thee, O man, that living and immortal foul of which thou art poffeft? Did not the almighty give it; a ray of his own luftre, a particle of divinity to dwell within thee, and direct thee? What conftant exertion of the fame goodnefs, my beloved brethern, has been requifite to preferve thofe fouls with which God has indued us? Through the journey of life, who has cared for you, and conducted you? When you firft faw the light, you entered upon a fcene befet with temptations, furrounded with dangers, and expofed on every fide to ftorms and tempefts. To all thefe, by

[D] REVEL. XV. 3.

your ignorance, inexperience, weakness, rashness, you have been a thousand times laid open. A ship this hour lies safe in the harbour; the sailors are all asleep. By some unforeseen accident the cables break, and upon a dangerous coast, the vessel is driven out to the raging sea, whose billows every moment are ready to overwhelm her, or dash her against the rocks; yet so deep a sleep hath seized the men, that none awake. This is an emblem, tho' a faint one, of many of the dangers of human life; and what but the watchful care of the universal Parent could preserve us in the midst of them!

But can you reflect upon no particular known, and striking interpositions of providence in your favour? Did you never in any instance see yourself so involved, that human aid (tho' even this is to be ascribed to God) could not have extricated you, and has not the deity appeared to relieve you? Was you never oppressed with such sickness and affliction, that your friends and physicians have given up every hope of your recovery, and yet you are alive at this day? Are there no parents here, who have despaired of their dearest child, whom yet God has been pleased to restore to them? Is there no husband who had the immediate prospect of shedding tears on the grave of the wife of his bosom, who yet lives in happiness with him? is there no faithful and affectionate wife, who yet retains the father of those children, whom her fears have represented overwhelmed with want, and plunged in calamity, when she thought she saw death striking the fatal blow,
which

SERMON VI.

which nothing but the divine goodnefs prevented? Obferve well your circumftances. Are you poffeffed of power, bleffed with riches, and favoured with health, happy in your friends, beyond the reach of your enemies? To whofe favour do you owe all thefe mercies? Who hath exempted you from adding one to the numerous family of the poor, the afflicted, the oppreffed, and the difconfolate? Ye fons of joy, amidft your profperity, obferve the hand which raifed you up; adore and love his goodnefs.

But the world and all its bleffings fade and difappear, when I furvey the miraculous difplay of mercy, which this facred book exhibits. Suppofe, my brethren, that fome perfon, who poffeffes a very large fhare of external enjoyments, whom his fellow-mortals rank among the few that are happy; but whofe views, as he is deftitute of the light of the gofpel, were moftly confined to the prefent life, and as to futurity, were dark, confufed, and uncertain, were to fit down and ferioufly confider his condition; would he not naturally entertain fuch reflections as thefe? I poffefs many of the enjoyments of life which I fee denied to numbers like myfelf. I poffefs eafe, and often enjoy pleafure, while others are oppreffed with labours, and tormented with pain. But in one thing I am on a level with the meaneft: I muft die as well as they. From undergoing this common lot of humanity, all my poffeffions cannot redeem me. When I die, whither I fhal go I know not; but experience informs me, that, whenfoever it is, nothing which I prefently

call

call mine can accompany me. I feel my own mind often difquieted by committing actions which I difapprove, and for which I greatly dread the difpleafure of the Author of my being, to whom I perceive myfelf accountable. When I leave life, perhaps his indignation, hitherto fufpended, may break out, and who knows how miferable I may be? This damps all my prefent joys, and how willingly would I part with all I have, in order to be afcertained of happinefs in that ftate which will fucceed the prefent, and which in all probability will laft much longer? Chriftian, learn to prize thy happinefs in being the difciple of a Mafter, who came to free thy mind from fuch uneafy reflections. For when involved in mifery there was no eye to pity us, providence interpofed, and the fcheme which to providence feemed fitteft for accomplifhing man's falvation, was by the facrifice of the fon of God. At the appointed time, Jefus, *the brightnefs of his Father's glory* [E], in whom dwelt the wifdom of the moft high, affumes our nature, appears among mankind, reveals a religion the moft pure and the moft perfect, and at laft, to propitiate the juftice of his Father, and to feal the truth of his religion, expires upon the crofs. Reflect upon the advantages which you derive from the religion of Jefus: acceptance with God, the pardon of tranfgreffion, peace of mind, and the hopes of everlafting felicity, and all this upon the eafy terms of trufting in God, acting like men, and living in conformity

[E] HEB. i. 3.

SERMON VI. 95

to reason and conscience. To persuade you to such a behaviour, what motives hath not Jesus laid before you? How plainly hath he delivered his laws? how strongly hath he enforced them? by what a perfect, and amiable example doth he excite you? and how frequently hath he assured you that the assistance of his Spirit is given to those who ask it?

OF purpose till now I deferred considering the evils of life, as an objection against the goodness of God, because the objection is most briefly and most satisfactorily answered from the christian religion. Do you then mourn under misfortunes opposite to the blessings I formerly mentioned, under poverty, oppression, loss of your dearest friends, sickness, and pain? See your Master suffering the greatest troubles, and yet not complaining: and shall the servant repine, when his Lord shares his fate? But farther, from the lectures of Jesus, observe what he hath often declared: *I go to prepare a place*[F] of repose and felicity for every follower, who patiently, as I did, endures the troubles of life. The righteous, tho' numbered among the dead, shall live with me, and their righteous friends shall meet them here, where the second death hath no power. To every sincere christian in this house hear him farther proclaiming in effect: The fleeting days of human life, my friends and followers, consider only as the entry to a divine and immortal life.

[F] JOHN xiv. 2, 3.

I have

I have marked out the road to glory. I have opened the gate of this heavenly kingdom. Struggle through the toils of a day, and an eternity of bliss with me your Master shall be your reward. Let worldly disappointments and losses teach you submission to your heavenly Father; let the blessings of life teach you gratitude. Lo here is the place where sorrow is no more, where tears are never shed, where friends never part, and where gratitude and love kindle such a flame in the human mind as is at once most pleasing to God, and delightful to man.

Has God, my brethern, given us his own son, and through his merits have we access to immortality? What is there then that is truly good for us which he will refuse us, after this proof of his mercy? Can you consider the supreme Being in those engaging lights, as your father, your friend, your surest guide through the temptations, dangers and difficulties of life, and your conductor to the mansions of everlasting felicity; and not be ready to own the reasonableness of love to him? Surely you do own it. But, christians, this is not sufficient. Do you feel it too? Does it now burn within you? Can you say with sincerity, My soul, O God, is thy workmanship, and with my whole soul I love thee!

If you are thus disposed, you will readily enter into the latter part of this discourse, which was designed to point out some of the reasons on account of which love to God may be termed the first and great commandment.

First

FIRST. It may be termed so, when we consider the feeling itself and its object. The former has something in it so disinterested, so generous, and noble, that experience teaches us (let the lovers of God bear witness) it gives an emotion unspeakably pleasing to the soul. It is the affection which, when regulated aright, is freer from alloy than any other. Fear damps the ardour of the mind. Humility gives it pain. Even gratitude itself, which I ever venerate, is attended with a sense of numerous wants. But love elevates the mind, expands the soul, takes us off from considering ourselves at all, and fixes us solely upon its object. And what is its object? Not power; for power may be unjustly exercised: not even wisdom; for wisdom may be sometimes employed in contriving the means of punishment; but goodness, and benevolence, and the highest degrees of these perfections, as they are exhibited in the character of the supreme mind.

SECONDLY, The great importance of love to God will appear, if we consider its effects. When this principle reigns in the mind, will it not produce universal obedience? What through the gospel of Jesus is always recorded as the natural effect, and what is always required as the surest proof of our loving God? Is it not obedience to his laws? *If ye love me, keep my commandments* [g]. *Ye are my friends, if ye do whatsoever I command you* [h]. *He that hath my commandments, and keepeth*

[g] JOHN xiv. 15. [h] JOHN xv. 14.

them, he it is that loveth me [1]. It cannot be otherwise. If we regard him as the best of beings, and love him as such, will we repine at any affliction of his appointment? Thus resignation is grafted on love. If this affection prevails in us, will we account any labour hard, any piece of duty too severe? Thus it becomes the parent of fortitude and patience. In one word, point out to me the man who is sincerely a lover of his Maker, I can assure you he venerates his laws, and though the infirmities of nature prevail sometimes over him, in general he obeys them.

Finally, Love to God is of the highest importance, as it is of the most extensive duration. There are many of the virtues and graces of the christian life which are designed only for the present state of mankind: the future state will not admit of their exercise. Here the wicked are ready to provoke and injure, and the christian ready to forgive and bless. Here faith must be cultivated as the firmest support of goodness and integrity of life: But there vision will come in its place. There the society will consist only of the good; the objects of resentment shall never be perceived, and where there can be no provocation there is no scope for forgiveness. Even the fear of God, while the vail of mortality prevents us from a more complete knowledge of him, continues to be mixed with something of the dread, which, when we shall see him as he

[1] John xiv. 21.

is, beneficent, gracious, and all benign, shall be ever excluded. But love shall ever abide, and ever increase in the human mind. God hath here planted the seed; the kindly influences of religion foster it. The cares of the world and the storms of life retard its growth; but in the hearts of good men it continues, though slowly, still to grow. At the death of the most pious it is only a tender plant; but when we shall arrive in happier climes, where no clouds overshadow the sun of righteousness, it shall take deeper root, and flourish with immortal verdure.

SERMON VII.

MATTHEW xxii. 39.

And the second is like unto it, Thou shalt love thy neighbour as thyself.

BLESSED *are the peace-makers, for they resemble God, and shall be called his children*; for ever blessed be the Saviour of mankind, who not only was, while he dwelt upon this earth, the greatest peace-maker himself, but also published a religion which was to descend to latest ages, the design of which is to expel enmity out of the world, and to make every man to consider his fellow-creature as his brother, and regard him with the same affection with which he regards himself.

In the verses preceding the text, a lawyer having enquired of our Saviour, *What is the first and great commandment?* he informs him, that it is to love God sincerely, fervently, and constantly, and that next to this the duty most important, is to love our neighbour. By our neighbour, according to the sentiments of our divine Lawgiver, is not to be underſtood, thoſe only who live in the ſame corner, or country, who are governed by the ſame laws, and ſubject to the ſame polity, but all who are connected by the ſame common tie of humanity. It is the command of this lawgiver, that we abound in love to all men, that we offer up ſupplications for them, and that we do good to every perſon as far as we have opportunity, *eſpecially to thoſe that are of the houſhold of faith.* Prejudices ariſing from education, from oppoſition of intereſt, from differences in religion, in the diſciples of Jeſus, muſt not reſtrain that univerſal good-will, which it is the very ſpirit of Chriſt's religion to promote. By his laws the Jews and Samaritans, tho' trained up with a peculiar degree of mutual rancour, were to conſider each other as neighbours and brethren. Thus every good chriſtian is what the philoſopher calls himſelf, a citizen of the world. Engraven upon his heart in indelible characters, which you may read in the tenor of his life, are piety and reverence to God, and love and friendſhip to the human race.

The law of univerſal benevolence preſcribed in the text, is indeed intended to comprehend thoſe private, but not leſs powerful affections, which regard a country, kindred, friends, benefactors, children, and the poor, from whence ariſe the virtues of patriotiſm, natural affection, gratitude, charity. Benevolence then may be conſidered as a leading principle of human nature, upon which all theſe are grafted. It may be compared to a venerable parent, whoſe numerous
offspring

SERMON VII. 103

offspring bear a strong resemblance to him, and are at once vigorous, healthy, and graceful.

But in order to give you a still more clear conception of the precept now before us, let us take notice of some of the most striking features in the character of that man who obeys it. The benevolent man wishes well to all; and though his own power is confined, he recommends them to that power that is unlimited. At the happiness of his fellow creatures he rejoices, and he is grieved for their misery. He shews the genuineness of these dispositions, by partaking in the joy of his acquaintance who happen to be successful, and by mingling his tears with those of the children of calamity. This fellow-feeling is not all. He uses his utmost efforts to promote the happiness of all within his sphere, and to prevent, or alleviate their sorrow. Not to defraud, or overreach, is but the least part of the praise which he deserves. In his commerce with men, those rules which others observe by constraint, and from dread of the law, he observes from inclination, from a pure heart and a good conscience. This is the character of a truly benevolent man. The benevolent christian attains a greater perfection in all these virtues by a steady imitation of that inexpressibly benevolent Mediator, who went about continually doing good, encouraging innocent chearfulness, wiping the tear from the eye of sorrow, restoring health to the diseased, and by every method promoting the temporal and spiritual advantage of mankind.

HAVING

HAVING thus explained the precept of loving our neighbour, I shall endeavour in the first place to point out the reasonableness of it. 2dly, Make some remarks upon the degree of this virtue required by our Saviour, *Thou shalt love thy neighbour as thyself*; and then endeavour to persuade you to the practice of it. May this discourse proceed from a heart overflowing with benevolence, and prove a means of impressing you with, or establishing you in this important grace of the gospel!

IN the first place, as briefly as possible, I shall endeavour to point out the reasonableness of the duty, the love of our neighbour. To discern the reasonableness of any duty there is no more needful, but a comparison of the nature of the being on whom the duty is enjoined, with the duty itself; and if it be found agreeable and congruous to that nature, it may be pronounced fit and reasonable. Now the most superficial view of human nature plainly discovers that benevolence is one of those principles of which it is compounded. It does not appear more evident that the eye is made for seeing, and the ear for hearing, than that the heart of man is so constituted, as to have an attachment to his fellow-creatures. If we saw a person take delight in hurting others, and involving them in misery without being prompted by any particular passion, but solely for the pleasure of doing ill, and becoming the author of misery, we should not hesitate to pronounce that person monstrous and unnatural. On the other hand, take any man and place him in society, we always expect

that

that where no contrary paffion that is more powerful interferes, he will be ready to delight in, and do good to the members of that fociety; and this without further view, than obeying the fimple dictates of his own mind. Read the hiftory of mankind, or narrowly obferve the actions which occur every day, and I think there is no poffibility of underftanding many fcenes in the former, or of comprehending many appearances of the latter, without fuppofing a principle of direct benevolence (that is, good-will to mankind) implanted in the human mind by its great Creator, abftracted from every view of private intereft, or even of public utility, into which fome have vainly endeavoured to refolve it.

WHAT has been faid is applicable not only to the general principle, but likewife to the particular virtues into which it may be branched out; fuch as love of our country, natural affection, gratitude, charity. We all acknowledge the reafonablenefs of thefe, by the applaufes we beftow upon thofe who poffefs them, and the high degree of difapprobation, of which we think thofe worthy who are deftitute of them. The man who betrays his country, who is cruel to his parents, ungrateful to his benefactors, or who hardens his heart againft the calls of mifery, we account a monfter. Such a perfon, as being deprived of the chief characterifticks of his kind, we call inhuman. He may poffefs the form, but he has fhaken off the nature of a man. Thus benevolence being a principle in our conftitution, the

reafon-reasonableness of the precept in the text is evident.

This would be farther established, were we to consider how absolutely and indispensably necessary, in a certain degree at least, it is for the very being and support of human life. For how long a period of life is man in a helpless condition, the most destitute of all animals, if his fellow-creatures did not give him their assistance! Exclude the principle of good-will in all its kinds, and the general lot of human life would be a short struggle with misery extreme; or rather without that principle there could be no such thing as human life: I am sure, not the least ray of human happiness. Add to this, that to the higher degree this second commandment is observed, man is in proportion so much the happier: and were it observed in perfection, the calamities of life would then be as few, as they are at present numerous. From these considerations, which might have been much enlarged upon, it is evident that the duty prescribed in the text, is truly fit and reasonable, becoming the nature, necessary for the condition, and productive of the happiness of mankind.

But the duty is not only prescribed, but likewise the measure of it pointed out. *Thou shalt love thy neighbour as thyself.*

It is the excellence of our religion, not only to propose the justest, and the best precepts with respect to our fellow-creatures, but also to afford us some marks, taken from what passes within ourselves,

SERMON VII.

in order to enable us to discern when they are rightly obeyed. Thus our actions are not only commanded to be honest, kind, and charitable, but also to be so in that degree, which we could reasonably desire those of others to be with regard to ourselves. *Whatsoever you would that men should do unto you, do ye also unto them* [k]. And in the text, we are not only commanded to wish well to others, and to love them, but also informed that our good-will then arrives at the christian degree of perfection, when it is in proportion to that affection which respects the individual; that is, the principle of benevolence ought to be as vigorous, as the principle of self-love. Desire to promote the good of mankind, equally with our own, is the elevated pitch to which christianity would exalt its votaries. A perfect disciple of Christ will be as tender about his neighbour's reputation, as he is about his own; as unwilling to spread a slanderous report of another, as he is uneasy to hear one of himself; as anxious to promote his brother's advantage, and as well pleased with the attainment of it, as he is joyful when something good happens to himself. When he is reproached, self-love leads him to justify himself; good-will prompts him to justify his neighbour whom he hears aspersed. Involve him in want, he feels pain and uneasiness, but religion and fortitude come in to his aid. If the case is his neighbour's, he not only feels pain and uneasiness on his account, but he employs all his efforts to relieve

[k] MATTHEW vii. 12.

him.

him. Let the firft difciples of Chrift bear teftimony to this character. They felt no want, but what was common. They knew no pain but what every one was willing to take his fhare of; no joy but what every heart made its own. They indeed confidered themfelves as *members of the fame body*, and acted in every refpect like thofe who believed the juftice of this allufion.

The reafonablenefs of our Saviour's precept of loving others as we love ourfelves may be difcerned if we attend to this, that benevolence is the principle by which we regard feveral individuals of the fpecies, felf-love that by which we regard one individual. When we confider the two feelings in this refpect, they appear directed to objects exactly alike, and therefore ought to be equal.

Before I leave this head, I fhall only make two remarks, as to the wifdom of fixing the degree of our felf-love as the meafure of our good-will to others.—In the firft place, as felf-love is generally a very ftrong principle in mankind, the precept, as delivered in our text, may prove a ftrong incitement to thofe who confefs the obligation of it, to increafe their good-will. Secondly, as felflove is very often apt to exceed its juft bounds, the confideration of its inferiority to our benevolence may lead us to endeavour, while we aim at increafing the latter, to bring the other to a more allowable pitch.

The nature of the fubject has drawn me into fome reafoning that may, to fome capacities, appear

pear rather too abstracted; though I have endeavoured to express myself as clearly as I could. The sum of what has been said is this: The love of our neighbour is altogether reasonable in itself, being conformable to that constitution which God has given us. Confined to no sect, party, or class of men; it ought to be universal. Besides this general principle of good-will, there are other separate principles, which attach us more strongly to our particular connections; but these are likewise comprehended in the text; and though they may encrease the force of the former with regard to those particulars, they ought not to weaken it with regard to the whole. By the perfect rule of our religion, a christian cannot rest satisfied with any measure of good-will to others, below what he bears to himself. O religion truly divine, which thus, by striking at the great root of our vices, an intolerable degree of selfishness, and a disregard to others, would at once cure us of them all, and render us like the angels in heaven, who in that happy clime, under the benign influences of the sun of righteousness, overflow with love and charity! Let me now, my beloved brethern, persuade you to the practice of the duty, upon which we have been discoursing, by presenting to you some of the most obvious and strongest motives.

In the first place, a generous, open, and benevolent heart, is ever attended with the most genuine pleasure; for to the exercise of love, gratitude, kindness, providence has annexed a most pure and unmixed joy. The mind of man
is

is defirous to grafp a large object, and pleafed with the conception of it; but are not the human race, our connection with them, a defire of their happinefs, truly grand and pleafing conceptions? Does the man, think you, whofe fituation puts it out of his power to extend his good deeds to mankind, feel no fatisfaction in dilating his foul, to wifh well to the whole, in recommending them to the univerfal parent, in fhedding the generous tear, when a tear is all he has to beftow, over the children of affliction? Afk himfelf. He will inform you, that the goods of this world fhould never be a bribe for him, to fteel his heart againft the calamities of the unfortunate, or deprive him of the joy of ranging through the great circle of God's creation, to wifh well to all rational beings. A contracted temper is always fretful, peevifh, and difquieted. The fources of its pleafures muft neceffarily be few and fcanty; whereas a benevolent difpofition is not only a fource of the higheft delight in itfelf, but it leaves a man open to the feveral gratifications of this life, and to all the innocent enjoyments that man is heir to. This temper both gives a relifh to a perfon's own proper pleafures, and appropriates to him thofe of his fellow-creatures. He rejoices with thofe that rejoice; and even when in the houfe of mourning he weeps with them that weep, there is a fecret charm which more than repays the forrow.

Again, would you wifh to act properly fo as to obtain the approbation of your fellow-creatures, and to appear amiable in their eyes? There is

not

not so effectual a method to procure the esteem and love of mankind, as to wish well to them, and to convince every one with whom you have intercourse, that you have their happiness at heart. Sympathy is the great bond of union among human souls. To raise any affection in the breast of another, the most direct course is to shew a similar one in your own. Thus the man possessed of the most generous and unlimited good-will, who considers his fellow-creatures as so many of his brethren, and is stedfast in all the offices of humanity, kindness and charity, is sure not only to be the object of approbation, but also the object of affection. Who is the sovereign that gains the affection of his people, the general that obtains the good-will of his army, the magistrate that attaches the regard of his citizens, the neighbour whom all that know speak well of? Is it not he, who shews that he deserves to be beloved, by first loving those with whom he is connected? Reflect upon the characters which always have been, and always are considered as the most amiable and engaging, and the circumstances which have made them be thought so; are they not those who have either been lovers of mankind, and of their country, or the friends of the fatherless and of the poor? Hath not history consecrated to immortality those who in heathen times impelled by a false religion, but with a view to save their country, willingly devoted themselves to destruction? Such an effect had this patriotism on those who were witnesses of it, that their veneration carried them beyond all reasonable bounds, in so much that they paid them

them divine honours. It muft be owned that with the greateft juftice the memory of thofe heroes is to this day highly regarded.

WHEN we read that Mofes abandoned the pleafures of a court, and of vice, for the fake of his people; when we confider his continual watchings for their happinefs, his prayers for their recovery after they had offended, his mild forbearance with their froward and rebellious temper; do we not behold him in the moft engaging view that man can be exhibited in? The fplendour of David's crown and the luftre of his royalty are quite eclipfed by the glory of the man, when we fee remorfe for his fin, and love for his people, prompting thefe generous fentiments. *I have finned; but for thefe fheep what have they done? Let thy hand be againft me and againft my father's houfe* [b]. How amiable is the character of the moft patient man, who in the depth of his diftrefs, was able to make this noble appeal to heaven. *Did I not weep for him that was in trouble? Was not my foul grieved for the poor* [c]? *I was eyes to the blind, and feet was I to the lame; the bleffing of him that was ready to perifh came upon me, and I caufed the widow's heart to fing for joy* [d]. But above all, how divinely engaging is the character of Chrift Jefus, who fhewed the moft illuftrious inftance of good-will to men that the world ever faw; for he came to be a ranfom for

---

[b] I CHRON. xxi. 17.   [c] JOB XXX. 25.
[d] JOB XXXI. 13. 15.

SERMON VII.

many, and to purchase their redemption; he led a life of unexampled sorrow, and suffered a death overwhelming to all the powers of humanity. *Greater love hath no man than this, that a man should lay down his life for his friends; but God commendeth his love to us, in that while we were yet sinners Christ died for us* [E]. O Jesus, let all nations bow down before thee, and let all people praise thee, for thy love to mankind is inexpressible!

But finally, brethern, consider, as a motive to engage you to universal good-will, and to all the offices of kindness and charity, that this is the only way truly to shew yourselves the disciples of Christ Jesus. *By this shall all men know that ye are my disciples, if ye love one another.* This, saith he, *is my commandment, that ye love one another, as I have loved you*; and again, *a new commandment I give unto you, that ye love one another* [F]. Deceive not yourselves; if the spirit of love dwelleth not in you, ye are strangers to the power of Christ's religion. You may wear the appearance of religion, but if you be addicted to ill-will, hatred, revenge, uncharitableness, though you should artfully endeavour to conceal them, in the sight of God you are at best but whited sepulchres, and to you the new testament applies all the woes pronounced against the Pharisees, those hypocrites of old, by the infallible Teacher of mankind. Above all things, then, my brethren,

[E] John xv. 13. Rom. v. 8. [F] John xiii. 34, 35.

have fervent charity, and remember that this commandment we have from Chrift, *that he who loveth God, love his brother alfo*^G. If you have any refentments, now lay them afide. If you have a contracted fpirit, give yourfelves no reft till you overcome it; *and put on, as the elect of God, holy and beloved, bowels of mercies, kindnefs, humblenefs of mind, meeknefs, long-fuffering, forbearing one another, and forgiving one another, if any man have a quarrel againft any; even as Chrift forgave you, fo alfo do ye; and above all thefe things, put on charity, which is the bond of perfectnefs*^H.

^G 1 JOHN iv. 21.   ^H COL. iii. 12, 13, 14.

SERMON VIII.

COLOSSIANS iii. 14.

And above all these things, put on charity, which is the bond of perfectness.

THE same word which in this verse, and in several other parts of the new testament is translated *charity*, is also frequently rendered *love*, Thus *Walk in love* [A]; *follow after righteousness godliness, faith, love* [B]. I may further remark to you, that the word is derived from that which our Saviour uses in the following passages, and many others of the same import. *Thou shalt love thy neighbour as thyself* [C]. *This is my commandment, that ye love one another* [D]. By this expression, *the bond of perfectness*, is meant, that this love or charity is the most perfect bond of human society, that it is that virtue which, if properly exerted, would retain men in the practice of all those duties which they owe to one another, and prevent

[A] EPH. V. 2. [B] 1 TIM. vi. 11. [C] MATTH. xix. 19.
[D] JOHN XV. 12.

those vices which occasion so much disturbance and present misery.

From these words I might properly draw several subjects of discourse; but I purpose only at this time to explain the nature and properties of christian charity.

Charity may be defined that disposition which inclines us to think and speak well of our fellow-creatures, and to deal kindly with them. Mere benevolence, or good-will, regards the beneficence of our actions, and our disposition to do good. Charity includes this, but respects more immediately the sentiments and affections which we feel towards others. Under the definition now given, are comprehended various virtues, to which in the ordinary intercourses of life we give different names. Thus it comprehends candour in our judgments, fairness in our actions, humanity and kindness in our whole behaviour. It also implies the absence of several of the blackest vices of human nature, malice, envy, falseness, deceit, cruelty, oppression, slander. Charity in this respect may be compared to a liberal fountain, giving rise to a large river, which in its course divides itself into several branches, and disperses health and plenty over the country thro' which it runs. And as this disposition of mind we are considering may properly be denominated the parent of many distinct virtues; so it may be remarked, that a small variation in the objects towards which it is exercised occasions its being called by different appellations. Thus, our love to mankind is termed

SERMON VIII.

termed benevolence; our love to our country, patriotifm; our love to our friends, friendfhip; our love to our kindred or families, affection. Neither is it furprizing that from the fame fimple original quality fhould proceed fuch various and extenfive effects. We may obferve in the natural world, that from the fame feed arife many ftalks, each containing many ears of the fame kind that was fown. From a fmall feed arifeth a tree with a trunk, branches, and leaves, between which and the feed depofited in the ground, the moft fharp-fighted can trace no refemblance, and which produceth in its turn many feeds of the fame kind. There is a likenefs and analogy between thefe things and the principles of our minds; or perhaps the qualities of the latter admit ftill of greater and more furprifing variations. The fimple, original qualities of our mind are probably not very numerous; but they are, as it were, feeds fown by the hand of the Creator, which gradully expand themfelves, grow up, and affume very various and diftinct appearances. The fimple quality itfelf requires fome abftraction and attention to obferve it; like a fmall feed, fcarcely vifible to the naked eye, but its effects are obvious to every perfon.

As charity therefore comprehends fo many virtues, and has fuch extenfive influence on the conduct of life, both in impelling to that which is right, and in reftraining from that which is wrong; it will be much more ufeful to confider it with refpect to its effects and confequences, than to regard it merely in an abftract light. And to render

der what I have to fay as practical as poffible, I fhall confider the influence of charity upon the mind and behaviour of a chriftian with refpect to the world; with refpect to his country; with refpect to thofe whom he is connected in the fame city, neighbourhood, or fociety; with refpect to thofe who differ from him in religious principles or opinions; with refpect to his enemies; and with refpect the vicious and abandoned.

First, Let us confider the effect of charity with refpect to the world. The furvey of the narrownefs of our prefent power and fphere of action, of the extent of our capacity of thought and perception, gives us the profpect of a contraft that is very wonderful. Our power of beftowing happinefs upon others, or procuring it to ourfelves is very limited; but our thought can range from one region to another, and travel with the lightning of heaven. Before we can move thofe clogs of mortality which we wear, from one ftreet to another, our imaginations are able to encompafs the globe, or to vifit the ftars. We find that the defires and affections of our nature are not fuited to our powers of action, but to our capacity of thought and imagination; and the man who entertained no wifhes, inclinations, or propenfions, but fuch as his prefent power could gratify or accomplifh, would be fcarce fuperior to a reptile, notwithftanding his form. When we compare our connections and acquaintance, thofe with whom we interchange mutual good offices, with the general body of mankind, they are limited within very narrow bounds, and confined to a ve-

ry

ry small number: but there is a strong law, the law of humanity, which connects us with all who are endowed with the same nature. No impassable mountains, no innavigable oceans, no inhospitable deserts, are boundaries to intercept the force and authority of this law. Like the sun it extends its heat and its influence to the utmost corner of the earth, and proves a connecting principle with all our fellow-creatures.

SUITABLE to this general and extensive law of humanity, christian charity requires that we wish well unto all, and offer supplications to God upon their account. *I exhort, therefore,* says the apostle to Timothy, *that supplications, prayers, intercessions, and giving of thanks be made for all men* [e].

BY our neighbour, according to our Saviour's religion, is not to be understood, one who lives in the same country, who is governed by the same laws, or subject to the same polity; but every one who is endowed with the same nature. To every such person, whether Christian, Jew, Pagan, or Mahometan, we are to abound in love, and to do good whenever we have opportunity. A good christian, when he thinks of the miseries, blindness, errors, and vices which prevail in the world, will surely out of a pure heart, and a good conscience, pray to the Father of mercy to remove them, and in the fervour of his spirit, and the sincerity of his love, with *that all the kingdoms of the*

[e] I TIM. ii. 1.

earth

earth may become the kingdoms of our God, and of his son Jesus Christ.

SECONDLY, Let us consider the influence of charity upon the temper and conduct of a christian with respect to his country. As the Almighty has divided men into kingdoms and nations upon the face of the earth, it is a part of the constitution of providence that we receive particular benefits from certain laws, governments, and tracts of country. This gives us a particular connection with certain communities, and in a well-disposed mind confers upon the principle of charity, the modification of love of our country. Now charity in this respect obligeth us to pray for the prosperity of our country, and to contribute to it as far as is in our power. It requires us to pay a deference to the laws, and to respect and obey our lawful governors, to contemn honours, power, or interest, when they cannot be obtained in a consistence with the laws; and to sacrifice private and partial views to the happiness of the state. These are general obligations upon every man: neither are they to be reckoned hard or severe; for in experience, I believe it will be found, that the love of our country, reverence and obedience to its laws, prove the surest path to the true happiness of individuals. And surely the consideration of the free and happy constitution under which we live, of the general justice and equity of our laws, of the security that is commonly possessed not only for our lives, but for our interests and property, ought to strengthen and increase in every Briton this sentiment of love to his country.

That what has been now advanced is entirely agreeable to the spirit and tenor of the scripture, is manifest. With what warmth does every Jew speak of the city of Jerusalem, and of that people who were separated by the Lord from all the nations of the earth? How affectionately does our Saviour speak of the same people, and what earnestness and anxiety does he discover for their welfare! But still farther; tho' at the time of his coming they were retained in subjection to a foreign power, so far from encouraging any rebellious sentiments against their conquerors, or using any means, as they imagined, that he would, to deliver them from their oppression, he teaches that it was their duty, *to render unto Cæsar the things that are Cæsar's* [F], and refuses not himself the jurisdiction of a court, where a governor of his appointment presided. The doctrine that is delivered in the 13th chapter of the epistle to the Romans is entirely conformable to these sentiments. *Let every soul be subject unto the higher powers*, (says the apostle) *for there is no power but of God: the powers that be are ordained of God: Whosoever therefore resisteth the power, resisteth the ordinance of God. Wherefore ye must not only be subject for wrath, but for conscience sake.* What has been before said relates to the duty of men in general with respect to their country. I may add, that the principle

[F] Mark xii. 14.

of love of our country lays particular obligations upon men in particular circumstances. Thus it is the duty of the statesman to consult and deliberate for the good of his country, of all officers of justice to administer equity impartially, of the soldier and sailor to encounter the enemies of the state with bravery, and of all who have any public trust to execute it with integrity.

Thirdly, Let us consider the influence of the law of charity with respect to those who live in the same city, neighbourhood, or society. There are many whose views are so narrow, and whose knowledge is so confined, that they scarcely form to themselves conceptions of the general body of mankind, or even of that large community of which they are members. We feel ourselves more ready to pity the ignorance, than to condemn the vice of such men. But there are none who have the natural use of reason, who are not sensible of their connection with their fellow-citizens, or neighbours, or with that particular society or order of men to which they belong. And here, if all the effects of love and charity were to be withheld, the foundations of society would be overturned. Our state would be much worse than that of those miserable savages who live in the woods, support themselves upon the fruits which nature spontaneously produces, and fear a foe in every man they meet. From the constitution of providence the boast of absolute independence, or even of independence upon our fellow-creatures is altogether vain and chimerical. In social life how could the rich be cloathed or fed, or have their

houses

houses furnished, or their numerous wants supplied, if it were not for the poor, the laborious, and the industrious? What is the title of a sovereign if he has no subjects, but an empty name? What arduous deed could a general perform, if he were deserted by all his troops?

In human life we are linked together by a chain formed by the hand of Omnipotence, and to this connection both duty and necessity should engage us to submit. With regard therefore to those of our fellow-creatures with whom we have immediate intercourse, the law of charity obligeth us to act with all fairness, honesty, sincerity, and kindness. It obligeth the rich to refuse the gains of oppression, to be mild, merciful, ready to relieve the wants of the indigent, and compassionate the wretched brethern of their nature. It obligeth those in an inferior station to be just and faithful in their service, submissive in their behaviour, and grateful for the good offices they receive. It obligeth all men to be candid in their interpretation of one anothers actions and intentions, to bear with one anothers frailties, and to forgive each others faults. Such behaviour every person expects, and thinks reasonable with regard to himself; and no rule can be more equitable, than to do to others as we would that others should do to us.

But in society the characters of men, and the relations on which we stand to them are so different, that the application of the law of charity is almost infinitely varied. To explain more fully the nature of this virtue, let us consider,

FOURTHLY, The effects it will produce with respect to those who differ from us in religious principles and opinions. Upon this subject there are two opposite sentiments; both of which seem to me to be erroneous.

FIRST, Some think, that error in religious principle is so fatal and damnable, that they can have no good thoughts of those men who entertain it, and cannot believe that any who are so unacceptable in the sight of God can be entitled to any particular offices of kindness or charity, and if they would speak out, scarcely to the common duties of humanity. Such sentiments shock all our feelings. Our Saviour disapproves of them in the strongest manner, when he rebukes the forward zeal of his followers who desired to destroy those that refused to admit him into their city, by calling for fire from heaven. Surely men who think in this way, know not what spirit they are of [G].

ON the other hand, many seem to think, that there is no necessity nor propriety in giving one's self concern about religious opinions, provided the practice be upright and honest. But certainly truth deserves our search. Just opinions influence our conduct in many degrees. In many

[G] LUKE ix. 54, 55.

SERMON VIII.

inftances, even in ways that we cannot now conceive, they may promote our future happinefs, or under the government of God, the want of them may occafion much future wretchednefs and diftrefs. To maintain pure, therefore, the faith that we believe to have been delivered to the faints, is our duty; and zeal in the propagation of it becomes a chriftian. But what is that zeal? Is it the zeal of a furious party-man, of an enthufiaft, or a perfecutor? No; thefe characters are deteftable. Is it not then the zeal of a reafonable enquirer, of an honeft and a good man, who truly believes, and firmly maintains his opinions, who at the fame time that he endeavours to rectify the errors of his fellow-creatures, yet pities thofe who are mifled by thefe errors, becaufe he knows himfelf to be expofed to error? Is it a zeal about modes, ceremonies, and the externals of religion? Or is it about matters of which the importance is obvious? Surely the latter. A man may properly think that nothing relating to religion is of fo little confequence as not to engage his attention; but the weightier matters of the law will employ his thoughts much more than the lefs weighty.

CHRISTIAN charity will then engage the man who is actuated by it to differ with temper, to reafon with moderation, to try to convince by the weight of his arguments, not by the violence of his paffions. He knoweth *that the wrath of man worketh not the righteoufnefs of God*[H], The

[H] JAMES i. 20.

fervant

servant of the Lord will not strive, but be gentle unto all men, apt to teach, patient, in meekness instructing them that oppose themselves [1]. As he will try to convince, so he will be ever open to hear, and to weigh the reasons of his adversaries. Sensible of the weakness of human nature, and in how different lights the same thing appears to different men, yea even to the same man at different times, he will still maintain his differences in the bond of peace. He will not assume the strange work of the Lord, or denounce the judgments of heaven; but rather hope that in some future period, both he himself and those that oppose him may be brought to see more clearly, and have all their errors dispelled. Let Mahometans employ the sword to bring men to the obedience of their prophet, and to reduce them to uniformity in religion; but O that christians never had forgot that the voice which ushered in their Master into the world proclaimed peace on earth and good-will to men, and that the weapons by which he establishes his kingdom are not carnal, but spiritual!

FIFTHLY, Let us consider in what manner christian charity should engage us to behave to our enemies.

THERE is no principle in human nature more apt to exert itself than resentment, when we meet with any treatment that we judge improper, undeserved, or severe. The first feeling is natural, unavoidable, and necessary in the present situation of mankind; but the due moderation

---

[1] 2 TIM. ii. 24, 25.

SERMON VIII.

and restraint of it commonly exposes us to one of the hardest trials that we meet with in life. Herein then consists the victory and triumph of the christian, that the greatest and most unprovoked injuries he always abstains from revenging. His honesty and his candour are too great not to let his enemy know, that he is sensible of the ill-treatment he has met with, but his charity and self-government are so great, that he suffers no injurious expression to pass his lips; and were his foe in his power, his first attempt would be to reclaim him by meekness, gentleness, and true greatness of mind; and upon his repentance, he would cordially be reconciled to him, and receive him as his brother. If that were rendered impracticable, the utmost length he would go would be to deprive him of the power of repeating the like injustice; or if his crime deserved the interposition of the magistrate, he might deliver him to the just punishment of the laws; but every impartial spectator might observe the uneasiness he felt at being compelled to such severity.

Do you think this pitch of virtue surpasses human nature? We sometimes, though rarely, see that pride produceth this forgiveness, as thinking the person who has offended below consideration: and shall the noblest virtue of the human heart be thought less powerful upon all occasions than a bad quality is sometimes? I am sure no duty can be more plainly required, or more strongly insisted upon, than this great duty is in the gospel. *If thy brother*, says our Saviour, *trespass against thee, rebuke him; and if he repent, forgive him;*

him; *and if he trespass against thee seven times in a day, and seven times in a day turn again to thee, saying, I repent, thou shalt forgive him* [k]. Upon every interpretation that these words will admit, they show that the christian must carry this temper of forgiveness to the highest pitch. Again, says our Saviour, *Love your enemies, bless them that curse you, do good to them that hate you, and pray for them that despitefully use you, and prosecute you* [l]. The same virtue is strongly recommended in that parable which is contained in the 18th chapter of Matthew, where the king is represented as taking an account of his servants, and punishing that one severely who shewed no mercy to his fellow. It concludes with these remarkable words, *So likewise shall my heavenly Father do also unto you, if ye from your hearts forgive not every one his brother their trespasses.*

LASTLY, Let us consider the influence of christian charity on our behaviour with respect to the vicious and abandoned. A hatred of vice is natural to an upright mind, and the feeling this is one of the strongest symptoms of a good disposition, and one of the surest guards of virtue. That we should incline to associate with the just, and feel a stronger attachment to them, and that on the contrary we should abstain from the company of the vicious, is surely lawful, prudent, and commendable. But there are many occasions in life, where unless, as the apostle speaketh, *we*

[k] LUKE xvii. 3.   [l] MATTH. V. 24.

were

were to go out of the world, we cannot avoid meeting with the impious, the unjust, and the intemperate. It would perhaps be neither good for them, nor for ourselves, that we resolved never to meet with them. The worst are still connected with us while in this world, by the great tie of humanity; and when we consider the misery of vice, and the future punishment that awaits it, a charitable mind is apter to commiserate than to detest.

In these instances, charity therefore obligeth us to take all proper opportunities of instructing, of admonishing, of reproving, of shewing our disapprobation of the crime, and yet our love of the criminal. Of all the weapons ever yet devised, to bend the wills, alter the temper, and subdue the hearts of men, severity, sourness, bitterness, anger, are the least agreeable to a good mind, and the least successful in themselves. Whereas meekness, gentleness, and yet firmness, the awe and authority of virtue, without the forbidding air of stubbornness, the soft and amiable charms of true goodness, the generosity of sympathy, the mild, yet penetrating words prompted by these dispositions, prove the most powerful means, and have the strongest influence in gaining sinners, in restraining them from vice, and in winning over willing subjects to the interests of true religion.

SERMON IX.

Psalm li. 17.

The sacrifices of God are a broken spirit; a broken and a contrite heart, O God, thou wilt not despise.

It is extremely probable that this psalm, in which the sentiments of a true penitent are so strongly expressed, was composed by David, after a sense of his guilt had been raised by the affecting parable of Nathan, which we read in the xiith chapter of the second book of Samuel, and of which the occasion and consequences are so well known. This whole composition discovers a mind overwhelmed with sorrow, agitated with remorse, earnest for mercy, and penetrated with all that variety of emotions, which the reflection upon flagrant crimes, when it is neither blunted by obduracy nor irritated by despair, so naturally inspires.

In compositions of this kind, we are not to expect a strict connection of thought. Such a connection would totally destroy their beauty, and be a sure proof that the passion of grief, and the feelings of penitence which they exhibit, were affumed, not real. Their true merit confifts in the correfpondence of the fentiments and expreffions, to that animated and varied tenour of foul, from which they are fuppofed to flow. Confidered in this light, the pfalm before us abounds with beauties that muft ftrike every fenfible reader. In the 14th and 16th verfes, David implores, in the moft fervent manner, deliverance from the guilt of that blood, which he had fo caufelefsly and bafely fhed, the recollection of which crime rendered him unable to addrefs the God of purity with confidence and freedom till he had received fome affurance of his pardon. *Deliver me from blood-guiltinefs, O God, thou God of my falvation, and my tongue fhall fing aloud of thy righteoufnefs. O Lord, open thou my lips, and my mouth fhall fhew forth thy praife.* The reflection upon his guilt naturally brings to his mind thofe facrifices which were commonly thought to be of an expiatory nature, but which, as we may learn from various places of the pfalms, David well knew to be of no value on their own account, and to be only fo far acceptable to God, as they were accompanied with fuitable difpofitions in the offerer. *For thou defireft not facrifice, elfe would I give it ; thou delighteft not in burnt offering* [A]. But he knew well that the fentiments of penitence, and the meltings of heart occafioned by them, had an intrinfic worth, and a natural propriety. The facrifice never failed to be acceptable, when attended with

[A] VER. 16.

SERMON IX.

such a temper; and without any external sacrifice, this temper was always a pleasing and efficacious offering. *The sacrifices of God are a broken spirit; a broken and a contrite heart, O God, thou wilt not despise.* The metaphorical expression of a *broken spirit* is readily understood, and the repetition of the sentiment, which in the latter part of the verse is thrown into the form of an address to God, not only leaves a stronger impression, but is extremely natural, as it marks that hope and comfort, which are intermingled with the grief of a penitent, when he reflects upon the mercy and placability of God.

It were needless to consume more time in explaining the proposition contained in the text, which is of itself so intelligible, namely, that a penitent disposition, or unfeigned sorrow for past offences is acceptable to the Almighty. But I think it may be both an agreeable and useful employment, to trace, if possible, some of those causes, on account of which repentance is reckoned in scripture so important a virtue, and declared to be so pleasing to God. This enquiry, if it is properly prosecuted, will discover to us the reasonableness, and the necessity of a penitent disposition, and furnish an opportunity of obviating those objections, which may be thrown out upon this subject.

I would only premise, that when we trace the reasons on account of which repentance, or in the language of the text, *a broken and a contrite heart*, is so acceptable to God, it is not necessary to suppose

pose that man is so constituted, as to be capable of discerning the whole, or even the principal of them. There may be relations and fitnesses of the most important nature, and those immediately regarding human characters, to which most men, perhaps the wisest, are entire strangers. And though an ignorance of the ends that are promoted, and of the manner in which they are promoted by a certain temper and behaviour, no doubt forms some presumption against the connection between the means and the end, yet this presumption may be overcome in many different ways. B t still it is to be remembered, that our Maker is pleased in most cases, not only to point out our duty to us, but also to lay open the reasons or grounds of its different branches; and when we plainly discern any part of our conduct, or any disposition of our mind, to be adapted to the general constitution of man, or productive of good effects, we are naturally led to conclude, that this fitness and tendency, though, as far as we see them, they may not be the sole or principal causes of the divine approbation, do yet in some measure determine the Deity to bestow his approbation. Let us therefore proceed to consider, with all humility and attention, what those circumstances are, in a penitent disposition, upon which its amiableness and usefulness depend, and which render it acceptable to God.

In the first place: I would observe, that when a person has violated the laws of heaven, and acted contrary to the dictates of his own conscience,

it

SERMON IX.

it is a part of his conftitution, that the reflection upon his guilt fhould fill him with remorfe.

It is a part of the duty of confcience, to condemn our evil actions after they are committed, as well as to warn us againft them before-hand, and excite us to avoid them. In giving way therefore to the natural feelings of the mind, when they are prompted by reafon, and have the fanction of confcience, there is, independent of the utility of fuch a conduct, fomething fo amiable in the eye of man, that we cannot but fuppofe it at the fame time acceptable in the fight of God.

In many inftances, the reftraining and moderating of the natural feelings of the mind, is one confiderable part of our duty; but the fuppreffing or counteracting of them altogether, though this has fometimes been the boafted aim of philofophy, is plainly reverfing the work of God, and diftinctly oppofing that intention which is difcovered to us in the conftruction of our inward frame. Were there nothing more in contrition and forrow of heart for paft fins, but merely giving fcope to that felf-reproach, which confcience excites on their account, we muft neceffarily approve the exercife of it. In like manner, we cannot but condemn the perfon who, though he has given the jufteft occafion for fuch fentiments of remorfe, is altogether a ftranger to them.

If it be objected, that what is paft cannot be recalled, that an action already committed cannot be altered, or cancelled by the tears that are now fhed shed for it: I answer, Because I cannot recall what is past, because my future conduct cannot cancel or obliterate my former sins, therefore disquiet and compunction take hold of my mind; and by indulging this compunction to a certain degree, I am sensible that I act in conformity to the best principles of my nature, and I approve of such conduct, as I do in many other cases, without reflecting upon the advantage with which it may be attended. When one hears the last groan of an only child, or lends a hand to close his eyes, the tear naturally falls, and grief takes possession of the soul. We approve of that tear, and sympathize with this grief: but will a river of tears recal to its ancient receptacle the departed spirit, or, as far as we know, procure the least benefit to that object of our affection for whom they are shed? Yet the man whose eyes are dry from considerations of this kind, we condemn as an unsusceptible and selfish being, who refuses to endure a pain which his nature prompts him to suffer, because it cannot contribute to the completion of his desires.

Thus the consideration that sorrow for our past offences is natural to the human mind, or, in other words, conformable to that constitution which God has given us, affords us just reason to conceive that they will meet with his approbation and acceptance. I have said that it affords us just reason to conceive, because I am sensible, that what has now been said, would prove too weak a foundation for supporting the assurance of his acceptance, if we had nothing to aid us in our research

SERMON IX.

research but the light of nature. But every one will observe that to investigate the reasonableness of a doctrine that is revealed, is quite a different thing from establishing the certainty of the same doctrine, if no revelation had been granted to us.

I HAVE not in this discourse used any arguments to prove that remorse is natural to a guilty mind: Every man is sensible that it is. We are surprized when we meet with any person, who is not filled with horror by the consciousness of an atrocious crime which he has perpetrated. Malefactors when they allow themselves to think, seldom fail to experience this horror, which is the first step to true penitence.

BUT the suitableness of a penitent disposition to the nature of man, is not the sole reason for supposing it acceptable to God. I proceed therefore to observe in the second place, that this contrition seems to be absolutely necessary, in order to produce a change of temper, and a reformation of conduct.

IF this shall appear to be the case, it will be one of the many instances which evince, that what is conformable to our natures, promotes at the same time the most important ends. Now if a person commits a crime, for which he feels no compunction, place him in the like circumstances, and what reason is there to think that he will abstain from repeating it? He was surely seduced at first by the violence of some passion, the force
of

of some appetite, or the desire of some end that perhaps had been allowable if it had been attained by lawful means. If the same passion assails him, if the same appetite urges him, or the same desirable end is to be attained by the like unlawful means, for what reason will he abstain from an action, the commission of which never gave him an hour's uneasiness? Cain slew his brother Abel in the field; and from the history it does not appear that at first he was touched with remorse. Was any thing more wanting but another brother, and the like envy and resentment, to induce him to repeat the crime? It is true, that though some considerable time elapsed, between David's first guilty step, and the message which God sent him by Nathan, he had only seduced one Bathsheba, and murdered one Uriah; but if like beauties had in the interval kindled like unlawful desires, and if other Uriahs had obstructed their gratification, what reason is there to think, that the sacredness of wedlock, or the respect for a brave and guiltless servant, would have restrained him? Attend to the matter as it is considered in common life. If a person commits an unjust action, for which he feels no shame or remorse, suppose a theft; will any person of common sense, who knows this, trust to his honesty in the like situation?

But where the feelings of penitence take possession of the mind, they naturally and unavoidably alter the disposition, and have a direct influence in reforming the conduct. The stings of conscience, the meltings of sorrow, the prayers for pardon, the solemn renunciations of sin and the

the refolutions of amendment, all which are included in penitence, prove fo many powerful arguments, to refift the violence of thofe paffions which have produced fo much pain. They will probably abate the ftrength and impetuofity of unlawful defires: they will certainly prove natural curbs and reftraints to prevent us from indulging thefe. They are evidently ftrong incentives to prefer for the future the peaceful and fedate enjoyments of virtue, and to abandon for ever the tumultuous, but difquieting pleafures of vice. After David had fo often *watered his couch with his tears* ᴸ, after he had in fuch bitternefs of fpirit compofed his penetential pfalms; how ftrongly muft his foul have been fortified againft the indulgence of a criminal paffion? How determined muft he naturally have been againft incurring the guilt of innocent blood, which had already occafioned in his foul fuch exquifite torments? Can it be reckoned unfair to conclude, that the remorfe which agitated the mind of Peter, when he *wept bitterly* ᴹ upon denying his Mafter, and the refolutions with which his penitence for a conduct fo daftardly and mean infpired him, contributed greatly to render him fo intrepid during the remainder of his life, fo daring in the time of danger, and fo unfhaken in the midft of the moft unjuft and violent perfecutions? In common life we always fuppofe (which is a ftrong proof of the natural tendency of repentance) that a perfon who has been guilty of a bad action, and fuffered

---

ᴸ PSALM vi. 6.   ᴹ MATT. xxvi. 75.

the

the compunctions of penitence, will avoid a repetition of that which caused them; and, in order to have a reasonable security for his good behaviour, and to dispose us to trust him, the chief difficulty lies in determining whether his penitence was feigned, or real. You will readily see, that by penitence, we here mean not those violent sallies of grief, which are to be discovered in some of the most fluctuating and variable characters, but that anguish of heart, that humiliation before God, those resolutions, and those efforts, which repentance is commonly understood to imply.

With regard to the curbs, or restraints which real penitence for particular crimes naturally lays upon the mind, it is further to be observed that, though they principally relate to those crimes, which occasioned the penitence, they are not confined to them. It is natural, almost unavoidable, that they should be extended to vice in general, and particularly to all vices that are of a more atrocious nature. A man who has deeply repented of an expression injurious to his neighbour, will not only have strong motives to guard against calumny in his conversation, but doubtless will be equally cautious of giving a false testimony against his neighbour in a court of justice. The thought is so obvious, it cannot fail to occur. If an injurious expression dropt in common discourse subjected me to such remorse, what will be the consequence, what must I feel, if in a public trial I give a solemn testimony that shall be equally false? This observation might be illustrated

trated by a thousand other instances, but I think it is sufficiently intelligible from what I have said.

Thirdly, In order to shew the importance of a penitent disposition, and the reason of its being so acceptable to God, I would remark, that it puts the soul in a proper frame for receiving the impressions of virtue in general. I only observed before, that it had a natural tendency to restrain us from vice, and to engage us to form resolutions against it. This leads a step farther. The mind of man has been compared to a soil, which requires preparation and culture before the seed can be thrown into it with advantage. In the same manner there are certain dispositions of mind which are friendly to the lessons of virtue, and to the precepts of religion. When the soul is softened with repentance, then is the hour to inculcate the maxims of purity and holiness, and to animate to a virtuous conduct. I do not say that it is the only season; but surely it will be allowed that it affords one proper opportunity for this purpose. If you had a pupil whom you were anxious to train up to virtue, when could you hope more effectually to inspire him with the love of mercy, gentleness, and equity, than when he repented of some rash, injurious, or severe action? If we were to inculcate a prudent and discreet behaviour upon any neighbour or friend, to whom we wished well, when could we choose a fairer occasion, than when he felt and lamented the ill consequences of a foolish step? In a word, when would we judge a person to have a proper degree of

tractableness

tractableness and sensibility, an aptness to imbibe instruction, and a disposition to retain it, if not when his heart is softened, his conscience alarmed, his abhorrence of guilt strong, and his purposes and aims already pointed to piety and virtue?

It was probable this natural tendency of a contrite spirit which induced our Saviour to make it an indispensible requisite in those who come to him. He called not the righteous, that is, those who had a high opinion of their own merit, but sinners, or those who were deeply penetrated with a sense of their own guilt. To the same purpose he declares that he is the physician not to the whole, but to the sick. Publicans and sinners resorted to him, and if they had obeyed the instruction of his forerunner, who admonished them to repent, they never were rejected. Many of the parables which our Saviour delivered, represent the same truth in the strongest manner. Penitence may therefore be considered as the ground-work of virtue, or the culture that prepares the soul for its reception.

In the fourth place, I observe, that as it has this tendency in general, so it is particularly calculated for the improvement and exercise of some of the most capital virtues of the christian life. If we consider any one virtuous disposition, as prevailing in the mind, it has probably a remote tendency to form a complete character of virtue and holiness, and lays a foundation for those virtues that least resemble itself. It has some kind of attractive quality with respect to every thing that
bears

SERMON IX.

bears the same general character: but the attractive quality becomes much more vigorous and discernible, with respect to those virtues, that are of the most similar and congenial nature. In that case the mind passes with the greatest facility and readiness from the former to the latter, and the force of the prevailing principle naturally spreads, and communicates itself. The application of this doctrine to the subject in hand will illustrate what has been said.

A PENITENT disposition has, as we have seen, a natural influence in preparing the mind for the entertainment and practice of virtue in general, but it has a more powerful and immediate influence, in cultivating some particular virtues of great importance. For instance, when a person repents of any act of injustice or fraud, he will be led to form direct resolutions of living honestly and uprightly. His penitence therefore will give a direct impulse to the mind to practice justice. This again may lead his attention to the other virtues, and give his mind an impulse to temperance and forgiveness, though the tendency in this case be only remote. But it is to be observed, that the penitent disposition we describe, from whatever occasion it has taken its rise, naturally inclines the heart to piety, meekness, moderation and charity. It will be acknowledged that these are virtues of the first class; and if it be absolutely necessary, as we are sure it is, that our minds be tinctured with these, in order to our acceptance with God, whatever contributes so largely to their improvement, must certainly be of the highest importance. The
attentive

attentive hearer will perceive, that I do not consider penitence, as the only instrument of our improvement in virtue, but as one among others, which by the appointment of providence, and the constitution of our nature, is rendered subservient to this end. And that this is the case, I imagine, can scarcely be disputed.

Repentance leads us to consider the supreme Being as highly displeased with sin, yet inclinable to mercy. And certainly no considerations can operate more powerfully to draw forth our reverence and our love, two of the principal parts of piety. Every one knows, that the softness and the sorrow of heart which repentance excites are nearly allied to humanity. As a proof of this, I need only remark, that the breathings of a contrite spirit are commonly intermixed with humane and generous sentiments. If a penitent were uttering a peevish, a discontented, a despairing expression, though it would be justly condemned as indecent and wrong, we should not yet question the sincerity of his repentance. But if we discovered a sentiment of cruelty, or inhumanity, we should not hesitate a moment in pronouncing it hypocritical. With respect to meekness, moderation, and charity, I shall only add, that nothing can tend more strongly to improve them, than the recollection of our own frailties and feelings, for which we ourselves stand in need of so many allowances. If any of us proposed to persuade another to be candid and charitable, what more direct course could we take, than to remind him in those instances, wherein he had

reason

SERMON IX.

reason to wish for the candour and charity of others? But penitence brings to remembrance things of this kind, with more force and energy than can be effected by the moſt accompliſhed orator. It is the very diſpoſition which ariſes from the deepeſt impreſſion of them.

Thus we have ſeen, that penitence, or *a broken and a contrite heart*, is adapted to the nature and conſtitution which God has given us; that it is the proper and powerful corrective of thoſe vices which occaſioned it: that it prepares the heart for the reception and culture of virtue in general; and that it has an immediate influence in exciting and increaſing our piety, humanity, meekneſs, moderation and charity. But ſurely what is ſo ſuitable to the beſt and nobleſt principles of the mind, and productive of ſuch eminent and peculiar advantages for the improvement of the character, muſt be highly pleaſing to God. *The ſacrifices of God are a broken ſpirit; a broken and a contrite heart, O God, thou wilt not deſpiſe.*

L.

SERMON X.

MATTHEW vii. 24—28.

Therefore, whosoever heareth these sayings of mine, and doth them, I will liken him unto a wise man which built his house upon a rock: And the rain descended, and the floods came, and the winds blew, and beat upon that house, and it fell not: for it was founded upon a rock. And every one that heareth these sayings of mine, and doth them not, shall be likened unto a foolish man which built his house upon the sand: And the rain descended, and the floods came, and the winds blew, and beat upon that house, and it fell; and great was the fall of it.

THE frequent declarations of the gospel and the experience of human life sufficiently convince us of a fact, which upon a bare consideration of the matter, we should scarcely suppose could take place, That the knowledge and practice of religion are not only often disjoined, but that men are very apt to consider the former as most essential, and so efficacious as to insure the favour of God, though the latter should be totally, or in a great measure

measure disregarded. When I attend to the feelings of my own heart, I am astonished that this depravity should be found in the list of human errors. When I read the gospel, I am still more astonished that it should prevail among christians, and that perhaps in as great a degree as it does among Pagans or Mahometans. The voice of nature commands us in the first place to act the part which becomes a man. The dictates of religion constantly teach us, *that if we know our duty, happy are we if we do it*. The verses which I have now read to you plainly inculcate this truth. It is the conclusion drawn from the general tenor of our Saviour's sermon on the mount, and in a particular manner from the passages which immediately precede. At the 15th verse he cautions his disciples to beware of false and deceitful appearances, and by an illustration taken from the trees and herbs of the field, he teaches this important doctrine, That human conduct and behaviour are the great characteristics of sentiments and dispositions. *Wherefore*, says he in the 20th verse, *by their fruits ye shall know them*. Then in a new paragraph, from the 21st to the 24th verse, he continues the same subject in that simple yet energetic manner which we naturally expect must have operated strongly, as we learn from the concluding verses of this chapter that it actually did, on the opinions and affections of his hearers. *Not every one that saith unto me, Lord, Lord, shall enter into the kingdom of heaven, but he that doth the will of my Father which is in heaven*. In the estimation of our Saviour, the power of foretelling future events, the power of ejecting demons, the

power

power of working miracles, which it seems were conferred sometimes in those days like strength, beauty, or external advantages, and possessed by men who abused them, were inferior to that piety and virtue which, though much neglected, are without doubt the noblest accomplishments of man. Our Saviour then sums up his reasoning upon this subject in the verses I have now read to you. In these the indissoluble connection which ought to subsist betwixt the knowledge and the practice of religion is plainly declared, and the wisdom of our maintaining this connection represented by a similitude taken from the prudence or imprudence of different characters in common life. An attention to the events which occur, and to those truths which may be learned from experience, constitutes the difference betwixt a wise man and a fool; and nothing leaves so strong an impression upon our minds of this difference, as a representation of both engaged in the same plans and operations, and of the various success which accompanies them, arising from the observance or neglect of some material circumstances, *Whosoever therefore heareth these sayings of mine,* &c.

In discoursing therefore from my text, it shall be my business at this time to lay before you some arguments which may shew both the wisdom and necessity of joining the practice of religion to the knowledge of it.

By living in a country where the gospel is published, by having the scriptures in our hands, by the frequent opportunities we enjoy of hearing the

the truths of religion explained to us, by the general sense that there is of moral obligation, and by the force of christianity in preserving and improving this sense, I think it may be asserted, that the knowledge of religion still prevails in a considerable degree among us. It is indeed difficult to conceive that accounts so simple and so interesting, truths so pleasing and so alarming, and revelations so well adapted to the various capacities of human nature as those contained in the gospel, should be read or heard with attention by those who believe the veracity of the author or relater, without leaving the principles of instruction and knowledge. Much have the learned men of this world to answer for, who, by glosses, interpretations, commentaries, and systems, have rendered obscure and intricate what the voice of heaven hath pronounced so plainly. But though the knowledge of religion is, or at least might be in our circumstances very general, I appeal to our lives, the test established by Christ himself, if this knowledge be not much disjoined from practice. We hear the sayings of Christ; but are we careful to do them? Let the intemperance of the young, the avarice of the aged, the oppression of the powerful, and the dishonesty of the indigent, serve for a reply to these questions. I am willing to judge as favourably of the world as possible; I wish rather to extenuate than to exaggerate the vices of my fellow-creatures: and while I see every man professing christianity, and so few even seeming to be anxious to live up to its rules, I am disposed to impute many of their sins to an error in judgment, that the profession and knowledge of

christianity

SERMON X.

christianity are important advantages in their favour, and that they will cover a multitude of transgressions. *We are Abraham's seed,* said the Jews upon every occasion, when they wanted to assert their relation to God, or distinction among men; and I cannot help thinking we too often resemble them. We are the disciples of Christ, the professors of the pure, reformed religion, abhorrers of the abominations of popery, of the errors of heretics, and so forth. Such pleas, being used by themselves, and unconnected with their natural consequences, give reason to believe that we place more weight in them than we are warranted to do, either from the gospel, or from common sense. I consider our confidence in them as a great foundation of our iniquities, and if I could but as certainly destroy the superstructure as I can shew the weakness of the foundation, I should certainly deserve well of mankind, and enjoy the sweetest of all rewards, the consciousness of having done a worthy action. With this view I proceed to shew the inseparable connection which should subsist between the knowledge and the practice of religion, or, in the words I used upon first proposing this head of discourse, to shew the necessity of joining the practice of religion to the knowledge of it.

In the first place; The necessity of this union will appear from the consideration that man is a being naturally formed and principally designed for action. Religion then, which is certainly intended for the support, consolation, and direction of man here, and for his preparation for another state,

state, wherein, in all probability, he is destined to be an active being, must be connected with the active powers of his nature, and designed for their culture. That man is a being designed for action, is plain from various indications of his nature. The manner in which our daily food is procured to us, the necessity of labour and exercise for the preservation of health, the helplessness of children, which requires the active exertions of the full grown, and that second childhood to which the decrepitude of age brings us, and which renders us dependent upon the care, and attention, and active endeavours of those, to whom we had been formerly obliged to lend a like attention in different circumstances; these all shew us that man is made for action, and that necessity forces it upon him. This is so true, that if perfect and entire indolence were to take place, death would soon overtake the vigorous and the robust; and the infant, whose cries seldom fail to excite our attention and our endeavours to help it, and the aged, whose grey hairs and exhausted vigour now command our respect and assistance, would feel the effects of an inhumanity, founded in the love of repose, more fatal than any that ever actuated the breast of the cruel and revengeful. Our state and condition then proves that we were intended for action and exertion. The general propensities and conduct of human creatures prove the same. A child no sooner begins to distinguish objects, than it shews some desire of moving towards them, or discovers a wish of having them brought within his reach. Ten thousand attempts he makes before he can use his limbs;

SERMON X.

limbs; but no sooner does he obtain the use of them than he is constantly exerting them. Except the season taken up in sleep, children are continually exerting themselves; and all that playfulness and useless labour, as we sometimes think it, but which was once so delightful to every one of us, are necessary to the increase of their growth, the strength of their bodies, the expansion of every corporeal and mental power. Before the age of reason and reflection, an inactive human creature is in that unfortunate condition which we must lament and pity, the condition of idiotism. Can any thing prove more strongly that action is natural to man?

When man grows up, the keenness, the warmth, the variety of his passions and affections keep him almost constantly employed; and if by the proper direction of these, he does not acquire habits of activity which remain with him at a less turbulent period of life; he feels the resentment of nature against his misconduct; and his listless days, and the discontent which never fails to be consequent upon them, sufficiently inform him how grievously he has erred. To judge of this matter, let us only appeal to what we have experienced. When employed in any innocent and useful occupation, or in the bringing to maturity any virtuous and praise-worthy plan, how short does the day seem, and how swiftly do the hours pass away! When the body is not employed, nor the mind exerted, when a man is half asleep, and reduced to that often desired state of having nothing to do, how compleatly miserable is he!

The

The present hour is tiresome, the reflection upon it is painful. Thus our earliest propensities, and consciousness of what we feel, and experience afterwards, coincide with the necessities of our state and the circumstances of our condition, to show us that man was made for action. Is it to be believed then that religion should be addressed only to what is secondary in our nature and state, and not to what is primary and most important?

In the 2d place; The necessity of joining the practice of religion to the knowledge of it, appears from the general analogy of nature with respect to all our pursuits, employments, and occupations. Arguments drawn from the general tenor of ordinary life, and applied to things that are of a more spiritual and exalted nature, certainly ought to have weight with us. They will have weight with all who are of a sober and attentive turn of mind, nor, as far as I can recollect, do I know of one general conclusion taken from the ordinary conduct of life, which when applied to us as religious and immortal creatures, would tend to mislead us. Let us then consider how the case stands as to our temporal pursuits and employment; and here we shall find, that if knowledge is considered as sufficient of itself, and not as the foundation for conduct and practice, it becomes even ridiculous, and renders the person indued with it, more contemptible than if he had been immersed in ignorance. Suppose that any of you called a physician to visit a parent, a child, or a domestick, and that he should talk to you

every

SERMON X.

every time of the nature and kind of diftemper with which his patient was afflicted, but applied nothing for his relief: What judgment would ye form of him, if the perfon diftreffed fhould die? You would no doubt think you had reafon to reproach the phyfician. And if in anfwer to your refentment againft his indolence and neglect, he fhould begin a learned differtation, and prove to you that he underftood the cafe thoroughly; would you not confider him as affronting your underftanding, and difgracing his own profeflion? If you had loft your caufe at law by the negligence of your advocate, who, to apologize for himfelf, fhould talk to you about the nature of fimilar rights, of evidence and probation; would you not believe the man to be a compound of knavery and impudence, without the leaft fpark of virtue, or the leaft fitnefs for his employment?

A MAN that could believe himfelf to be a hufbandman, becaufe he could defcribe all the utenfils in hufbandry, and difcourfe learnedly on the nature of foils and manures, and every time his crop mifgave him, fhould think he fufficiently vindicated his own management by giving an ingenious defcription of a plough or a harrow, we fhould all be tempted to efteem a fool, notwithftanding the wifdom of his words.

IF a merchant fhould difcourfe of all the articles of commerce, defcribe the countries whence they come, the cafieft and beft method of importing them, and yet never have any thing in this fhop, but goods that were extravagant in their price,

price, and bad in their quality, he might impose upon a silly man in a coffee-house, but no discreet master or mistress of a family would ever choose to deal with him.

If a woman who had children to educate, and a family to manage, should discourse about all the best plans of education that were ever formed, and the most effectual ways of treating servants, and yet exhibit in her own house a scene of disorder and bad management, she would never obtain the praise of a worthy woman. If a young woman in a superior station of life, should, upon any particular occasion, speak very properly about the propriety and decorum of dress, about the charms of elegance and softness, and the attraction of modest diffidence, and yet show herself always tawdry, and assuming, and loquacious, her very words would render the contrast of her manners the more observable and more odious.

If again, a servant should be able to speak of all the duties of his station; of the attention, activity, and observance that are requisite, and yet act directly contrary to them; the people in his own rank would not value him, and no man in a superior station would choose to employ him. I might illustrate this subject by examples brought from every state and condition of human life. And if we disregard the general conclusion which all these examples force upon us, we discover a degree of folly, of which we in vain expect that the Almighty, in his course of administration, will not make us feel the bitter consequences. Is

there

there any reason to think that man, as a religious creature, is not under the same method of government which takes place with respect to him as a living, intelligent agent in this world? Is there not all the reason in the world to believe the contrary? How many analogies from ordinary life does our Saviour make use of to instruct men in the truths of his kingdom? But how could they be brought with any propriety, if these two, our business in common life, and our business as religious creatures, differed in the most essential and capital circumstances? Thus he teaches us, by allusions to the dignity and duties of kings, the occupation of husbandmen, of shepherds, of labourers, of masters and servants, of parents and children, of builders, of a company of virgins preparing for a marriage, of dependants receiving the commands of their superiors, and acting in consequence of them. His instructions upon these points frequently begin with these or such like expressions. *The kingdom of heaven is like unto a certain king. The kingdom of heaven is like unto a certain housholder. The kingdom of heaven shall be likened unto the virgins.* If action and conduct were most essential in the one, but speculation, knowledge and belief only necessary in the other; we can hardly suppose that our Saviour would have run the comparison, and argued from our duty in the one case to what it is in the other.

In the third place; the necessity of joining the practice of religion to the knowledge of it, appears, from considering the real and principal object of our approbation in judging of human characters. It is dispositions, manners and conduct

duct that we chiefly attend to in judging of men; and they are certainly the moſt natural objects of attention. This is ſo true, that even when people have adopted ſome ſtrange and unaccountable ſcheme of religion, yet the natural feelings of their heart often predominate in their manner of judging of others, and they forget thoſe ill-founded rules which they had eſtabliſhed for themſelves.

The wildeſt enthuſiaſts, the impious decriers of good works as derogatory to the honour of God, if any-how connected with ſalvation; in how many inſtances do they agree in their judgments with thoſe whom they conſign to damnation for their hereſies? Uſe all the means poſſible to expel nature and common ſenſe, yet they will often recur; and neither the worſt habit, nor the moſt abſurd opinions will be able conſtantly to warp and influence our judgments. Let us attend to experience, that guide of human life, and muſt we not all feel that it is the active conduct, the tenor of the life, the diſplay of the humane, the amiable and the reſpectable virtues of our nature, that fix and aſcertain the character, and draw forth a permanent and ſteady approbation? To judge candidly and impartially, we muſt abſtract from a number of circumſtances, and attend to a variety of others. If we would become acquainted with the figure and preciſe colour of many external objects, we muſt view them in different poſitions, for fear of a deception from an unfavourable ſituation, or a falſe light. It is neceſſary to uſe the ſame precautions with reſpect to to characters. If we hear any man difcover much knowledge and exalted fentiments, we approve of him: but our approbation does not depend upon his knowledge and fentiments merely, but upon thefe as difcovering fymptoms and indications of a fimilar character. For if we hear a man talk in this manner, and yet know that he is a tyrant to his wife, or cruel to his fervants; will his difcourfe make the leaft impreffion in his favour, or will it not rather add to our diflike and abhorrence? Let the zeal of Peter and the eloquence of Paul flow from the mouth of a preacher: but if intemperance, or lafcivioufnefs, or cruelty, or revenge ftain his character, he will be an object of refpect and approbation to thofe only who are ignorant, or uncertain of his vices. *For enquire, I pray you, of the former ages, and prepare yourfelves to fearch of your fathers. They fhall teach and tell you, and utter the words of truth.* In what age or nation was not virtue principally approved? if it is wanting, is not the femblance of it abfolutely requifite to procure reputation from the prefent age, and fame from fucceeding ones? Is it not by means of virtue, and of an active faith the foundation of virtue, that thofe who are celebrated in fcripture, and *now dead, yet fpeak to us?* This is truly the cafe from the days of Abel, and will continue to be the cafe while human nature remains the fame.

But remove the charm which virtue beftows, and all our praife becomes languid, and all our feelings become dead. I hear with reverence the divine difcourfes of Jefus: They penetrate my
inmoft

inmost soul. But the beneficence of his temper, the mildness of his demeanour, the condescension, the mercy, the magnanimity, the heroism which he discovers, still affect me more. It is his conversation with, and attention to his disciples, his active exertion of his benevolent inclinations and affections, his readiness to pour wine and oil into the wounds of the distressed, his acceptance of, and kindness to sinners, his conduct in Pilate's hall, his behaviour at Calvary and on the cross, his resignation under afflictions that were quite overwhelming, his treatment of his enemies, his constant superiority to the world, and his respect for all the divine appointments; it is these that fix the diadem upon the head of Jesus, and oblige every man who feels the force of all-conquering virtue to bow down before him and to cry, *Hosanna to the son of David! blessed be he that cometh in the name of the Highest!*

In the fourth place; I would prove the necessity of joining the practice of religion to the knowledge of it, from the general strain and express declarations of the scripture. When a person peruses any book, besides the particular facts it contains, and the doctrines it inculcates, there are some general and leading principles which run through the whole of it, and of which it leaves a strong impression upon the mind of the reader. The two points which the reading of the scriptures appears to me to fix most strongly upon the human mind, are, a sense of the divine perfection and administration, and a conviction of the necessity, beauty and dignity of piety and virtue, or

moral

moral conduct in general. These two subjects are often blended together, and are equally pointed out to us in the accounts of the primæval state, the fall and the recovery of man. This matter must be referred to every man's own feelings and discernment. The view however I believe to be natural, because it has often struck me, and an attention to it has always confirmed my first sentiments. Let every one judge for himself. But upon the supposition of the justice of the remark now made, it is plain that this general impression which the reading of the scripture conveys, will prove beyond all contradiction their moral tendency. To one who feels this strongly, the producing particular instances and passages may seem a vain labour. But general impressions do not equally strike all; and there is a great class of mankind whose observations are mostly confined to particular and detached passages. Let us then attend to some of the express declarations of scripture upon this subject: and instead of multiplying quotations, I shall take notice only of a few that are most apposite and striking. In the fourth chapter of Genesis, the history of Cain and Abel is related to us in a very simple and affecting manner, and the Almighty is introduced as declaring this eternal truth to mankind, that his favour could only be ensured by a life of virtue and integrity. *And the Lord said unto Cain, Why art thou wroth, and why is thy countenance fallen? If thou dost well, shalt thou not be accepted? But if thou dost not well, sin lieth at the door.* Upon the occasion of Balak king of Moab sending for Balaam to enquire solicitously how the God of Israel might be rendered propitious to his ambitious and unjuft views, Balaam gave this memorable anfwer, recorded to us by the prophet Micah: *He hath fhewed thee, O man, what is good: and what doth the Lord require of thee, but to do juftly, and to love mercy, and to walk humbly with thy God?* There is an appofite piece of hiftory to our prefent purpofe recorded of Samuel and Saul, in the fifteenth chapter of the firft book of Samuel. Saul, inftead of obeying the exprefs appointments of heaven, partly perhaps from avarice, and partly from the view of gaining the hearts of the foldiery, had only deftroyed among the Amalekites all that was vile, but had faved the beft of the oxen, and the fatlings, and the lambs, and all that was good. Upon being queftioned about his procedure by Samuel, he endeavoured to fcreen the difobedience of his conduct under a religious pretext, as if all thefe things had been preferved with a view to offer facrifice unto the Lord. The prophet's rebuke is contained in ver. 22. and places in a ftrong light the propriety and neceffity of active virtue above every other confideration. *And Samuel faid, Hath the Lord as great delight in burnt offerings and facrifices, as in obeying the voice of the Lord? Behold, to obey is better than facrifice, and to hearken than the fat of rams.* The admonitions, rebukes and exhortations of the prophets in general breathe entirely the fame fpirit with the reply of Samuel. It is fcarcely poffible to read a chapter of the new teftament without perceiving that it inculcates the neceffity of joining together the knowledge and the practice of religion. Nothing can be more to our prefent

purpofe

purpose than the words of our text and some of the preceding and subsequent verses. It is evident that the intention of some of the parables is to teach us this truth. Our Saviour himself only explains a few of them; and in some of those explications this doctrine is expresly maintained. Thus, Matt. 13th chapter and 23d verse, *But he that received the seed into the good ground is he that heareth the word, and understandeth it; which also beareth fruit, and bringeth forth some an hundred fold, some sixty, and some thirty.* We are informed in the eleventh chapter of Luke's gospel, the twenty-seventh verse, that a certain woman, struck with the divinity of our Saviour's discourse, cried out, *Blessed is the womb that bare thee, and the paps which thou hast sucked.* Our Saviour laid hold of this opportunity to include the principles now under consideration. *But he said, Yea rather blessed are they which hear the word of God and keep it.* It was upon the occasion of exhibiting an extraordinary instance of condescension, and pressing an imitation of his own virtue upon his followers, that he ends his exhortation with these words, in the 17th verse of the 13th chapter of John's gospel; *If ye know these things, happy are ye if ye do them.* The evil propensities of human nature are always ready to discover themselves; and as our Saviour himself speaks in the highest terms of faith, or a sincere belief in religious truths, and several of the apostles have done the same; some enthusiasts arose who endeavoured to separate the knowledge and the practice of religion, and considered the former as alone necessary. This pestilent heresy gave occasion probably to the writing of the epistle of James; in which he particularly insists on the insufficiency of faith without works.

Faith, says he, in the 17th verse of the second chapter, *without works is dead*. In the following part of the chapter he shews the necessity of uniting these two principles, and the natural and easy manner in which they coalesce and support each other. *But wilt thou know, O vain man, that faith without works is dead? Was not our father Abraham justified by works, when he offered up his son Isaac upon the altar? Seest thou how faith wrought with his works, and by works was faith made perfect?* And then he concludes in the 26th verse; *For as the body is dead without the spirit, so faith without works is dead also*. Several things that are of the utmost importance to christians may be deduced from this discourse.

In the first place; it has a natural tendency to give us a practical conviction of the connexion between knowledge and practice. This connexion there are few of us, I believe, that would be disposed directly to deny. But the facts and analogies from common life, and the declarations of scripture, may engage us to attend to it more seriously. Truth is so suitable to our feelings, that, when simply proposed, it is commonly acknowledged; but the impression it makes, and the practical use of it, depend much upon the variety of attitudes in which it is represented, and the arguments by which it is confirmed. Let what has been said excite us to hear attentively and to do carefully the will of God.

In

SERMON X.

In the second place; Let us remember that the great design of religion is to make us better men, and that the duties it requires, and the instruction it gives, are all intended for the improvement of the character. The sacrament of our Lord's supper, for instance, is not a mere formal piece of respect, or a transient exercise of love to God, gratitude to Christ, or charity to men; but such an exercise of these and other devout affections as truly exalts the mind, transforms the heart, and improves the temper. If upon this occasion you admire and adore the goodness of God in sending his Son into the world, your admiration becomes a man. If you think with gratitude on the matchless love of your Redeemer, the emotion is approveable. Who would be a stranger to such a pleasing affection? If the sense of your guilt and unworthiness, and the view of those sorrows which they occasioned to an insulted, suffering, expiring Saviour, prompt the tear of penitence and sympathy; let the tear flow: it would be graceful upon the hero's cheek. But why are all those affections proper? Because they are suitable to our nature, correspondent to our circumstances, and perfective of our characters. I approve of them: I beseech you, give scope to them; but at the same time pray that they may be converted to the improvement of your lives. Preserve the temper they infuse, the manners they inspire, the views they confer in common life; and shew that the doctrines, the life, the death, and the resurrection of Jesus, are the means of raising you up to newness of life, and holiness of conversation.

SERMON XI.

PSALM xxiv. 3, 4, 5.

Who shall ascend into the hill of the Lord? and who shall stand in his holy place? He that hath clean hands, and a pure heart; who hath not lift up his soul unto vanity, nor sworn deceitfully. He shall receive the blessing from the Lord, and righteousness from the God of his salvation.

IT is commonly supposed, and it appears extremely probable, that this twenty-fourth psalm was composed by David, in order to be sung by himself, the priests, the Levites, and the people of Israel, when the ark was removed from the house of Obededom to mount Zion [A]. That the procession upon this occasion might be the more striking and solemn, it was accompanied with a variety of musical instruments, such as psalteries, harps, timbrels, cymbals, cornets, and trumpets. These were played upon in concert with the sing-

[A] 2 SAMUEL vi.

ers, whom Cheneniah the master of the song had previously instructed in their several parts.

The sixty-eighth psalm was composed at the same time, the recital of which, together with the musick adapted to it, probably continued till the procession came near to mount Zion, when this twenty-fourth psalm was begun.

While the two first verses were rehearsing, they approached the foot of the hill. Then the king, who had laid aside his royal robes, and assumed the dress of a Levite, advancing, we may suppose, a few steps before the rest, with a voice equally musical and distinct, asked, in the hearing of the whole assembly, *Who shall ascend into the hill of the Lord? and who shall stand in his holy place?* The answer was returned by the first chorus, in these expressive words, *He that hath clean hands and a pure heart*; and with equal spirit continued by the second; *who hath not lift up his soul unto vanity, nor sworn deceitfully.* After this the king, the priests, and the Levites, transported with joy, lifting up all at once their voices in concert with the musical instruments, might sing the following verse; *He shall receive the blessing from the Lord, and righteousness from the God of his salvation.*

How grand this procession must have been, and how elevating the musick with which it was attended, I leave every one to imagine, and I shall only observe that, in this instance, we find musick under the care of one who was so perfect a master

SERMON XI.

a master of it, employing its irresistible power to excite all those sublime and devout emotions, which tend to raise and purify the minds of men. That we may more fully enter into the spirit of that part of the psalm which is to be the foundation of our present discourse, the following observations may be useful.

IN a variety of passages of the old testament we discover the respect and awe which filled the minds of the sacred writers, and of the Jews in general, when they mentioned the hill of Zion. Upon this mountain the ark of God, who dwelt between the cherubim, the authentick symbol, and sure pledge of the divine presence, was now to be deposited, and here it remained for a considerable time. For this reason it was called *the hill of God, the holy hill, the mount which the Lord had chosen, where he was to dwell, because he had desired it* [b]. The house of their king was also built upon the same ground; the most stately towers were erected upon it, and it was defended by the strongest fortifications. Thus at once the seat of beauty, and of strength, the habitation of divine power, and the mansion of earthly majesty, it became peculiarly venerable; and the very name of Zion naturally excited the fervours of religion and the zeal of patriotism. These sensations, awakened at this time by the novelty and solemnity of the procession, and enlivened by the presence and participation of their sovereign, must

[b] PSALM CXXXii.

have

have risen to a degree of enthusiasm, which, when well placed and happily directed, conveys such rapture, I had almost said such innocent, tumultuous joy, that the man who hath never felt it may be justly considered as an object of pity. When therefore the inspired monarch spoke and said, *Who shall ascend into the hill of the Lord? Who shall stand in his holy place?* every word must have roused attention, and every look communicated reverence.

The general practice of those who live in warmer climates, the whole system of Jewish manners, the particular ablutions and purifications prescribed to that people, the distinction of their meats into clean and unclean, gave a natural tendency to express whatever was perfect in its kind, by the metaphors of cleanness and purity; and though in every language these phrases, *cleanness of hands* and *purity of heart*, are sufficiently intelligible for denoting a general rectitude of conduct, and honesty of intention, yet in the Hebrew language they had a peculiar degree of force and vivacity. By reminding the assembly of those ceremonies and distinctions which were so expressly pointed out by their law, and so religiously observed by their nation, they conveyed the ideas now intended, with more than ordinary advantage. *We* acknowledge that the expressions are proper; *a Jew* felt that they were nervous. When the first chorus replied to the king, *He that hath clean hands, and a pure heart*, not an honest and a worthy man present, but must have rejoiced in the secret gratulations of his own

heart;

heart; and not a thief, a robber, a cheat, or a hypocrite, but muſt have perceived his joints begin to tremble, and his heart to fail him as he proceeded.

As the firſt chorus gave the general character of a good man, the ſecond ſeems to have warned againſt thoſe particular vices to which the Jews long diſcovered a moſt aſtoniſhing propenſity, and from which the Almighty uſed every method to guard them.

In the language of ſcripture the falſe gods which the nations worſhip are frequently called vanities: the worſhip of them is frequently ſtiled *following after vanity*; and putting confidence in them is termed *truſting in vanity*. As the Jews were ever ready to join in the idolatry of their heathen neighbours, to impreſs on their minds a ſenſe of that crime, and to excite a reſolution againſt it, was extremely ſuitable to the deſign of their preſent aſſembly. The ſuperſtitious rites of the Jebuſites, their ſacrifices to their idols, had perhaps been performed in the very ſpot where the ark of God was to be placed. It was unavoidable to remember their abominations: it would have been improper not to have pointed out, in this inſtance, the difference which ought to ſubſiſt between the deſcendants of Shem, and thoſe of Canaan. The man that boweth his knee to an idol is not worthy to call upon the name of the Lord. The Iſraelite was only to lift up his ſoul unto God.

In the days of primitive simplicity, before avarice, vicious refinements, and deceitful reasonings had corrupted the hearts of men, an oath was accounted the most sacred and inviolable of all obligations. An appeal to the Most High was reckoned so awful and solemn, that the rocks, the mountains, or the heavenly bodies, were sufficient vouchers of its authenticity, and no man was called as a witness to engagements which scarce any man thought of infringing. The piles of stones so often erected in Judea, the trees with which the country abounded, gave testimony to the piety and fidelity of its inhabitants. In these circumstances, the breach of an oath must be generally looked upon with particular abhorrence; and therefore as the man that *swore to his own hurt, and changed not*, was among them a character of the first consideration, it was a necessary consequence, that the deceitful swearer should be an object of the greatest detestation. Perhaps too, just before this period, David may have made the people enter into one of those covenants, so common among the Jews, by which they bound themselves in the most solemn manner to adhere to the worship of the true God. On this supposition, there is a singular propriety in the words added by the second chorus immediately after those pronounced by the first; *Who hath not lifted up his soul unto vanity, nor sworn deceitfully.*

Thus enlivened by the presence of a splendid assembly, soothed and animated by the chorus of sacred musick attending the ark of God, who was distinguished among them by the title of *the Lord of*

SERMON XI.

of Hosts, ready to enter a city which had long been possessed by their foes, in the view of a sovereign who was the father of his people, every eye would sparkle with joy, every heart aspire to perfection, and every voice be ambitious to join in the general choir. Struck with the character of the righteous man every one would be interested in his favour, and every one would offer up a prayer for his prosperity. In this situation, the words which David had taught his attendants must entirely correspond to their own feelings; and with one heart, and one voice they would pronounce, *He shall receive the blessing from the Lord, and righteousness from the God of his salvation.* The voice of the Omnipotent seemed to re-echo in every year, *Blessed shalt thou be in the city, and blessed shalt thou be in the field. Blessed shall be the fruit of thy body, and the fruit of thy ground, and the fruit of thy cattle, the increase of thy kine, and the flocks of thy sheep. Blessed shall be thy basket and thy store. Blessed shalt thou be when thou comest in, and blessed shalt thou be when thou goest out* [c]. Those who had more enlarged, and elevated views, looked for still nobler blessings, and trusted that the period of their perfect joy was to begin, when that which so fully satisfied others was terminated.

These observations may assist us not only to apprehend the meaning, but to enter into the spirit of the passage now under consideration.

[c] DUET. xxviii. 3, 4, 5, 6.

Its

Its application to the intention of our present meeting is so obvious, that it scarcely needs to be pointed out: The character which was requisite in order to make a proper approach to God under the law, is surely not less requisite in order to make a proper approach to him under the gospel. If the everlasting God was ready to bestow blessings on the righteous posterity of Abraham, he will not be less ready to bestow them on the sincere disciples of Christ.

In discoursing therefore from this portion of scripture, I propose, in a dependance on divine grace, to consider the character which is necessary in order to fit us for waiting on God in his ordinances; and to conclude with some reflections.

First, I propose to consider the character which is necessary in order to fit us for waiting on God in his ordinances. It is thus described in the words of the text; *He that hath clean hands, and a pure heart; who hath not lift up his soul unto vanity, nor sworn deceitfully.*

In every character which would gain the approbation of thinking men, much more in that which would find acceptance with the all-wise God, an inoffensive behaviour is the least thing required. The rapacious wretch, whose house is filled with the gains of oppression, with the goods of the widow and fatherless, or the provision which the poor man had laid up for his subsistence; the unrelenting miser, and the secret defrauder, may assume the appearance of religion,

and

and practice some of its duties; but the voice of reason loudly exclaims against their vain pretensions. By fallacious reasonings, foolish distinctions, and a violent zeal, they may impose upon themselves. The deceitfulness of sin may partly blind them; but their characters cannot so much as bear the inspection of men like themselves. How then can they stand before the judgment of God? Listen to the first dictates of nature, to the awful voice within you, which, when permitted, never fails to speak the truth; attend to the plainest precepts of the gospel, and be persuaded that without integrity of life, and decency of conduct, all pretensions to religion are perfectly frivolous. Is this truth so manifest, that it needs not be insisted on? Common sense says it is, but the practice of men seems often to assert the contrary. Did the Pharisees blush, when they joined in the exercises of religion, though they robbed widows houses, and practised all manner of injustice? Do not multitudes at this day, who dare not openly avow it, whisper it to themselves as a ground for their security in sin, that the performance of some positive duties will serve as an atonement for the neglect of many moral ones? But let heaven and earth bear witness, that he who is an enemy to man, cannot be acceptable to God. This then is the first branch of the character we are now inquiring into, a freedom from all open and secret injustice, from every enormity, and indecency in outward conduct.

But the utmost circumspection with respect to the external behaviour is far from being sufficient to render us acceptable worshippers to God. Man sees only the actions; he can discover no more of the disposition than these lay open. It is the prerogative of God to *search the heart*, and to *try the reins*. The secret motives which actuate the soul are perfectly known to him who formed it; and unless they are upright, in vain do we look for his acceptance. *Blessed are the pure in heart, for they shall see God*ᴰ. They alone are approved by him, and they only are capable of enjoying him. If you present a book to an illiterate person, fairly printed, and elegantly bound, he estimates its value from its outward appearance; but a wise man looks into its contents, considers these, and pronounces accordingly. The heart is a book which God alone is able perfectly to read, and he pronounces with unerring judgment and impartiality. *As the flag that groweth up without water, whilst it is yet in its greenness, withereth before any other herb, so the hypocrite's hope shall perish. His hope shall be cut off, and his trust shall be as the spider's web* ᴱ.

Yᴇ are called in Christ Jesus to be *the temples of the Holy Ghost* ᶠ. The request of our Saviour is, *My son, give me thy heart*. And if it is possessed of the riches of this world, corrupted by its pleasures, or engrossed by its vanities, will you presume to present it as a suitable oblation to God? How pious, how benevolent, how pure ought

---

ᴰ MATT. v. 8. ᴱ JOB. xiii. 11, 12, 13, 14.
ᶠ 1 COR. vi. 19.

SERMON XI.

his intentions to be, who deliberately fubjects himfelf to the infpection of that eye, which is more quick and penetrating than the lightning of heaven! Is the feat of corruption a fit habitation for the Spirit of God? Is the heart which is the flave of a harlot, a proper offering for the Son of God? Will he who calls himfelf in fcripture the *jealous God*, endure any rival in your affections? You never had an inclination to bow before an image; to offer facrifice to Baal, or to worfhip any of the gods of the heathens, never entered into your thoughts. Can you be faid then never to have *lifted up* your *foul unto vanity*? Alas! the attention which is commonly paid to gold and filver, the facrifices of truth and honefty, virtue and humanity, which are made to attain them, fhew fufficiently in what veneration they are held by their votaries. Are they not properly the idols before which the covetous bow? Have malice or revenge, or other irregular paffions, ever ruled over you, and fubjected you to their fway? If they have, remember the voice of truth hath fpoken it, *Ye are his fervants whomfoever ye obey*ᴳ. *Let no man deceive you* with vain words: *He that doeth righteoufnefs is righteous, even as God is righteous* ᴴ.

In our defcription of the man who can ftand before the the Lord, we have not yet taken notice of a principal part of his character drawn in my text. It is added, he *hath not fworn deceitfully*.

ᴳ ROM. vi. 16.   ᴴ 1 JOHN. iii. 7.

When I look back to ancient ages, I see almost whole nations of Pagans, among whom an oath was a pledge of fidelity scarce ever broken. Even a dissolute heathen poet who was favourable to so many other vices, hath expressed the greatest abhorrence of this. How shameful is the degeneracy of nations called christian! Thou Sovereign Father of the universe, forgive their depravity, and convert them. Let the best example, the most wholesome laws, and the strongest motives, unite in making those who profess this religion, the best of men. I should be unworthy, altogether unworthy of my place or office, if I feared to tell the highest among my hearers, that even the common oaths still practised by many, however trifling they may appear to the thoughtless or the debauched, shock the ears, and kindle the indignation of every serious christian, and render the man who is addicted to them, totally unfit for approaching to God, whose name he affronts, and whose authority he despises. But I should be unjust to every principle of virtue and religion, if I hesitated to declare, that the riches of the Indies, purchased by one false or equivocating oath, are bought at too dear a price. I hail as the disciple of Jesus, the poorest man who can say, I have lost this world's goods, but by the grace of God, I have preserved my integrity. Much hast thou gained, thou happiest victor; and insignificant are the toys which thou hast lost. But the man who is wealthy or powerful, by unjustifiable methods, who has not scrupled to perjure himself, or to involve others in that horrible crime; my soul, enter not into his secret, dwell not in his habitation. He
is

SERMON XI.

is a corrupter of the society of men: how detestable must he be in the sight of God!

Thus keeping my text in view, I have delineated some features of that character, which is necessary to fit us for waiting on God in his ordinances. I have pointed out some of those virtues which should adorn it, and laid open some of those vices which ought never to stain it. It may still be proper to be more particular; and as the display of real characters has a tendency to convey instruction more forcibly than general descriptions, it may not be unallowable to paint a few; such as I hope will be found in life, and such as I am sure we ought to imitate in those duties which suit our situation, if we wish to be acceptable in the sight of God.

First of all then, figure to yourselves an eminent merchant, who had enjoyed the happiness of a religious and virtuous education. From his infancy the sentiments of piety were wrought into his mind, and they were strengthened with his years. He was not exempted from the temptations that are incident to youth. He had often resisted them, but with sorrow he found that they had frequently been too powerful for him, or that he too easily yielded to them. Yet with humble hope, he betook himself to the mercy of God, thro' the mediation of his Saviour. His heart was open to that divine influence, which is never denied to such as ask it. After many severe conflicts with his passions, he was happily confirmed in religion, and an established character amongst all who knew him. His fellow merchants, in every exigency, were ready to confult him, and to follow his advice. It was always dictated by integrity and good fenfe. The poor bleffed him. To no public fpirited defign that lay within the reach of his abilities, did he ever refufe his aid: neither his friends, his family, nor the ftate, had ever reafon to reproach him. The regularity of his public devotions, and the chearfulnefs of his temper were equally remarkable. No man fufpected that he was remifs in the private duties of religion; but he was fo fecret in the performance of them, that the feafons he fet apart for this purpofe, were fcarcely known to thofe who lived in the fame houfe with him. A variety of incidents would occur in fuch a man's life, that could not fail to difcover his religious temper. It may be inftructive to fpecify a few.

A NEIGHBOUR who was the father of a numerous family came to him one day, and told him that by his interpofition he could receive a fupply of a certain kind of merchandize which would be a mean of faving his credit, and preventing the ruin of his family. He happened to have a large quantity of the fame goods on hand. The bringing more muft hurt his profit confiderably; but humanity and religion did not fuffer him to hefitate a moment. He granted his requeft. The embarraffed circumftances of another neighbour made him willing to difpofe of certain effects below their real value. He made the offer to the man whofe character I am now delineating. He paid him at the common rate, and fufpecting that vanity

vanity might partly have prompted him, almoſt condemned himſelf for ſaying, I never yet took advantage of any man: God forbid that I ſhould begin with you. To recount all the good offices of ſuch a man, whoſe life was dedicated to virtue and religion, were endleſs. There was ſcarce a day of his life, in which ſome generous or friendly, ſome charitable or pious action would not be told of him by his neighbours; and no evening would ever paſs away, in which he was not ready to ſay, I proſtrate myſelf, O God, before thy throne; Lord be merciful to me a ſinner. To this man we may perſuade ourſelves the favour of heaven would not be wanting. Temperance and activity would naturally conduce to his health; nor will ye wonder that his affairs proſpered in conſequence of his induſtry and prudence, joined to the bleſſing of God, and the confidence of thoſe with whom he was connected in buſineſs. It would rather be ſtrange if in his caſe the obſervation of Solomon were not verified: *In* wiſdom's *right hand is length of days, aud in her left hand are riches and honour* [1]. I reverence this character; and were I in company with ſuch a perſon, I ſhould be apt in the overflowing of my heart to cry out, Peace is in the dwelling of the upright, and the favour of God ſhall not depart from him. I ſhould be ſolicitous to know the ſecret emotions of his ſoul. I believe him to be a ſaint, and I ſhould not be ſurprized if he ſpoke to me in ſuch terms as theſe. " I am conſcious that the world,

[1] PROV. iii. 16.

" often

" often unjuſt to better men, aſcribes to me more
" than I deſerve, On a thouſand things in my
" paſt life, I look back with regret. I am not
" inſenſible to the pleaſures of goodneſs, but can-
" not help at the ſame time feeling and lamenting
" the diſorders of my heart, and the errors of my
" conduct. I adore the all-perfect Being, and
" humble myſelf before him in duſt and aſhes.
" In the meritorious obedience, the unſpotted ſa-
" crifice, and the powerful interceſſion of Jeſus,
" I place my only hope." Would to God, that in
moſt of its features, this character were a juſt repreſentation of many in this aſſembly.

HUMAN life, my brethren, is a diverſified
ſcene. A ſingle character gives but a confined
repreſentation of it. My profeſſion calls me to
the practice of many duties, and to the exerciſe of
ſome virtues, which are not ſo immediately neceſſary in your ſtation. You are ſubjected to many
difficulties, and expoſed to many ſnares, from
which my lot in the world has exempted me. To
give therefore a more extenſive view of the man
who will be acceptable in his approaches to God,
let us ſubjoin ſome other characters.

IN the ſame place, we ſhall ſuppoſe, there
lived a perſon very different in ſeveral reſpects
from him we have already deſcribed. Let thoſe
ſcenes which marked his early days, and which he
now laments, be for ever buried in oblivion.
Being afterwards the father of a numerous family,
he was by ſome of the ſeverer domeſtic afflictions
led to conſideration. Conſideration produced repentance;

pentance; and by the grace of God, repentance for the paſt ended in a thorough reformation for the future. A train of evils however ſeemed ſtill to attend him. At firſt his faith wavered; but often tried, it grew ſtronger every day. Perhaps too great ſeverity ſucceeded his former diſſipation; but the regrets he felt, and the calamities he ſuffered, rendered this very pardonable. Of many it has been remarked, that age, other purſuits, and different cares have produced a change to the better: But concerning him every one was ready to ſay, How powerful is religion, and how viſible are the effects of divine grace! The reflection upon his own failings rendered him wonderfully mild in his judgment of others, but engaged him in many acts of mortification, which were termed ſuperſtitious by the uncandid, but which he apprehended to be neceſſary in his caſe, and therefore of religious obligation. A ſeries of diſtreſs ſtill purſued him. Deprived at laſt of the conſolations he was wont to receive from a virtuous and affectionate wife, bereft of many hopeful children, ſunk into poverty by unavoidable diſaſters, ſo many misfortunes brought wrinkles on his countenance, and gave an early greyneſs to his locks. With his eyes lifted to heaven, whilſt the tears flow down his cheeks, imagine you hear this ſon of affliction thus addreſſing himſelf to his Creator; O my God, pity and ſupport me. My ſufferings are not equal to my ſins, yet, merciful Father, remember I am duſt, lay not on me more than I am able to bear. But whatever it may pleaſe thy providence to inflict, preſerve me from repining, and have mercy on me for his
ſake

sake who was acquainted with grief and suffering, and who came to seek and to save that which was lost. Nothing can strike that is not particular; let us attend then more narrowly to this man's character. It was distinguished by patience, self-denial, and fortitude. After his reformation, no man could hear him say, I have done every thing, but Providence frowns upon me. Being pressed to receive benefactions from some who knew his situation, he who in his better days had given liberally, would reply to this purpose: " When I can " struggle no longer, I will readily and gratefully " accept the assistance of others; but while my " health and capacity remain, I shall never re-" ceive what ought to be bestowed on the more " indigent and helpless." Suppose him at length on the bed of death, in full possession of his reason, would it not be natural for him to express his sentiments in some such manner as this; O my friends, love God.' Adhere to the laws of Jesus Christ, and know that your labour shall not be in vain. You behold me worn out with age, and overwhelmed with calamities; but without the consolations of religion I had been utterly wretched and undone. My warfare is now accomplished. Gracious God, forgive the errors of my youth, and the sins of my riper years. My soul revives within me. The grace of my redeemer gives me new strength. O conduct me from this valley of tears to the regions of glory and felicity. Come Lord Jesus, come quickly. Who is not ready in such a case to say in the words of Balaam, *Let me die the death of the righ-teous,*

teous, and let my last end be like his [k]? But to proceed,

In the sight of God, my brethren, no station is mean. In his view it is not rank, but conduct only, that can dignify or disgrace. Let us suppose then a person, whose birth, education and natural endowments confine him to one of the lowest spheres of life. While he serves his fellow mortal, he shews himself the servant of God. The ordinary duties of his station are not very extensive or very numerous, but he is thoroughly conscientious in the performance of them. His integrity and assiduity are irreproachable: Uncorrupted by the vices of others, he neither purloins his master's goods, nor permits his interest to suffer by his negligence. The maxims of honour and meanness which depend upon a commerce with the world, and which are not without their use, do not actuate him, he is influenced by nobler and more rational motives, he acts from singleness of heart, fearing God whom he knows to be no respector of persons. He considers himself as one who is bought by the blood of Christ, in whom there is no distinction of rich or poor, or bond or free; and that gratitude and duty bind him to obey his laws. He knows that every faithful disciple of Jesus is an heir of eternal happiness. This raiseth him above the world. Satisfied with the humble greatness of a good conscience, he

[k] NUMB. xxiii. 10.

deserves more respect than thousands that are clad in purple and fine linen.

But to imprefs your minds with a sense of those virtues which are required in the worshippers of God, why should I have recourse to such descriptions as these? The scripture itself has in various places in the strongest and liveliest manner described the conduct that is necessary for fitting us to appear before the Lord. Let us select some of the most remarkable passages where this subject is treated. The whole of the fifteenth psalm is taken up in describing a citizen of Zion. It begins with a question exactly the same with that in our text, *Lord, Who shall abide in thy tabernacle? Who shall dwell in thy holy hill?* Attend carefully to the answer which is given.

The import of the enquiry in the sixth chapter of Micah is the same; and the answer is coincident. There is a strange tendency in the corrupted nature of man, to apprehend that he can please God by mere external observances. This is strongly exemplified in the Jews, and no less strongly exposed by the prophets, who never fail to insist on the necessity of a holy and beneficent life. *Wherefore*, says the Jews, *have we fasted, and thou seest not* [L]? And what says the prophet? *Wash ye, make you clean, put away the evil of your doings from before mine eyes, cease to do evil, learn to do well, seek judgment, relieve the oppressed, judge the fatherless, plead for the widow* [M].

[L] Is. lviii. 3.   [M] Chap. i. 16.

The doctrine of our divine mafter, who came not to deftroy the law or the prophets, but to fulfil them, entirely correfponds to this. In his fermon upon the mount, none are termed bleffed, but thofe who were poffeffed of the feveral virtues there recommended. No man could be a difciple, or, according to the phrafe of fcripture, *enter into the kingdom of heaven* whofe *righteoufnefs* did not *exceed the righteoufnefs of the fcribes and pharifees* [N]. The whole tenor of the gofpel declares, that *in Chrift Jefus circumcifion availeth nothing, nor uncircumcifion, but a new creature* [O]. Such of his parables as moft fully difplay the mercy of his difpenfation, particularly thofe of the pharifee and publican, and of the prodigal fon, do likewife fhew the neceffity of an humble fpirit, and a right temper, in order to acceptance with the fupreme judge. There is not a greater blafphemy againft the Son of God, than to fuppofe that he meant by his doctrine to loofen the obligations of virtue and purity, of which he exhibited in his life fo perfect a pattern, and which in his teaching he recommends with fo much warmth and energy. I might alfo infift on the example of thofe, whofe hiftory the fcripture records for our inftruction. I might defcribe the righteoufnefs of Abel, of Noah, of Abraham; the virtue of Jofeph, the meeknefs of Mofes, the integrity of Samuel, the patience of Job, the fortitude of the prophets, the zeal, the charity, and the magnanimity of the apoftles. To illuftrate

[N] MAT. V. 20.   [O] GAL. vi. 15.

the

the fame point, I might difcourfe on the penitence of David, the contrition of Peter, and the happy confequences with which they were followed. In fhort, the whole of the bible from beginning to end would confpire in confirming that antient oracle of heaven, *If thou doeft well, fhalt thou not be accepted? And if thou doeft not well, fin lieth at the door* [p], and in teaching this important principle, That *the prayers of the wicked are an abomination to the Lord* [q]; but that the cry of the righteous reacheth to the throne of God, and that the lifting up of their hands is as acceptable as the *morning and the evening facrifice*.

I shall now conclude with a few reflections. In the firft place, fince the character which is requifite for rendering us acceptable worfhippers of God, is fo pure and holy, how careful fhould we be to inquire whether it is ours? We are fo conftituted, that the prefence of a fellow creature gives us a defire of appearing to him in a favourable light. This defire is fenfibly felt before an equal, but it exerts itfelf more ftrongly before a fuperior. Even the moft virtuous are not without a wifh to know by what honeft means they may render themfelves agreeable. If this is natural, how inexcufable muft it be to approach precipitately the prefence of that Being, before whom the angels cover their faces with their wings? Need I fay, that his approbation is of more importance than that of the world? Need I fhow that his

[p] GEN. iv. 7.   [q] PROV. xxviii. 9

favour

favour is life, and his loving kindnefs is better than life? How folicitous then fhould we be to know, whether we are the objects of it? Let us therefore attend to the language of our conduct, and examine the difpofition of our hearts. This is not a work to be gone about flightly; it ought to be performed with the utmoft ferioufnefs and ftrictnefs. If we find that the love of God and man has been the main fpring of our actions, let us give God the glory, and refolve, that by his grace ftrengthening us we will perfevere, and go on to perfection. To ferious refolutions let us add fervent prayers to God, addreffing him in the words of the pfalmift, *Search me, O God, and know my heart: try me and know my thoughts. And fee if there be any wicked way in me, and lead me in the way everlafting* [R].

FINALLY, fince that conduct and temper which God requires in thofe who approach him, is fo blamelefs and holy, what reafon have we all to humble ourfelves in his fight, and to acknowledge and deplore our unworthinefs? *We have all finned and come fhort of his glory* [S], *and were he ftrict to mark iniquity, we could not ftand before him, nor anfwer for one of a thoufand* [T]. The beft men are far below the ftandard of perfection, and too fenfible of their defects to plead their virtue at the tribunal of juftice, or to challenge as their right the friendfhip of the fupreme. And how far are we below the character of the beft? With what

[R] PS. CXXXIX. 23, 24. [S] ROM. iii. 23. [T] JOB. ix. 3.

contrition

contrition should a review of our past offences fill our minds? and what humility should the consciousness of present frailties inspire? Happy is man who has been early led into the paths of virtue, and pursues his journey towards perfection with unremitting steps. Happy in the next degree the sinner, who, pierced with a sense of his guilt and misery, flees from both by a speedy repentance, and implores pardon in the blood of Christ. If you, my brethren, perceive the beauty of holiness, if you love it, and if you resolve to practise it, come to God in humble confidence of his mercy thro' Jesus your redeemer, by whom we are warranted to assure you that ye shall not be rejected. It is your Saviour's character, that he *will not break the bruised reed, nor quench the smoaking flax* [u]. If you are sick of sin, and weary of its bondage, be not afraid of applying to him who is the physician of the sick, and the deliverer of the captive. With the outstretched arms of unbounded compassion he will receive you as his brethren, and his friends. *Ye shall receive the blessing from the Lord, and righteousness from the God of your salvation.*

[u] MAT. xii. 20.

SERMON XII.

LUKE xv. 11—24.

And he said, A certain man had two sons: and the younger of them said to his father, Father, give me the portion of goods that falleth to me. And he divided unto them his living. And not many days after, the younger son gathered all together, and took his journey into a far country, and there wasted his substance with riotous living. And when he had spent all, there arose a mighty famine in that land; and he began to be in want. And he went and joined himself to a citizen of that country; and he sent him into his fields to feed swine. And he would fain have filled his belly with the husks that the swine did eat: and no man gave unto him. And when he came to himself, he said, How many hired servants of my father's have bread enough to spare, and I perish with hunger! I will arise, and go to my father, and will say to him, Father, I have sinned against heaven, and before thee, and am no more worthy to be called thy son: make me as one of thy hired servants. And he arose, and came to his father. But when he was yet a great way off, his father saw him, and had compassion, and ran, and fell on his neck, and kissed him. And the son said unto him, Father, I have sinned against heaven, and in thy sight, and am no more worthy to be called thy son. But the father said to his servants, Bring forth the best robe, and put it on him, and put a ring on his hand, and shoes on his feet. And bring hither the fatted calf, and kill it; and let us eat and be merry. For this my son was dead, and is alive again; he was lost, and is found. And they began to be merry.

THE company to which our Saviour addressed his discourse at this time, consisted of men who had very different characters, and who, to outward appearance, were very unlike in their manners. The publicans, who were the collectors of the taxes imposed by the Romans, and who were extremely disagreeable to the Jews, both on account of their office and their behaviour in the execution of it, with many others equally notorious for their vices, made up one class of his hearers. The other class consisted of the scribes and pharisees, whose pretences to purity and sanctity were very high, who treated those who differed from them with the most supercilious contempt, assuming an exclusive privilege of being accounted holy; while at the same time their hearts were altogether vitiated and corrupted.

THE parables recorded in this chapter are admirably calculated for instructing the former of those classes in the extent of the divine mercy, and thus engaging them to fly to its protection,
and

SERMON XII.

and for reproving the uncharitableness and self-sufficiency of the latter. In the two first parables, that of the lost sheep and that of the lost piece of silver, we may discern the address of our Saviour as a teacher. The strongest reasons for hope are explicitly conveyed to the publicans and sinners: but the rebuke to the scribes and pharisees is oblique and concealed. Thus the attention of his audience is roused, and their affections gained: and by the force of truth, delivered in the most engaging manner, the murmurings of the pharisees on account of our Saviour's keeping company with sinners are made gradually to subside. In the third parable, which begins at the eleventh verse, in a narration the most simple and natural, all those circumstances are united, which, while they enlighten the understanding, are at the same time proper for touching the heart. We here discover this divine teacher shewing, with equal clearness, his enlarged mind, his compassionate heart, his awful authority, and his nervous eloquence. I have confined myself at present to that part of this parable which chiefly presents to us the misery of vice, the disposition of a true penitent, and the mercy of God. The decorum and propriety with which our Saviour conducts his allegories, and their excellence, not only as sources of moral instruction, but as patterns of just and fine writing, are very remarkable. Instead of darkening a plain passage by a tedious critical commentary, I choose in the present case to justify the remark I have now made by the following observations.

SERMON XII.

It is the younger of the two sons who is impatient of his father's restraint, and asks for a portion of his goods. His youth and his inexperience plead some excuse for his levity, his impatience, and the rashness of his request. The haste with which this young man, as is observed in the 13th verse, collected all he had, in order to fulfil his designs, is extremely agreeable to the fire and impetuosity of youth, and to the violence of eager and ungratified passions. There is also a circumstance taken notice of in the same verse, which interests the reader in his favour, and prepares us in some measure to expect his recovery: it is, that *he took his journey into a far country.* By this it is hinted that, though bent upon vice and resolved to indulge himself in it, yet he was not lost to shame, nor to the force of every other virtuous principle. The eye of a father would have proved too severe a check upon him, and his authority too great a hindrance to his unlawful pursuits. Beyond the reach of that eye which would have inspired him with reverence, he therefore resolves to live, and the interposition of that authority which his nature would not have suffered him to have contemned, he determines by his distance to render impracticable.

The intention of our Saviour's discourse discovers the propriety of his relating briefly the manner in which this young man squandered his fortune. It was not his design to render him too much an object of detestation. He therefore does not paint his vices in those strong colours, in which we know from other descriptions that he
was

SERMON XII.

was so able to draw them. It is sufficient at present to denote them by the name of riotous living. It is natural to imagine, that extravagance will be the parent of want: but it is also natural to suppose, that influenced by some timely warning, one may be brought to reflect and to recover himself before he is plunged in the very depth of misery. This supposition, the history in the present case for a little seems to favour, and the intimating all at once the extremity of the wretched, forlorn and despicable condition of this thoughtless youth, more strongly excites the feeling of surprize and sympathy, from the mixture of which we receive those emotions of sorrow which the human mind approves of and upon the whole delights in. *He joined himself to a citizen of that country,* but alas! *he was sent into the fields to feed swine, and he would have been glad to have filled his belly with the husks which the swine did eat; and no man gave unto him.* These expressions convey to every one the ideas of a mean and servile employment, and extreme indigence. But they impressed a Jew still more strongly. These animals whose flesh the Jews were not allowed to eat, and whose carcases they were prohibited to touch, this young man, who once had so different prospects, was now obliged to attend as a keeper, and even envied them the food which they devoured. On account of his wretchedness he is forced to give up the rights of his birth, the prerogative of his former station; and want conquers that antipathy which his education, his prejudices, and his religion had so deeply rivetted in his nature.

O 2   BUT

But affliction produced in him sober thoughts. In the 17th verse we are told that *he came to himself.* Vice and immorality is one species, and perhaps the worst species of madness. And therefore in antient languages, wisdom and virtue are often considered as signifying the same thing; so in like manner are vice and folly, or madness. I think in this there is great propriety. For madness, according to the general acceptation, means such an extravagant deviation from the ordinary apprehensions and actions of men, as discovers either the want, or total derangement of some of the principal faculties which men daily exercise in common life. Now vice is the same deviation from the established constitution of nature, and the same violation of its laws as madness is of the ordinary practise of mankind.

Every thing in this parable is animated. No tedious descriptions, nor tiresome relations. The whole is transacted, not narrated. The speech with which the prodigal resolves to accost his father, paints in the most expressive language, the wretchedness of his state, and the penitence and humility of his heart.

In the 20th verse we read, that *when he was yet a great way off, his father saw him, had compassion, and ran and fell on his neck, and kissed him.* Does not every circumstance display the character of the tender parent? The eye which age and affliction had rendered dim, notwithstanding the squalid and miserable appearance of the traveller, at a distance recognizes his own son. Affection warms
the

SERMON XII.

the father's blood, gives fuppleness to his joints, and fpeed to his feet. The interruption which the father makes in the 22d verfe to the premeditated difcourfe of his fon, relieves from the languor of a repetition, and difcovers in a moving manner, the ftrong affections and overflowing fympathy of the father's heart. In the charge given to the fervants, and the reafons by which it is enforced, are ftrongly marked the generofity of the father's difpofition, the naked and miferable condition of the prodigal, the unfeigned joy at his return, and the gracious manner in which he was received.

Upon the whole, this parable appears to me one of the moft fimple, natural and animated pieces of compofition. But its excellence in thefe refpects conftitutes the leaft part of its merit. What may be termed the body of the difcourfe, the language and the incidents, are elegant and ftriking: and the foul, the fentiments and the moral inftruction which it conveys are fo juft and important, that they entirely correfpond. Let us now confider it in this latter light.

I need not inform any perfon, that the father is intended to reprefent the Almighty, who is the univerfal parent of heaven and earth, *who openeth his hand, and liberally fatisfieth the want of his creatures:* or that in the younger fon, is figured the character of a finner, who regardlefs of the ties of duty and gratitude, forfakes the laws of God, and follows the corrupt devices of his own heart. All this is extremely obvious: and yet fcarcely any thing more is neceffary for making us fully comprehend

prehend the moral inftructions that are juftly founded on this parable; for we are not to fearch for the moral of every circumftance. Such difquifitions are generally harmlefs, and may fometimes be ufeful; but they rather tend to withdraw our attention from the chief end of parables. The propereft way of treating them feems to be, to obferve and enforce the general purpofes for which they were fpoken: and to point out thefe, does not require much acutenefs or penetration. They are for the moft part extremely evident. For inftance, does not every one fee that the portion of the parable now under confideration is principally calculated for the purpofes I formerly hinted at, to reprefent to us, 1ft the fatal confequences of rafhnefs, folly and vice; 2dly the difpofition and temper of a true penitent; and laftly, the mercy of God, and his readinefs to receive every returning finner. Keeping thefe three objects in our view, I fhall again review the hiftory of this prodigal fon, and apply what may be faid as we go along.

UNEASY under the reftraint which a father's prefence impofed, this young man is anxious to leave his own country, and to fulfil all the defires of his heart. Having obtained from an indulgent parent, a fhare of his eftate, he immediately undertakes his journey. At this inftant, let us contemplate him, young, healthy, unexperienced, elevated with the prefent, fearlefs of the future, his eye indicating the rapture of his heart; his foul prognofticates the higheft joy, and he thinks himfelf the happieft of mortals. What fcenes of pleafure sure does he revolve in his mind! and he longs for nothing but the day in which he shall gratify all his wishes. But why should he fear the presence of a father? why fly from the sight of a man, whom he knows to be the object of reverence? His heart even now sometimes misgives him, and virtue offers her sacred admonitions. But the the flattery and intoxication of vice push him on, and regardless of every wise and sober reflection, he hastens to his ruin. His money becomes the mean of his destruction. His appetites grow every day more irregular and rapacious, and he purchases every object that can gratify them. The light of reason sometimes rises in his soul. He extinguishes it by plunging in vice. Many a time has conscience offered to be his monitor: by the most infamous debauchery he checks her admonitions, till for a season, she has relinquished her office. Why should I recount all the dishonest deeds, the impure thoughts, and the unworthy pleasures of a man, who follows the corrupt inclinations of his heart, and is deserted by God? A companion of profligates, tyrannized over by his lusts, avoided by every good man, he must soon feel the misery, which, though contrary to his intention, he has so directly and assiduously earned. *He wasted his substance, and he began to be in want.* How great and how fatal was this change! Accustomed to eat before he was hungry, to drink before he was thirsty, never to suffer the call of any appetite to remain unanswered, how wretched does he now feel himself, deprived not only of the superfluities, but of the very necessaries of life! Where are now the companions of his bet-

ter

ter days, the partakers of his riotous and unholy pleafures! Where is the friend in whom he trufted, the miftrefs with whom he fquanderd, or the fervants that were obedient to his call? They are all fled; the blaft of winter is come; and thofe infects that only wantoned in the funfhine of summer, are for ever vanifhed. The extremity to which he is reduced, obliges him to fubmit to the meaneft and moft defpicable employment.

OBSERVE him now, and remark the alteration which fin has produced. What hopes and expectations did his look betoken when he left his father's houfe? What joy did it exprefs, when he was rioting in wantonnefs? behold now, what dejection, and what defpair? The niceft art was employed in preparing garments to fet off his youth and beauty to advantage: behold now, rags fcarcely protect him from the cold; the beggar and he wear the fame attire. The beggar, who was never in a better ftate, receives with gratitude every morfel, and taftes it with pleafure: to this youth, the remembrance of the paft imbitters the prefent. Removed from a paradife to a wildernefs, from a falfe paradife to a real wildernefs, the fharpeft arrow of affliction pierces his breaft, and the tears he fheds difcover a heart overwhelmed with the bittereft grief. I almoft forget his fins, and I compaffionate his fufferings. But we have not feen the half of them. His outward mifery ftrikes the eye, but it is only the fhadow of his inward anguifh. How fhall I paint to you the remorfe that preys upon his heart, and the agitations that diftract his foul! Fortune, thy
attacks

attacks are severe, but the attacks of guilt are intolerable. Bodily infirmity may be borne, *but a wounded spirit, who can bear? When the arrows of the Almighty stick fast in a man, then indeed is he troubled, and bowed down mightily. He is feeble, and sore broken: He roareth by reason of the disquietness of his heart. His heart panteth, and his strength faileth him.* In what a different light does the prodigal now view his immorality, his debauchery, his impiety? A thousand thoughts present themselves: but every one is more excruciating than another. All his vices pass in review before him. They are like the ghosts of the murdered, and they seem to intreat that the vengeance of heaven may overtake him. Is this picture too much heightened? I really believe it is not: and could we look with impartial eyes at the havock which sin makes in a human soul, I am persuaded we should confess the justness of this portrait. We enter into a lazar-house, and we see our fellow-creatures oppressed with some inveterate and unremitting distemper, or smitten with one universal sore. Nature shrinks at the sight. Oh! for the eye of angels properly to discern the diseases of the soul, to perceive the blackness of guilt, the horror of an awakened conscience! Then every sight that is now sickening would become almost pleasing in comparison of the loathsomeness of these. Vice repeated and persevered in, is the the only object which makes angels relinquish the charge of mortals, and fly from their society as we fly from the place infected with the plague.

BUT

But there is no room left for repentance, no place for pardon? To all the evils of sin is that last and most intolerable one to be added, the despair of a recovery? No, my brethren, it is not. This history discovers to us the disposition of a true penitent; and our Saviour, who relates this history, presents this disposition at the throne of God, and irresistibly pleads for its acceptance.

The evil of sin lies in the soul. Before it is removed therefore the soul must undergo some alteration. It is in vain to imagine, that true penitence consists in external observances or costly offerings. If you could sacrifice *thousands of rams*, and make an oblation of *ten thousand rivers of oil:* if you should give *your first-born for your transgressions; the fruit of your body for the sin of your soul*, still you might be a stranger to that temper which gained the prodigal so welcome a reception. When one receives a wound, we do not apply bandages and ointments to his garments, but to the part affected. The diseases of the soul in like manner are not cured by extrinsic and foreign applications, but by something that is inward and congenial. Now repentance is that medicine which, by the blessing of God and the operations of his spirit, cureth the soul of sin; and it consists in a serious sense of our transgressions, a deep humility on account of them, a sincere contrition of heart, accompanied with an ingenious confession, and an unshaken resolution of amendment.

All these particulars are either expressed or implied in the temper of the returning prodigal.
I will

SERMON XII.

I will say to my father; Father, I have sinned against heaven and before thee, and am no more worthy to be called thy son; make me as one of thy hired servants. He has such a strong sense of his past folly, that he acknowledges he has forfeited the rights of his birth. He asks not the privilege of a son, but the protection of a servant. His whole speech discovers the genuineness of his sorrow, and the deepness of his contrition; far from endeavouring to cover or palliate his transgressions, he confesses them in the most open and affecting manner. The expression of his resolution of amendment is the only thing which seems here to be wanting; but this very circumstance gives us a new occasion to observe the wonderful propriety and inimitable beauty of our Saviour's discourses. The prodigal had been engaged in such scenes of wickedness that the reflection upon them quite overwhelmed him. He scarcely durst promise upon his own treacherous heart. And having so far and so causelessly offended, he blushes to declare his resolution of amendment. He leaves it to his look, his manner, the whole spirit of his discourse, to speak the secret but firm purpose of his soul. Is not this a conduct at once the most engaging, becoming, and noble? and does not the representation of it discover to us one of those delicate strokes of description which distinguish a master?

I MIGHT expatiate upon each of the particulars implied in repentance, shew their connection, and explain how one one of these naturally leads to another, in the order I have mentioned them. Without a sense of sin, it is plain, we cannot feel
the

the first emotions of penitence. But a sense of sin seriously entertained, is a natural source of humility; for when we consider our corruptions and vices, we cannot esteem ourselves, but are ashamed and abashed on account of them. In this state, our heart, formed to discern and and aspire after what is excellent, is affected with a feeling of its own defects. Overwhelmed with grief, we find no ease but in an honest confession; and from this very act we are formed to derive some consolation. Resolution of amendment is the natural consequence of these previous steps; and indeed the only course which remains for us to take. Your time will not permit me to insist more fully upon these particulars. Let me only produce a few texts of scripture, to show that the disposition now described is the only acceptable sacrifice to God, and indispensably necessary in christians. It was a prevailing error among the Israelites, that God would be pleased with a variety of oblations: their prophets are careful to correct this error, and to lead them to just sentiments upon this subject. *Hear, O my people. and I will speak; O Israel, and I will testify against thee. I am God, even thy God. I will not reprove thee for thy sacrifices or thy burnt-offerings, to have been continually before me. I will take no bullock out of thy house, nor he-goat out of thy folds. For every beast of the forest is mine, and the cattle upon a thousand hills. I know all the fowls of the mountains, and the wild beasts of the field are mine. If I were hungry, I would not tell thee; for the world is mine, and the fullness thereof. Will I eat the flesh of bulls,*

SERMON XII.

bulls, or drink the blood of goats [A]*?* To the same purpose, David in another place says, *Thou desirest not sacrifice, else would I give it: Thou delightest not in burnt-offering*; and immediately after declares, agreeable to our doctrine, *The sacrifices of God are a broken spirit; a broken and a contrite heart, O God, thou wilt not despise* [B]. *He that confesseth his sins, and forsaketh them,* saith the wise man, *the same shall find mercy; but he that covereth his sins, shall not prosper* [C]. And in the new testament, destruction is denounced against all who do not repent. *Except ye repent, ye shall all likewise perish* [D]. In the parable of the pharisee and publican [E], the latter, who was ashamed on account of his sins, who stood at a distance, and beat upon his breast, and said, *God be merciful to me a sinner: went down to his house justified, rather than the other.*

BUT in the third place: In this parable is represented to us the mercy of God, and his readiness to receive every returning sinner. This is the perfection of the divine nature, in which, as offending creatures, we are principally interested. By his goodness he is the object of the love and veneration of angels. From its emanations they receive their felicity, and, dwelling at the fountain of joy, they know no sorrow. But goodness itself, strict impartial goodness, is the object of terror to a weak imperfect creature like man, con-

[A] PSALM l. 7—14. [B] PSALM li. 16, 17.
[C] PROV. xxviii. 13. [D] LUKE xiii. 3. [E] LUKE x.

scious of his sins, and repeated offences. Goodness engages the being that is possessed of it, to be beneficent, to bestow the means of happiness, but not to restore them if they have been misapplied or squandered. When I survey the justice of the Divinity, I tremble in his presence; and were I ignorant of every other moral perfection of his nature, I should pray to be reduced to nothing. When I view his goodness, I admire and adore it; but I envy the angels who never fell, and who are the objects of its complacence. But when I see him cloathed in his mercy, I glory in my lot as a man, and raise my eyes to immortality. Now it is this attribute which is represented to us in this parable. When the prodigal had wasted all, when he was ruined and undone, and was obliged to return to that father whom he had disregarded and dishonoured; we read, *while he was yet a great way off, he had compassion, and ran and fell on his neck, and kissed him.* Does not this teach us that, *like as a father pitieth his children, so the Lord pitieth* every repenting sinner. Even under the severity of the old dispensation, the Omnipotent had declared himself *the Lord, the Lord God, merciful and gracious, long-suffering and flow to anger, forgiving iniquity, transgression, and sin. With him*, it was at that period declared, *there was mercy, that he might be feared, and plenteous redemption; and he remembered the frame* of mortals, *that they were but dust.* But still clearer declarations of the mercy and placability of God are afforded to us under the new dispensation, in which Christ himself is the law-giver. The heavenly voice at his birth proclaimed, *Peace on earth,*

earth, and good-will to men: as if all that had yet been known, was only to be compared to some scattered rays which preceded the rising of the sun. One great part of our Saviour's employment, during the whole of his ministry, was to display the divinity in his mildest aspect, and by this means, to *heal the broken in heart, and to bind up the wounded in spirit.* And finally, this Saviour, by an unspotted obedience, and a meritorious death, made *mercy and truth to meet together, righteousness and peace to kiss each other.*

Having now considered the fatal consequences of vice, the disposition of a true penitent, and the exuberant mercy of God; let us in a few sentences apply what has been said.

Is vice the direct road to misery and ruin? Does not daily experience convince us that it is? While the common accidents of life slay their thousands, this evil alone killeth her ten thousands. Let this teach us to consider it as our greatest enemy. If there were a general reformation in a country, I could scarcely number up the train of diseases, misfortunes, and afflictions which would disappear at once by its means: for trace our calamities to the source, and it will be found that vice is the chief one. *Let the wicked man forsake his ways, and the unrighteous man his thoughts*, and let all who are not yet initiated in sin, beware of it, *for verily it bringeth a snare to his soul.*

Secondly, Since the disposition of a true penitence is so pleasing in the sight of God, what reason

reason has every one of us, to endeavour to obtain it! The Almighty shews the value he has for a human soul, by preferring its renewal to every other sacrifice. There is a strange propensity in corrupt man, to endeavour to please God in some different manner; but this is the only way that is acceptable. *To what purpose is the multitude of your sabbaths, your new-moons, and your oblations? Wash ye, make ye clean, put away the evil of your doings, cease to do evil, learn to do well.* What occasion we all have, for this, let our lives and our manners testify. Does that piety, integrity or purity prevail among us, which become the gospel? Is that love to God, and regard to his laws, which the gospel enjoins, the ruling principle of our lives? Would to God it were! after all, there should remain sufficient defects to lament. But as it is otherwise, how deep ought our humiliation to be! Let us acknowledge our transgressions, and be diligent to search out the plague of our own hearts, and *turn unto God, who will have mercy; and unto our God, who will abundantly pardon.*

Lastly, this mercy of God which is displayed in the scriptures, ought to be the object of our praise and adoration. We are enabled to view God, and yet we are not confumed. *Bless the Lord, then, O my soul, and all that is within me, bless his holy name; bless the Lord, O my soul, and forget not all his benefits; who forgiveth all thine iniquities.*

He

SERMON XII.

He will not always chide, neither will he keep his anger for ever: he hath not dealt with us after our sins, nor rewarded us according to our iniquities; for as the heaven is high above the earth, so great is his mercy toward them that fear him: as far as the east is from the west, so far hath he removed our transgressions from us. Bless the Lord, O my soul.

SERMON XIII.

MATTHEW xi. 29.

Take my yoke upon you, and learn of me, for I am meek and lowly in heart, and ye shall find rest unto your souls.

IN the primitive ages of christianity, there could be no inducement for any one to assume the character of a christian, but his being persuaded of the truth of the gospel, and of its efficacy to procure salvation to those who obeyed its precepts. Men at that time very rarely engaged in any of the external exercises of religion, but from a sense of the obligation they lay under to purity and integrity, the ultimate ends of all religion. But now the case seems to be much altered for the worse. While the pious frequent religious assemblies out of devotion, regard the name of christian as the most honourable appellation, and confess that their profession of faith in Jesus lays them under the strongest obligation to obey his laws; a very considerable number assemble with these from different motives, consider the name of christian only as a proper badge in a christian land,

and profess themselves believers only through custom, or to obtain some temporal advantages with which the profession is attended, or to avoid some inconveniences which renouncing it altogether might occasion. Though they join in the forms of religion, they never consider this as laying them under an obligation to comply with the precepts of it, or seem to apprehend that they are guilty of hypocrisy, or what the scripture calls a mocking of God, for the pretence which they make of honouring him outwardly, when they feel no reverence for his perfections, and no regard for his will.

THERE is however one institution of religion, a participation in which is still considered, in this country at least, as a solemn avowal of the obligation to observe the laws of christianity; an institution from which the abandoned generally abstain, and in which, while he rashly engages, the heart of the hypocrite will scarcely fail to smite him. As you therefore of this congregation have it so nearly in view, to celebrate this sacred institution of the Lord's supper, the participation in which is considered as an acknowledgment that we are bound to receive the yoke of Christ, I have made choice of the words now read, as a proper foundation for the present discourse.

IN the 27th verse of this chapter, our Saviour had asserted his divine commission, his authority and power, and his intimate knowledge of his father, and near relation to him. *All things are delivered to me of my father: and no man knoweth the*

SERMON XIII.

the fon but the father, neither knoweth any man the father, fave the fon, and he to whomfoever the fon will reveal him. Then he who fo well knew how to unite the characters of juft dignity, and winning condefcenfion, immediately fubjoins one of the moft affectionate invitations, which he ever addreffed to mankind. Of this my text is a part. *Come unto me, all ye that labour and are heavy laden, and I will give you reft: Take my yoke upon you, and learn of me, for I am meek and lowly in heart, and ye fhall find reft unto your fouls.*

The yoke of Chrift is a metaphor to fignify his laws and commandments; and the taking of this yoke upon us denotes a fubmiffion to thefe. To learn of Chrift, comprehends a general attention to the doctrines he teaches, as well as to the precepts he enjoins, and has alfo a reference to the example he exhibits. The two following claufes, *For I am meek and lowly in heart, and ye fhall find reft to your fouls,* may be confidered as motives to engage our compliance with the exhortation in the preceding part of the verfe. Our Saviour takes notice of his being *meek and lowly in heart*, both for the tendency which thefe difpofitions would have to conciliate affection and confidence, and for diftinguifhing him from the Jewifh doctors, who affected a difgufting pride and fuperiority; qualities which, to fay the truth, human learning, when it is not conducted with a fpirit of fober enquiry, and made fubfervient to the purpofes of virtue and religion, is apt to infpire. By the *reft of the foul*, is meant that ftate of quiet compofure and ferenity, which ought to be the chief purfuit

of

of a wife man: and this expreſſion muſt have been eaſily underſtood by thoſe who heard our Saviour, eſpecially as it had been uſed in a ſimilar manner by one of their prophets. *Thus ſaith the Lord, Stand ye in the ways, and ſee, and aſk for the old paths, where is the good way, and walk therein, and ye ſhall find reſt to your ſouls* [A].

In proſecuting this ſubject, after ſaying a few things upon the nature and extent of the chriſtian law, which is here called the yoke of Chriſt, I propoſe to lay before you the obligations we are under to ſubmit to it, and confirm the ſenſe of theſe obligations by ſeveral arguments, eſpecially thoſe ſuggeſted in the text. We ſhall be the beſt able to diſcover the nature of the chriſtian law, by attending to the deſign for which it was publiſhed. Now it was puliſhed with this view, to recover the fallen race of mankind, and to reſtore them to the image of God, by rectifying their irregular appetites, by cultivating in their minds every diſpoſition that is virtuous and praiſe-worthy. The excellence of this law therefore conſiſts in its fitneſs to anſwer theſe ends. As Chriſt came to deſtroy the kingdom of Satan, and to *purify to himſelf a peculiar people zealous of good works* [B], his rules and precepts are all calculated for reſtraining vice, and promoting holineſs; or, to uſe the words of an apoſtle, *to teach us, that denying ungodlineſs, and worldly luſts, we ſhould live ſoberly, righteouſly, and godly* [C].

[A] Jeremiah vi. 16. [B] Tit. ii. 14. [C] Tit. ii. 12.

SERMON XIII.

THIS law, which is pure, as the nature of God, the fountain whence it proceeded, is as extenfive as the principles of our nature would allow, or as was neceffary to fit us for a more perfect and comprehenfive ftate, to which the prefent is preparatory. Thus it comprehends all the duties we owe to God, every branch of piety, as love, gratitude, reverence, fear; all the virtues of humanity, juftice, charity, meeknefs, forbearance, with a variety of other duties that arife from different fituations and circumftances in life; the virtues of temperance, fobriety and chaftity, to which we are fo powerfully excited, by being reprefented as *temples of the living God*[D], *as habitations of God through the Spirit*[E].

THE law of the Lord Jefus extends not to our actions only, but it engages thofe who comply with it to regulate their words, and to preferve purity in their moft facred and retired thoughts. Like a medicine, which not only operates upon the larger organs, but penetrates the nerves, and affects the fineft fibres, the chriftian law extends to the niceft movements of the foul, and is intended to influence every principle by which the foul can be actuated.

I PROCEED now to lay before you fome of the obligations you are under to fubmit to the law of the gofpel, or to take upon you the yoke of Chrift. May I fpeak in the fimplicity of the

[D] 2 COR. vi. 16.   [E] EPH. ii. 22.

gospel, and may the Spirit of Christ aid me in declaring your duty, in exciting you to comply with it!

In the first place then, you are under the strictest obligation to submit to the law, or yoke of Christ, because its reasonableness approves itself to your own minds.

When God formed man at first, he did not leave him to act in any manner that humour or passion might prompt him, but constituted him so, that when he should discern any thing to be reasonable or proper to be done, even supposing he should be willing to forego the advantages with which the doing it might be attended, or to suffer the evils in which the omitting it might involve him, yet this should not satisfy him, but a departure from his duty should moreover be attended with a present sense of guilt, or ill-deserving, independent of the consequences. When any scheme of religion is laid before a man, which he acknowledges to be reasonable, and with which notwithstanding he refuses to comply, he no longer uses the liberty of a man, but is domineered over by some appetite, or passion, or habit of subjection for which his own heart condemns him. Suppose therefore, that there were nothing more in christianity, but a simple detail of the different branches of our duty, we should be under the strictest obligation, from the very constitution of our nature, to comply with it; and our refusing to comply would upon reflection have filled us with uneasiness. Man is not left, like the brutes,

to

SERMON XIII.

to follow the present strongest impulse of his mind, but has another superior faculty, which claims the privilege of a lawful master, and is entitled to have its commands obeyed. The question with man ought not to be, which is the strongest propension, but which is the most reasonable. In this licentious age, it is necessary to insist upon this obligation, because many satisfy themselves in their impiety and irregularities by saying, that they are under no formal obligation to comply with the laws of religion, having done nothing to ratify the engagements into which others may have entered on their account. I am sure this is not the language of a man who uses his reasonable faculties. Your obligation to religion does not arise from the vow of your parents, or others, though it may be strengthened by that vow, but from the nature which God has given you. Before you disown this obligation then, renounce your nature. Acknowledge at once, that the boasted powers of reason and of conscience, you undervalue and contemn. Forsake the society of men. You claim the privilege of indulging every appetite and passion, without restraint: Herd with the beasts of the field: in similar pleasure you spend your days. Degraded man! O that I could sufficiently discover you to every eye as a monument of folly and of vice, that you might be pointed at by others, and that the contagion of your example might not spread. No! rather like Nebuchadnezzar may your understanding return to you, and with him, may you learn to praise and honour and extol the King of heaven and earth, who hath not left you at liberty to reject his holy law without self-condemnation.

Thus the very declaration of the moral duties of the gospel to those who must, and do confess that they are reasonable, lays them under the strongest obligation to practise them. The eye is not more formed to discern a difference between white and black, or the taste to distinguish between sweet and bitter, than the mind is to perceive the distinction between good and evil: nor is it more absurd, to call black white, or bitter sweet, than it is unnatural to reject the good and choose the evil.

But the obligation of christians to take upon them the yoke of Christ, does not arise merely from its reasonableness. This obligation is enforced by the highest authority, no less than that of God himself; for to the christian religion God hath given the strongest attestations, having appeared at various times, and in divers manners, to establish the law, the prophets, and the gospel; so that refusing to receive them is refusing to acknowledge the authority of God.

The different appearances of the Almighty are recorded for our instruction; and since they are sufficiently attested, they ought to produce a similar effect upon us, to that which they would have done, had we been witnesses of them. When God descended upon Mount Sinai in thunder and lightning, and the *voice of the trumpet waxed exceedingly*

ceedingly loud[F], it was to deliver that moral law, which Christ came not to destroy, but to confirm; and when we hear it as delivered by the Almighty, do we not tremble at his word, and reverence his authority? *Let all nations bow before him, and let all people serve him.* The same eternal Being who appears thro' the old testament as the God of majesty and glory, appears also, tho' in a different manner, and adds his sanction to the new. He who under the former dispensations, had discovered himself in his terrors, as an emblem of the law, condescends under the gospel, to shew himself less in the light of majesty than of love, as an emblem of the mildness of this latter dispensation. His Spirit descended on his Son like a dove, and he declared, *This is my beloved Son; hear ye him*[G]. Here no fire is called from heaven to destroy a rebellious race, no immediate judgment is inflicted for dishonouring, not the servant, but the Son: on the contrary, the most marvellous works of beneficence and mercy, which required the immediate interposition of heaven, are performed. And are not these so many proofs, that the religion which we profess, comes recommended by the divine authority? *The works that I do,* saith our Saviour, *bear witness of me, that the Father hath sent me*[H],

To the still, small voice of God therefore, which speaks within our minds, and enjoins obedience to the laws of piety, justice, and charity,

[F] EXOD. xix. 19.   [G] MATT. xvii. 5.   [H] JOHN v. 36.

there is fuperadded the clear declaration of the fame God in the fcriptures, enjoining us to honour and obey the Son, as we ought to honour and obey the Father. Do I fpeak to an affembly of men, who defpife, and daringly reject this authority? Will you join with the impious king who hardened his heart, and faid, *Who is the Lord, that I should obey his voice? I know not the Lord, neither will I hearken to him*[1]. Surely not, my brethren: you reverence the authority of God. Remember then that it is the fon of God, by the authority of his Father, who fays, *Take my yoke upon you, and learn of me.*

But I proceed to confider our obligations to fubmit to the yoke of Chrift, arifing either from explicit, or implied acknowledgments: and on this fubject, there are feveral things which I will throw together as briefly as poffible. When you were baptized, did not your parents, or fome others, become bound to train you up in the religion of Chrift, and to inftruct you in its principles? and have you not always confidered this as a virtual engagement in your name? I know you never renounced it formally; but did you ever really endeavour fo much as to fatisfy your own minds for your neglect of it? Or when you deliberately reflect on this engagement, and your departures from it, do you not feel a fecret conviction informing you that you are blameable? What is the language of your religious profeffion, of your

[1] EXOD. V. 2.

retaining the name of christians, of your claiming the outward privileges belonging to such? Every time that you address God, either in public, or in private, is it not a confession that you ought to obey his precepts? If you ever commemorated the death of Christ, or if you now propose to do it, is not this a solemn ratification of your baptismal vows? If you call him Lord, Lord, and yet do not the things which he prescribes, must you not own that your behaviour is altogether unworthy and inconsistent? For can any conduct be more inconsistent or contradictory, than to call him master, and yet refuse his authority? May he not justly say to you, *If I be a master, where is my fear? and if I be a father, where is my honour* [K]? Whenever you join therefore in any act of religion, and yet refuse obedience to the laws of the gospel, you acknowledge the justness of an authority, to which, notwithstanding, you refuse to submit; a conduct which your own hearts can certainly never approve of.

Having thus laid before you some of the obligations which we are under to receive the yoke of Christ, arising from our nature and constitution, from the regard due to the authority of God, and from our own explicit or implied engagements, let me endeavour to confirm the sense of these obligations by several motives; and this may be considered as a continuation in some measure of my former subject; for to a reasonable creature,

[K] MAL. i. 6.

a just

a juft motive is a proper ground for action, and lays him under an obligation to act accordingly.

In the firft place, my brethern, the fervice to which you are bound, by fubmitting to this yoke, is both reafonable and eafy. As chriftians, we are not loaded with the yoke of rites, ceremonies, and external obfervances, which was fo heavy upon the Jews, that neither thofe in the days of our Saviour, *nor their fathers were able to bear it* [L]. The dominion of Chrift, tends to free us from the flavery of fin, from the power of Satan, from the tyrannic fway of our own lufts, and to make us obey the beft principles of our nature, and yield to their dictates. The religion of the Lord Jefus is therefore called *the perfect law of liberty* [M]. By engaging in his fervice, we are faid to be *delivered from the bondage of corruption, into the glorious liberty of the fons of God* [N]: and chriftians are exhorted to *ftand faft in the liberty wherewith Chrift hath made them free* [O]. Our Saviour alfo declares immediately after the text, that his *yoke is eafy*, and his *burden light*. The objection which arifes to this from the weaknefs and depravity of our natures, I fhall take occafion to obviate afterwards.

At prefent, I proceed to perfuade you to comply with the advice in the text, from a review of the character of that Mafter, into whofe fervice

[L] ACTS XV. 10. [M] JAMES i. 25. [N] ROM. viii. 21.
[O] GAL. V. I.

SERMON XIII.

you are here called. I shall chiefly confine myself to the consideration of those circumstances in his character, which are marked in the text. We are there told, that he is *meek and lowly in heart*; and how perfectly his actions correspond to this character, let his whole life testify. Can my foul ever forget his condescension to his disciples, his forbearance to his enemies, his patience under his afflictions, and the numberless good offices, by which he alleviated or removed the miseries of men? To display him fully in this character, need I bring to your remembrance, that night in which *he rose from supper, and having laid aside his garments, girded himself with a towel, and washed his disciples feet* [p]? Need I recall to your minds the compassionate manner in which he spoke to the daughters of Jerusalem, and desired them to reserve their tears for their own miseries, when they were pouring them out for his? What sinner did this meek and merciful Master ever reject, if he came with a penitent heart? It was foretold to be his character, and he still retains it, that *he will not break the bruised reed, nor quench the smoaking flax* [q]. How striking, and how beautiful is the prediction concerning him, and how fully did he accomplish it! *He shall feed his flock like a shepherd, he shall gather the lambs with his arm, and carry them in his bosom, and gently lead those that are with young* [r]. When you consider your weaknesses, your irresolution, your follies, and your

[p] JOHN xiii. 4. 5. [q] ISA. xlii. 3. MATT. xii. 20.
[r] ISA. xl. 2.

vices

vices, are you not sensible that it would be impossible for you ever to please an austere master? or could any other be a fit Lord for you but he who has a *fellow-feeling of* your *infirmities* [s] ? Your meek and lowly Master imposes upon you no tasks which he himself did not submit to. He is not like the pharisaical doctors who *said, and did not,* who *bound heavy burdens, and grievous to be born, and laid them on other mens shoulders, but would not touch them with one of their fingers* [t]. In the severest instances of our duty, he left us an example, that we should follow his steps. In what school can we learn, where the instructor would be so ready to bear our frowardness, to pardon our neglects, and forgive our faults? If you refuse this Saviour, where will you find one like him? for there is no encouragement that he refuses, no assistance that he denies.

This leads me to consider, as another motive to induce you to take his yoke upon you, which will likewise obviate every objection from the depravity of our nature, the gracious aids of his holy Spirit, which he will vouchsafe to all who sincerely ask them, and rely upon them. Our Saviour did not leave this world, till he had promised that the Comforter, which is the Holy Ghost, should come to teach and assist his followers. Whatever difficulties therefore we may meet with in our christian course, by the aid of the divine Spirit we may be rendered superior to them. If the combat

[s] HEB. iv. 15. [t] MATT. xxiii. 3, 4.

in

SERMON XIII.

in which we engage, in order to subdue our irregular appetites, be severe, from the Spirit we may derive that strength which shall render us victorious. Do we labour under any disease whatever of the mind? By the help of that Physician who formed the heart, and knows its maladies, surely it may be cured. And, christians, though *we wrestle not against flesh and blood, but against principalities and powers, against the rulers of the darkness of this world, and against spiritual wickedness in high places* [u], yet by his Spirit who conquered the powers of darkness, and who overcame the world, all these may be resisted by us; and with such divine assistance, his *yoke* may be termed an *easy* one, and his *burden light*.

FINALLY, my brethren, attend to the promise that is here made to those who obey this exhortation. *Learn of me, for I am meek and lowly in heart, and ye shall find rest to your souls.* What is there in this world that is so desirable, as a quiet, a contented, and a resigned spirit? Tell me who is the happy man; he who arrives at the top of his ambition, and tramples upon his foes, but is domineered over by his lusts? he who wallows in luxury by means of his ill-acquired riches, but has no government over himself; or he who in this transient state, feels that internal satisfaction which the world cannot give, nor take away? Ye soft gales of peace, which proceed from the Holy Ghost, and are kept up only by an unremit-

[u] EPH. vi. 12.

ting virtue, be you my choice, and do you still refresh my soul. But where is that serenity and felicity to be found, except by submitting to the yoke of Christ? At the creation of man, religion was his companion, his perpetual attendant; and no care ruffled his brow, nor sorrow disquieted his breast; his eye beheld the lovely form, and his heart never strayed from her laws. But when he fell, his understanding was darkened, he lost sight of his true good, and pursued an imaginary happiness in a thousand delusive shapes. The experience however of every age has sufficiently proved that even the imperfect share of happiness which we are now capable of attaining, is no where to be found disjoined from religion. *Wisdom's ways are ways of pleasantness, and all her paths are peace*; and besides that natural peace which a pious conduct is immediately calculated to produce, the christian has moreover that supernatural quiet and consolation to depend upon, which is promised by his Master, for composing and solacing his spirit. *Peace I leave with you: my peace I give unto you: not as the world giveth, give I unto you. Let not your heart be troubled, neither let it be afraid* [x].

[x] JOHN xiv. 27.

SERMON XIV.

Psalm iv. 4. laſt part of the verſe.

Commune with your own heart upon your bed, and be ſtill.

THAT the royal prophet, by theſe words, enjoins retirement from the hurry and the tumults of human life, in order to give ourſelves time deliberately to conſider the wiſdom, the juſtice, and the goodneſs of the divine adminiſtration, and ſeriouſly to reflect upon our own actions, and the motives of them, will, I imagine, be readily admitted by every hearer. *Commune with your own heart upon your bed, and be ſtill.* At leiſure, uninfluenced by the ſpecious opinions, unbiaſſed by the corrupt practices of others, deaf to the enſnaring voice of pleaſure, and only open to the ſober dictates of reaſon, and the awful commands of conſcience, frequently meditate upon the perfections of God, and learn to reverence the ways of his providence. Often before-hand conſider the courſe of conduct which it becomes you to follow; and often review what you have thought and acted. You will all acknowledge that the nature and condition of man difcover religious retirement and recollection to be highly proper and ufeful. When we confider our wants, our weaknefs, our dependance, the dangers to which we are expofed, the hopes and the fears, as well as the immediate happinefs and mifery which our conduct occafions; they all confpire to force this acknowledgment. But how feldom our practice is influenced by it, let our confcience and our actions bear witnefs. For if the man who is of opinion that a frequent and ferious confideration of one's own behaviour, his difpofitions, and the awful account he muft render, might, by the blefling of God, prove a remedy for many vices, would but vifit the market-places, the taverns, and crowded, or private companies; or inquire into the cafe of the oppreffed, or lend an ear to the wailing of the poor; or obferve the cheats in bufinefs, the chichanery of law, the haughtinefs of men in high ftations, or the envy of thofe below them, the unreafonable violence which occafions quarrels and divifions, the immoderate keennefs in the purfuit of things temporal, and the remiffnefs in feeking after things eternal; he could not fail to be perfuaded, that the direction in our text, though heard with fome kind of reverence, is far from being devoutly, or commonly obeyed.

In my difcourfe to you therefore at this time, I propofe to explain the nature and defign of religious retirement and recollection, and to endeavour to perfuade you to the practice of thofe duties.

I ADDRESS

SERMON XIV.

I ADDRESS myself to every one in this house; but I consider the subject as more especially suited to those who have so immediate a prospect of commemorating the death of Christ in the Sacrament; for surely it is particularly fit that our hearts should be purified by meditation and prayer, when we are in so solemn and public a manner to profess ourselves the disciples of Jesus. I propose then in the first place to explain the nature and design of religious retirement and recollection. When the illustrious writer of this psalm, who had such a deep insight into the diseases of the human heart, and could so ably prescribe salutary remedies, here recommends religious retirement and recollection, it seems evident that he has no design to say any thing in commendation of a total seclusion from the world. The words by no means import any thing of this nature. A recess from the world and its cares can never be the object of a general precept. In conformity then to the intention of the text, I am to consider that kind of retirement which is proper for men engaged in the business of life, and which is necessary, in order to support the social character usefully and honourably. Whether a total seclusion from the world, a resignation of all the endearing ties of friendship, affection, love, a departure from all the duties which our present state requires, and of which providence seems to allot every one a share, be agreeable to the commands of God, or deserving praise of men, or a fit preparation for a state of happiness in the heavenly kingdom, where there is a society united by the strongest bonds, I will not at this time inquire. If they are ever allowable,

allowable, the circumstances which call to them are very peculiar; and I cannot hesitate to say that the most worthy of all characters is the man who maintains his station in life, ever animated by a fervent piety, and ever guided by an inviolable integrity. To cherish a spirit of piety, and to assist him in supporting an uniform uprightness of intention and action, religious retirement and recollection will be of the greatest importance. We will discern this if we consider in what the exercise of them consists.

It consists in devoting a portion of our time for the most valuable purposes, for conversing with our own hearts, for the consideration of our behaviour, and comparing it with the perfections of God, for inquiring after and applying the means of regulating every unlawful desire, and of moderating every unreasonable wish. In religious retirement, we are employed in pouring out our hearts before the giver of our life and our mercies, in imploring his assistance to improve our characters, in admiring and adoring the perfections of his nature, and in expanding the powers of our minds to receive the most gracious influences. The dispositions chiefly to be exercised in the hours of retirement are, sincerity in the consideration of our own characters; impartiality in the examination of our lives; a devotion of heart kindled by the contemplation of unerring wisdom, undeviating goodness and unlimited mercy, especially as these are discovered in our Lord Jesus Christ; humility of mind, and contrition of heart, so unavoidable when we are reviewing our own faults,

faults, and adoring the all-perfect God. The exact portion of time that should be devoted to religious retirement and reflection, or how often the seasons for these exercises ought to recur, cannot be precisely determined, as the circumstances of mankind differ so widely. But surely there is no occupation of life which does not admit of some intervals. And shall christians be less zealous about the interests of virtue and religion than the philosopher who enjoined his followers every night, before sleep sealed their eyes, to call themselves to an account for the actions of the past day. Besides this, by professing our belief in the oracles of God, we look upon one day in seven as particularly dedicated to religion. And by the views many of you have, and your attendance here, you profess a degree of reverence for other seasons set apart for this purpose. To the busiest of us, I will venture to say, neither time nor opportunities for retirement and reflection are wanting. To excite you to lay hold on these, I now proceed to propose some arguments, which I shall endeavour to lay before you in such a manner, that they may not only serve as motives to engage compliance with the psalmist's advice, but likewise, that they may convey to the attentive hearer some farther instruction, as to the method in which we may most advantageously spend the hours of retirement.

May God grant to you the hearing ear, and the understanding heart; and to the preacher, the power of persuasion!

IN the firſt place then, Religious retirement and reflection have a very direct tendency to reclaim and reſtrain from vice, and to improve in virtue. Man is compounded of ſeveral diſtinct powers and faculties, all neceſſary for human life and happineſs, provided there is that regular ſubordination preſerved among them, which nature points out, and without which, experience ſhews, that neither the individual, nor ſociety can ſubſiſt. It is evident from our very frame, that God has conferred an authority upon reaſon and conſcience. In the narrow empire of the human mind theſe claim a right to ſway the ſcepter. But who knows not, that man is apt to be miſled by the influence of his paſſions, that are ready to act as rebellious ſubjects againſt the juſteſt and beſt of ſovereigns? To break the bands of reaſon, and to obey the lawleſs dictates of irregular paſſion, the tumult of life, the ſuggeſtions of the gay, and the example of the vicious, prove like ſo many evil counſellors. They are the movers of ſedition: and their chief way of moving it is not by offering arguments, but partly by hurrying us away with the ſtream, and partly by raiſing ſuch an uproar around us, that the voice of reaſon, which may be compared to the ſtill, ſmall voice of God, which ſpoke to Elijah, is conſidered as a whiſper, from which we turn away our ear, as if we heard it not. If conſcience offers its threatening admonitions, the mixing more deeply in the circle of the diſſipated, the buſy, and worſt of all, the debauched, proves an opiate for that time to lull it aſleep. And thus the wretched man proceeds, till, like the haughty king, who, having

times

times without number trampled upon the divine laws of his nature, loft his underftanding, and was fuffered to partake of every grovelling and degrading pleafure. Is this declamation? Alas! it is fact. O thoughtlefs man, how often haft thou eagerly engaged in a fecond diverfion to drive away the reflection, the painful reflection which the guilt contracted in a former occafioned! I fee the cup in the drunkard's hand, and he greedily fwallows the poifon, in order to drown the remorfe of his mind for laft night's intemperance. The unwary youth, once initiated into finful pleafure, unwilling now to hear the counfel of virtue, but unable to reprefs it, feeks for the witneffes and advifers of his tranfgreffions, and from the laugh of levity, and the madnefs of impiety, he believes wifdom overcome, and acquires new fpirits to rufh upon his ruin. This day you begin to take undue advantages of your neighbour: you begin without daring to refolve that you will perfift. When you impofe upon your fecure brother, your tongue falters, and a fmall degree of attention, (but honefty is always unfufpicious) would difcern the alterations in your countenance. But to become more expert, you herd with the more experienced in villainy, and never allow yourfelves a moment to reflect, till you be a proficient in that worft of trades, in which at firft you was a backward fcholar. Thus hurrying from vanity to vanity, and from vice to vice, the wicked multiply acquaintance, and attach companions in iniquity, ftrangers, utter ftrangers all the while, to what it behoves them moft to know, ftrangers to themfelves. Ye fons of of folly, fain would I introduce you to a new acquaintance, fain would I engage you to take pleasure in a new kind of conversation. Cultivate an acquaintance with your own hearts, and I will change your name, and with reason: listen to the improving language of your consciences. Though you should meet with rebukes, prefer them to the flattering voice of those foes to your improvement, peace and happiness, which approach you under the insinuating, but false appearance of pleasure. For in the religious retreat, with every passion stilled, and every desire quieted, behold holy reason seated on her throne, and exerting her full power. Here you form just judgments of your own conduct, and of that of others, of the proper and lawful pursuits of life, and the means of attaining lawful ends. When, removed from the eye of the world, we converse with our own hearts, then every man is upon a level. The external marks of dignity are removed, power is suspended, and riches make no difference. These things which are so apt to intoxicate the human mind, being absent, the sins which we committed in the hurry of life are remembered, considered and lamented. Then is it that recollection executing the office of the prophet of old, can thus address the man in the most exalted station, *O King, let my counsel be acceptable to thee. Break off thy sins by righteousness, and thy iniquity by shewing mercy to the poor, if so be it may be a lengthening of thy tranquillity.* Let but the unjust judge review the sentence for which his injured brother complains of him; and will not the remorse this occasions prevent him from pronouncing a like one?

Ye

Ye who spend the night in revelling and drunkenness, whom the morning sun (which the children of temperance rise to behold with rapture, and which enables them to pursue the various, honest occupations of life) just shines upon as you are finishing your debauch; tell me seriously if you are not persuaded, that you would curb your licentious appetites, and walk in the paths of sobriety, if you set apart but ten minutes of every day for reflection, meditation and prayer? Would ambition ravage the world, or engage men in projects for pulling down states, ruining families, or reducing to misery particular persons, if those who feel its impulses would often calmly consider the vanity, uncertainty and short duration of temporal enjoyments? If this were the case, would ambition be any other thing in the human breast, but an honest desire of obtaining the means of promoting public, or private happiness? Would avarice hoard by every infamous method, if due scope were given to meditation, in order to convince us of the worthlessness of those riches which often *make themselves wings*, of the folly of purchasing the accommodations of a pilgrimage at the risque of losing an everlasting citizenship? It is in retirement that objects lose the false glare with which passion colours them, and that our own characters appear in a just point of view. Man will no doubt be partial to himself. I allow that the vanity of individuals is great. I allow that the blindness of man with regard to his own vices is astonishing: but let any person, considering himself under the awful influence of God, and praying earnestly to him that he would open his eyes

eyes to make him discern his faults, but once seriously reflect upon his temper and practice, and I maintain that he will not remain so vain, or so blind as he was before. Had David obeyed his own direction before Nathan came to him, he had not heard so apt an allegory without sparing the resolute but charitable application, *Thou art the man*. Whence proceeds it, but from want of serious consideration, that if I were to ask your characters at the most candid of your neighbours, and mark down what they told me, that I should present you with a list of several vices which you could readily apply to some of those with whom you converse every day; but before you discerned that they belonged to yourself, it would be necessary directly to inform you, ye are the men. The pharisee whom our Saviour describes in the parable was a stranger to his own proper character, because, though he seemed to be religiously employed, yet he had not sufficient impressions of the holiness of that Being *in whose sight the heavens are not pure*, because he turned his view to his good qualities, rather than his faults, and because he estimated his worth not from God's law, but from a comparison with others. In one word, I really cannot discern a vice in human nature which levity does not foster: and I am not sensible that there is any one vice which reflection and consideration would not at first tend to restrain, and by degrees to cure. I said likewise, that recollection and religious retirement tended to improve us in every virtue. By proving remedies for vice, they effect this in a considerable degree, but they have still a more direct tendency.

EVERY

SERMON XIV.

EVERY one is sensible, that resolutions to be virtuous have great influence to form a virtuous character. But resolutions entered into in retirement, and upon reflection, are those to which we most steadily adhere in action. In retirement we can best collect and most deliberately resolve to apply the maxims which the knowledge of the world is calculated to teach. Then occur all those religious and moral considerations which prove the fences and guardians of virtue. Consideration discovers the many failings and errors of which we have been guilty; and thus it promotes charity towards others, and forgiveness of injuries, at the same time the strictest circumspection over one's * * * * * * * * * * * * * * * * *

* * commanding situation he surveys the beauties which the chearful spring or fruitful autumn spreads round him, feels the most pleasing emotions diffuse themselves over his whole frame? While walking along the sounding shore, does agreeable amazement fill the soul at beholding these animated forms erected by the Almighty's hand, the towering precipices, the vast ocean, or the boundless canopy of heaven. If these things are so; and that they are, let experience attest, how reasonable is it to believe that the religious mind contemplating the everlasting Nature, before whom the sun is darkness, the earth an atom, and who treadeth upon the stars, should feel an expansion of its powers inconceivably great? and in this situation, will not he that delighteth to dwell in the upright and pure, *manifest himself as he does not to the world?* more especially, when the

the soul is enraptured with surveying the miraculous scheme of redemption, admiring the infinite love of that Saviour, who, *though rich, yet became poor, though high, yet humbled himself*, and by a course of actions most grievous and painful, opened the gates of glory to his followers; when we view him suffering, dying, rising again, when, as Elisha beheld his master, we behold him taken up into the superior regions, and are ready to cry out, *My God, and my Father*, will he refuse that a double portion of his Spirit should rest upon us? When piety prompts such expressions as these, *My soul thirsteth for God, for the living God: As the hart panteth after the water brooks, so panteth my soul after thee, O God*; Is it not reasonable to think that present experience should confirm this truth? *The eyes of the Lord are on the righteous; his ears are open to their cry.* I do not deny, my brethern, that much has been advanced about this doctrine of communion with God, with more zeal than knowledge. The manner in which the Spirit operates, we have the best reason to conclude, is often concealed from us, and inexplicable by us. But speaking the words of truth and soberness, it appears quite reasonable to ascribe the greatest part of that peace, joy and elevation which the truly religious man feels in his retired and devout hours, to the secret, though not less immediate or powerful, operations of that Spirit.

HAVING shewn the usefulness and the pleasure of religious retirement; If I were not convinced that with mankind often, where more generous and noble arguments fail, pleas from necessity engage

gage to action, I should scarcely urge, as an argument to comply with the advice in the text, the unavoidableness of suffering retirement often, of being often obliged to reflect by many of those accidents and afflictions, which are the lot of humanity.

The sun of prosperity has as yet shone upon you. But think ye, will he never be overclouded, or will he never withdraw his beams, by which means levity will be banished from your soul; and reflection, from which you fled as from an enemy, be forced upon you? Will that river on which you descend, and which terminates in the ocean of eternity, be always equally placid and serene? Are there no rapid streams where you will find the greatest difficulty to manage that small skiff in which you are conveyed? Are there no water-falls, many fathoms deep, where you will be in the utmost danger of being overwhelmed? Will no violent gusts, descending from between the hills, be ready to overset you? In that period of time, which is consumed in the voyage of human life, will there be no stormy days, nor dark nights? Will there be but three seasons in the year, and those of the gentlest kind, spring, summer, and autumn? Or will never winter appear, surrounded with all his storms? Vain mortal! *Man that is born of a woman, is of a few days; they are full of trouble.* Though you have as yet always attended the house of feasting and mirth, yet you know not what sorrow may remain behind. At the table of the former, I know reflection is seldom admitted as a guest, and men who
frequent

frequent their houfe, rarely ever retire; or when they do, they are taken up with the pleafures, or the bufinefs of to-morrow. They never confider their hearts, their lives, or their tempers. Even in the houfe of God, which they frequent for cuftom's fake, or perhaps to prevent their being alone, their affections and their defires are ftill with the world, ruminating upon the guilty pleafures that are paft, or looking forward to joys of the like nature. You have faid to yourfelves then, perhaps in the pride of your hearts, *My houfe fhall never be moved.* But I will make fome fuppofitions, that are often verified in life, which may perhaps convince you of the neceffity of reflecting in time. I will fuppofe that you yet retain the virtue of natural affection, and that you have friends and children who are dear to you. God fees fit to fend the rod of affliction, and to take them out of life. Attending upon their funeral, when every eye is ready to drop a tear, will you ftill allow thoughtleffnefs and inconfideration to poffefs your hearts? Perhaps you may here be able to boaft of your fuperiority. But know, that by folly many have been *brought to a morfel of bread*, and by unforefeen accidents, this hath fometimes been the fate of thofe in whom the wifdom of this world has been remarkable If you are fent then to the chearlefs hut of miferable poverty, dependent perhaps upon the charity of thofe whom you formerly defpifed; will your former companions now vifit you, to fill up every vacant and lonely hour? Upon the very ftreet, they would pafs you without feeming to know you. Though in the days of your plenty, they fquandered profufely with you

you at the debauch or entertainment, yet they will now treat you, as reflection perhaps will inform you, you treated the beggar who was shivering at your door, while you was wallowing in plenty. Finally, I will suppose those afflictions which befal many, pain, disquiet, sickness, shall befal you. And no matter whether you are rich or poor, for it will make very small difference. Can you then believe that the goblet, sparkling with wine or strong drink, is the banisher of care? Will your vicious companions sitting at your bed-side, prevent a visit from these strangers, thoughtfulness and recollection? Then indeed, in any of these or the like circumstances in which you may be, they will lay hold on you, and you can neither banish them, nor fly from them. They might have come to your aid and support, like guardian angels: but now they come like an armed force to bind you, and deliver you up to the tormentors. Therefore, my brethren, consider the situation in which you are, the misfortunes to which you are liable, which will oblige you to think and reflect, even in spite of yourselves; be persuaded now to accustom yourselves to these, that you may meet recollection and retirement, when they are necessary, with peace and satisfaction. As you would wish to abstain from vice, to improve in virtue, to enjoy the pleasures of devotion, not to render sickness, or poverty, or death intolerable, comply now with the advice of the Psalmist, *Commune with your own hearts upon your bed, and be still.* Believe me, my brethren, by following this advice, you will live the more harmoniously in the same society, and neighbourhood: you will love one another the better, be more willing to overlook each others frailties and faults. You will be the more faithful ministers, the more diligent teachers, the more upright merchants, the more honest artificers, the more affectionate parents, the more dutiful children. In a word, you will be the more perfect in all the relations and circumstances of life in which you may be placed.

SERMON XV.

Luke vii. 36—48.

And one of the pharisees desired him that he would eat with him. And he went into the pharisee's house, and sat down to meat. And behold, a woman in the city, which was a sinner, when she knew that Jesus sat at meat in the pharisee's house, brought an alabaster box of ointment, and stood at his feet behind him weeping, and began to wash his feet with tears, and did wipe them with the hairs of her head, and kissed his feet, and anointed them with the ointment. Now when the pharisee which had bidden him, saw it, he spake within himself, saying, This man, if he were a prophet, would have known who, and what manner of woman this is that toucheth him: for she is a sinner. And Jesus answering, said unto him, Simon, I have somewhat to say unto thee. And he sayeth, Master, say on. There was a certain creditor, which had two debtors: the one owed five hundred pence, and the other fifty. And when they had nothing to pay, he frankly forgave them both. Tell me therefore, which of them will love him most? Simon answered and said, I suppose that he to whom he forgave most. And he said unto him, Thou hast rightly judged. And he turned to the woman, and said unto Simon, Seest thou this woman? I entered into thine house, thou gavest me no water for my feet; but she hath washed my feet with tears, and wiped them with the hairs of her head. Thou gavest me no kiss: but this woman, since the time I came in, hath not ceased to kiss my feet. Mine head with oil thou didst not anoint: but this woman hath anointed my feet with ointment. Wherefore I say unto thee, her sins which are many are forgiven, for she loved much: but to whom little is forgiven, the same loveth little. And he said unto her, Thy sins are forgiven.

FROM many principles of the human constitution, it might easily be shewn, that there is no method of instruction so pleasing and powerful, as that which is derived from a just delineation of characters, and an affecting representation of facts. These take a ready and fast hold of the memory, and the conclusions to be drawn from them, being similar to what prudence teaches every man to draw in the ordinary conduct of life, are easily apprehended, and leave a lasting impression. The sentiment which has obtained such universal approbation, *I am a man, and I think nothing belonging to man foreign to me*, is deeply engraved upon every heart: and while the soundest abstract reasoning, or most wholesome general rules are disregarded, virtue scarce ever fails to insinuate itself, and to gain ground where it is recommended by those examples which discover the natural

and

and amiable feelings of the heart. They attract our love. They operate on our sympathy. They convince us, that what was once practised, is still practicable: and thus while they attach, they as it were transform the soul. On the other hand, the deformity of vice is best represented in a living object. It becomes more odious by being contrasted with virtue. Its pernicious effects are most obviously displayed, and the sentiments of approbation and abhorrence are mutually heightened by opposition. We can scarcely turn to any discourse of our Saviour's, which does not serve to illustrate these observations.

The passage I have now read represents to us, in the character of the pharisee, a proud, haughty and rigid temper, and discovers to us the dangerous nature of those vices, which may lurk in the breast of a man, and influence his conduct, who is at the same time ignorant of them. The sincere marks of sorrow and attachment exhibited by the humble penitent, work upon our compassion, and interest us for her recovery. The humane and generous conduct of the great Instructor of mankind, soothes and revives her dejected spirit: and we partake of these pleasing emotions. The acceptance of her humility, repentance and love, dispels all those doubtful and solicitous thoughts, which the sting even of forsaken guilt would otherwise occasion, and diffuses that sacred serenity and joy over the human heart, which meet with the approbation of conscience and of heaven. Such sentiments as these, I believe, naturally present themselves to a religious mind, on reading

this

this paſſage. On account of its perſpicuity and plainneſs, it does not require a long commentary; a few remarks, however, will not be improper.

The phariſees were a ſect of the Jews, who pretended to a peculiar ſanctity and virtue. They valued themſelves on a ſtrict obſervance of the law, and an entire conformity to all its ceremonies. The merit they aſſumed to themſelves on this account, expreſſed itſelf in a ſupercilious haughtineſs of behaviour, and an avowed contempt of others. It is natural to imagine, as it in fact happened with the phariſees, that a religion which conſiſted ſo much in externals, ſhould often be made a cloak to conceal the carnal purpoſes of the heart. One of this ſect, whom we may reaſonably believe to have had as much candour and charity as moſt of the order, invited our Saviour to his houſe; and agreeably to the uſual condeſcenſion and courteouſneſs of his behaviour, he readily accepted the invitation. The excluſive privilege which the phariſees claimed of being accounted holy, had introduced a diſtinction that could not fail to be attended with very pernicious effects. If a man was not admitted into their ſect, if he did not conform to every trivial obſervance, if he filled an office which happened with them to be unpopular, or diſhonourable; in one or all of theſe caſes, he was regarded as a ſinner. Thus men, who in the eſtimation of the ſtricteſt ſect among them, went all under the ſame denomination, being unreſtrained by any regard to character, readily fell into thoſe vices, an abſtinence from which would not have altered their general

general reputation. Uninfluenced by the hope of honeſt praiſe, or the fear of deſerved reproach, it was no wonder if the real vices, which an injurious and political diſtinction had chiefly occaſioned, and from which the phariſees could boaſt they were free, ſeemed to juſtify the appellation which they gave them. Pride and prejudice had carried the antipathy againſt them ſo far, that to hold any communication with them, or to eat with them, was accounted a ſtain; and a good office performed to them was ſcarce reckoned one of the duties of humanity. Our Saviour, whoſe native virtue and unſtained integrity rendered no mean compliance with the prejudices of the times neceſſary, and the overflowings of whoſe benevolence were, like the rays of the ſun, diffuſed to all, never avoided their company, notwithſtanding the offence it gave, and the contempt and malice it produced: but by the apteſt admonitions, and the moſt merciful declarations, infuſed into their minds, the obliterated principles of virtue; and by inſpiring them with the hopes of the divine favour, recovered them from deſpair and guilt, to penitence and reformation.

It happened that while our Saviour was at meat with the phariſee, a woman of the city who belonged to the claſs we have been ſpeaking of, and who had probably been notorious for her vices, came into the houſe; and having brought with her an alabaſter box of ointment, while our Saviour reclined on the bed, ſtood at his feet and wept. The grief of her heart, and the fervour of her affection made her tears flow in ſuch abundance,

dance, that she washed his feet with them, She moreover wiped them with the hair of her head, and anointed them with the ointment. I will not enter into any curious inquiry who this penitent woman was, whether Mary the sister of Lazarus, Mary Magdalen, or some other; or whether the history before us relates to the same event which is recorded by the other evangelists, as happening immediately before our Saviour was betrayed. It is sufficient to say, that the first is a point of mere curiosity, which it is neither easy nor necessary to determine, and that the relation we are considering, differs so much from those of the other evangelists referred to, both in order of time, and a variety of circumstances, that it appears extremely probable to me that they are not founded on the same transaction. It may be proper to make some remarks upon the signs of penitence and attachment which are here described.

There are some expressions of our passions natural and universal. There are other indications of them, which may be ultimately founded in nature, but immediately derived from the particular manners and customs that prevail in a country. Accidental circumstances too, in the former part of one's life, may give an additional and peculiar expression to some tokens of sorrow. Thus the effusion of tears is the natural and universal indication of grief, the genuine expression of a soul melted with sorrow and penitence. The washing the feet of a stranger was an antient mark of hospitality, as we may see from Abraham's address to the angels, whom he invited to come into

SERMON XV.

into his tent. The custom spread over the east, and prevailed also among the antient Greeks. It had been retained by the Jews, and might naturally come to be considered as a token of regard, which is a sentiment so nearly allied to hospitality. I might here therefore remark, that, when our Saviour washed his disciples feet, it was an instance both of condescension and regard, very suitable to the manners of the country. A salutation, in almost all ages and nations, has been considered as a token of good-will and friendship. And this very circumstance adds an infamy to the treachery of Judas, and a severity to our Saviour's question, *Betrayest thou the son of man with a kiss?*

The hair of her head, which this penitent had probably been so careful to braid and attire, in order to set off her beauty to the greatest advantage, to gratify her vanity, or seduce the unwary, now hangs loose, unadorned and dishevelled. She uses it to wipe the feet which her tears had bathed. The contrast of her former life and manners renders the negligence of her dress, and the instance of her humility more striking testimonies of the sincerity of her sorrow, and the purity of her purposes.

Ointments and perfumes were used in those days by way of ornament and neatness, and were often offered at entertainments to the guests. The practice of using them gave occasion to our Saviour to exhort his disciples, when they fasted, not to disfigure their faces as the Pharisees did, but to wash them, and anoint their head. What had formerly served for the decoration of her person,

son, the penitent now employs to anoint our Saviour's feet.

The compassionate Jesus saw and received these natural, genuine and striking tokens of remorse, repentance, and regard with complacence. But on this the disposition of the pharisee immediately appears, *for he said within himself, If this man were a prophet, he would have known who, and what manner of woman this is; for she is a sinner.* The vices which this remark discovers, I shall have occasion to mention more particularly afterwards. At present I only explain the history. Our Saviour, who judged not by the seeing of the eye, nor the hearing of the ear, but who discerned the secret sentiments of the heart, that he might obviate the objection, which was evidently the result of pride and self-confidence, makes use of a short, but apposite story. *There was a certain creditor which had two debtors, &c.* [A]. Simon, who perhaps did not know that the question had any relation to his own suspicions, answers according to the natural and first feelings of his heart. *Simon answered and said, I suppose that he to whom he forgave most* [B]. In the 44th, 45th, 46th, and 47th verses, our Saviour applies the conversation to Simon and the penitent; the whole is to be taken together, and the meaning appears to me to be this, that as the generosity of a creditor, in the judgment of the pharisee himself, is the more to be praised the larger the debt he remits,

[A] VER. 41, 42.   [B] VER. 43.

SERMON XV.

so the mercy of God is the more to be admired in the pardon and acceptance of a notorious sinner: and as the gratitude of a debtor rises the higher, and is on this account more the object of our approbation, the greater the sum that is remitted him, so the gratitude and love which the remission of many sins kindle in a true penitent, are so strong and fervent, that the condescending Father of goodness regards them with a particular degree of approbation.

The opposition between the conduct of the pharisee and the woman sets both in the strongest light. I would only add, to what I have already observed, upon the circumstances that occur here, that the customs of giving water to wash the feet of their guests, of salutation and presenting them with ointments, which had formerly been marks of general respect and hospitality, had, by the spirit of party and the mutual hatred of sects, been converted into tokens of more particular friendship and connection. The conduct of the pharisee to our Saviour at this time, which is tacitly blamed, renders this probable. The same also appears from our Saviour's observation in his sermon on the mount. *And if ye salute your brethren only, what do more than others? do not even the publicans the same*[e]?

After these observations, let us now attend to those reflections which this passage suggests to us.

[e] MATTH. V. 47.

Let

Let us, in the first place, consider the character of the pharisee, whose vices are not expresly mentioned, but are left to be collected from the general strain of the history. There is no reason to think that he was among the most corrupt of that sect. We may suppose that he was no stranger to those virtues which the pharisee claims in the xviiith chapter of Luke, and that he was unstained by those vices, from which he glories in being free. He might have thanked God that he was neither *an extortioner, nor unjust, nor an adulterer; that he fasted twice in the week, and gave tithes of all that he had.* Fraud and oppression he had never countenanced; and we may allow that the ordinary uprightness of his behaviour was irreproachable. Ye men of the world, would ye desire a better character, or wish for a more blameless reputation? Strangers to the lovely and alluring form of virtue, you mistake for it a lifeless image which only bears a resemblance in a few features. From the history now before us, let us examine this character more minutely, and point out its defects.

First, The unjust suspicion which the pharisee's heart suggested, at seeing our Saviour receive the kindness of the penitent, without shewing any marks of displeasure, evidently discovers a high degree of pride and self-confidence. The whole history also shews that he had no sense of his own imperfection, nor the least apprehension of his own demerit. There is not a vice more unbecoming human nature, considering its frailty and imperfections, than an overweening opinion of ourselves: as if we were exempted from follies and faults. When it is observed in the ordinary transactions of life, it is a proof of great weakness. But in the concerns of virtue and religion, it plainly discovers that we have no just and elevated sentiments of the standard of virtue; that we think of the supreme Being, the source and centre of all perfection, in a manner that is unworthy of his purity and holiness, and that the culture and improvement of our own hearts and temper are the least object of our attention. With respect to our fellow-creatures, this temper has the worse effect. It gradually weakens and confines our virtue, and at last almost destroys the sentiments of humanity, kindness, generosity and compassion. If it should not happen entirely to corrupt and deprave the heart, it at least deadens all the best and most amiable affections of our nature, and prevents the exercise of every great and exalted virtue. Will the man who has indulged and cherished his pride, till it has become the prevailing and ruling passion of his heart, and blinded him to every frailty and fault in himself, be ready to forgive injuries? Will he return good for evil? Will he be patient under afflictions? Will he bear opposition? Will he spare the wretch that has incurred his resentment, and lies at his mercy? Will he shed the soothing tear of pity, or speak the words of kindness to quiet the distress of a troubled heart? Will he bind up the wounds of his poor inferior, and pour wine and oil into them to heal them? Ah no? Triumphing in the virtues, at whose defects the heaven-born soul would blush; and glorying in his being free

from

from flagrant vices, he despises his fellow-servant, and even approaches heaven with an assured countenance, and says to the humble and fearful, but devout worshipper, *Stand by, I am holier than thou.* This pride and self-confidence, by which man is most directly allied with the spirits who fell, is thus not only heinous in itself, but may properly be considered as a source of many other vices. Like a plentiful, but impure fountain, it emits a variety of streams equally turbid and impure. Being the quality most remarkable in the pharisaical character, the indignation which our mild and charitable Saviour expresses against this sect, may shew its enormity. By assuming an appearance of a conscious superiority, of a high regard for virtue, of a detestation of the abandoned, it screens itself from the censure of the world, and not rarely from the knowledge of the very man who is a prey to it. Thus being a foe equally powerful, secret and pernicious, its attacks cannot be too cautiously nor diligently guarded against. And the declarations in the gospel, that are so frequently repeated against this vice, are a most awful and alarming warning to christians to attend particularly to their characters, and not to rest satisfied, as men are but too apt to do, if their consciences reproach them with no positive guilt.

Secondly, I have the longer insisted upon this vice, because I consider it as the source from which others discovered to us in this history do flow. And as they are capable of being distinguished from it, let us particularly attend to them.

It

SERMON XV.

It appears then, in the second place, that he was either devoid of the virtue of humanity and compassion, or that the vice which has been already named had so overpowered him, that it prevented its exercise. When the penitent came into the house, she discovers the strongest and most evident symptoms of sorrow and distress. This language, which is the language of nature, never fails to rouse, and to interest the heart. And to be ignorant of it, or inattentive to it, is the surest sign of an unfeeling soul. Yet the sorrowful appearance, the tears and the humble conduct of the penitent, so far from attracting the attention, and exciting the pity of the pharisee, only afford occasion for a captious and ungenerous reflection. Knowledge of the world, and the false appearances that are to be met with in it, may render a man cautious and discerning: but if it steels the heart against every tender and compassionate feeling for a real sufferer, though almost the most worthless of men, let my soul remain in ignorance. The woman here described was, it is true, a sinner. But did the most unfeigned and expressive sorrow carry no plea for pity? Rigid and unrelenting virtue, is this the lesson thou teachest thy votaries? No. The virtuous heart is ever humane. At the sufferings of guilt it softens and melts, but with the tears of honest sorrow and penitence it mingles its own, and with the most attracting and endearing sympathy sooths their pains, and mitigates their anguish.

Thirdly, Another fault with which the pharisee is chargeable, is this: It appears that he must have

have entertained very low and groveling notions of the divine purity and perfection. He harbours not the least fufpicion that his own worth is defective, or the least doubt that the divine favour may be withheld: he feems on the contrary to confider it as his due. What muft this man think of that everlafting One *in whofe fight the heavens are not clean, and who charges his angels with folly?* While he extravagantly exalts his own merit, how muft he have debafed the Father of lights, whom the cherubims cannot behold without vailing their faces? Could his divinity be really the powerful, the jealous, the merciful, the glorious God of Mofes and the prophets? or was he not rather the imperfect, the weak, the partial being of his own imagination? Think not, my brethern, that in this his underftanding was merely defective. Juft opinions of the Deity fcarce ever fail, efpecially where revelation is vouchfafed, to arife in the mind that is difciplined by virtue, and governed by good affections. The proud and the vicious, on the contrary, are fhut out by their own folly from the knowledge of God, and have no difcernment of the Moft High. *The Lord hateth a proud look, but he giveth grace unto the lowly* [D]. Thus an attention to the character of the pharifee fhews us, that he was ruled by pride, and a confidence in his own merit; vices moft unbecoming the nature and condition of man: that his heart was infenfible to the language of forrow, and eftranged from the feelings of humanity, and that

[D] PROV. vi. 16, 17. iii. 34.

SERMON XV. 257

his conceptions of the supreme Being were altogether unsuitable and unworthy of his nature.

LET us now attend to a very different character, I mean that of the penitent woman. Her humility and penitence render her the object both of our regard and instruction. This woman, who had been a sinner, brought an alabaster box of ointment, and while our Saviour was at meat, stood behind him weeping, and began to wash his feet with her tears, and to wipe them with the hair of her head, and kissed his feet, and anointed them with the ointment. These indications of her love and attachment, her humility and purposes of amendment found such acceptance with our Saviour, that he said unto her, *Thy sins are forgiven thee.*

FAIN would man hope, even without revelation, that the tears and cries of a returning sinner would bend the justice of the divinity, and incline him to mercy. Fain would nature lead us to ascribe a relenting temper to the Governor of the universe, like to that humanity, pity and compassion which we discover in man. But the trembling pinion of reason fails, when she soars to such sublime heights: and the report she brings is various, uncertain and confused. After the longest deliberation, the most sensible and most natural prayer which a man suspended between hope and fear would offer to his Maker upon this subject, would be some such one as this. " O thou Sovereign of the universe, pour
S " thy

" thy confolation into a heart that is racked with doubts and difquiets, and dares neither diftruft thy mercy, nor rely on thy favour." It is revelation that properly defcribes the nature, and affures us of the efficacy of true repentance. Thefe important and confolatory doctrines are difplayed to us in the inftance we are now confidering.

SERMON XVI.

MATTHEW xxvi. 36——44.

Then cometh Jesus with them unto a place called Gethsemane, and saith to his disciples, sit ye here, while I go and pray yonder. And he took with him Peter and the two sons of Zebedee, and began to be sorrowful, and very heavy. Then saith he unto them, My soul is exceeding sorrowful, even unto death: tarry ye here, and watch with me. And he went a little further, and fell on his face, and prayed, saying, O my Father, if it be possible, let this cup pass from me: nevertheless, not as I will, but as thou wilt. And he cometh to the disciples, and findeth them asleep, and saith unto Peter, What, could ye not watch with me one hour? Watch and pray, that ye enter not into temptation: the spirit indeed is willing, but the flesh is weak. He went away again the second time, and prayed, saying, O my Father, if this cup may not pass away from me, except I drink it, thy will be done. And he came and found them asleep again: for their eyes were heavy. And he left them, and went away again, and prayed the third time, saying the same words.

SERMON XVI.

Though it be universally acknowledged, that the example of Christ is intended for the imitation of Christians, yet we seldom take sufficient pains to delineate the several virtues of his life, and to impress our own hearts with a sense of their dignity and importance. The solemn institutions of religion, however, have a direct tendency to bring these objects to our view; and the insisting on them, when we meet for public worship, must probably have the advantage of falling in with the natural current of our feelings and sentiments.

The knowledge of the characters of those persons whom history represents to us, is chiefly derived from observing the manner in which they acted in the capital and most interesting scenes of life. In these the leading qualities of the mind concenter, and exert themselves; and they are marked so distinctly, and represented, as it were, so luminously, that we can ascertain them with precision. But of all the circumstances in which man can be placed, that of calamity and affliction proves most directly the vigour and the dispositions of his mind; and such as this situation discovers him to be, such he generally is.

The passage of scripture which I have now read, represents our Saviour overwhelmed with such a load of sorrow and suffering, and overpowered with such a variety of melancholy prospects, that, supposing the truth of his history, even his enemies cannot fail to believe, that upon this occasion,

casion, the natural and the genuine feelings of his mind must have broke forth, and that now, when all art must have been disconcerted, he truly appeared what he actually was. Every word therefore which he speaks, and every emotion he discovers, strongly indicates the nature of his character, and, as it were, sets the seal to it. The former transactions of his life must be tried by this touchstone; and in every instance wherein they correspond to what he spoke and acted in these critical moments, we must consider them as the exhibitions of an uniform and consistent character. But before we enter on this view of our subject, let us attend to the preceding part of the evangelist's narration, and to the facts that are here represented to us.

As the time of our Saviour's suffering drew near, he gave more direct intimations of it to his followers, and pointed out the very person who was to betray him into the hands of sinners. After the institution of his supper, he had departed with his disciples to the Mount of Olives, where he again declares to them his own impending sufferings, the general consternation in which they should be involved, and their desertion that was to ensue. After this, our text informs us, that he went to Gethsemane, and his particular attachment and affection engaging him to make choice of some of the disciples for companions in that mournful hour which was to follow, he accordingly selected Peter, and James, and John, and retired with them to a small distance. To them he opened the calamitous and distressed

state

state of his mind, in that plain and unaffected language which is so natural to distress. *My soul, says he, is exceeding sorrowful, even unto death.* And while he knew that it was appointed for him to *tread the winepress alone, and that of the people there should be none with him* [A], yet the infirmity of nature so far operated as to make him hope for some assistance from the presence and sympathy of his friends. He therefore entreats them to tarry, and to watch with him. Then he went a little farther, and in the bitterness of his soul, he fell on his face, and implored his father's aid, in these words, equally expressive of his piety and his resignation, his sufferings and his fortitude: *Father, if it be possible, let this cup pass from me: nevertheless, not as I will, but as thou wilt.* Upon returning to his disciples, he finds them asleep; and addressing himself to Peter, who, but a little before, had so confidently promised upon the fidelity and steadiness of his service, *What*, says he, *could not ye watch with me one hour?* At the same time he gives a gracious admonition against any future defection, and points out the means of avoiding it, *Watch and pray, that ye enter not into temptation:* and with the same mildness and benignity which ever distinguished his character, he commends their affection, and palliates their error. *The spirit indeed is willing, but the flesh is weak.* In the utmost agony of mind which forced the sweat through every pore like great drops of blood, as Luke informs us, he reiterates the same

[A] ISAIAH lxiii. 3.

fervent

SERMON XVI.

fervent and refigned prayer, and again finding the difciples afleep, he retires the third time, and prays to his father, ufing the fame words.

From what caufes this forrow proceeded, which our Redeemer felt, is not precifely faid. But the whole hiftory fhews us that it was extreme and overwhelming. It certainly confifted chiefly in thofe views which arife from a dark and depreffed ftate of mind, and which the foul that feels, knows to be more poignant than all the tortures that can be inflicted on the body. The future calamities of a city whofe overthrow he frequently laments in fuch pathetic terms, the wretched ftate of a perifhing world, the inconfiderable effects his divine inftructions had hitherto produced, the falfenefs of a pretended friend, the infirmity of a few felect difciples; all perhaps wrought upon his compaffionate heart, and filled him with inexpreffible anguifh. The forefight of fufferings which humanity fhrinks from, of pangs which an imagination full of fenfibility clothes with more terror than the actual fufferings inflict, was perhaps too powerful to be borne in that fituation in which thefe ideas prefented themfelves. Add to all thefe, the confcioufnefs that thofe divine aids on which he had always depended, and which had been fo liberally communicated, were now for a feafon withdrawn; and that alone, and unfupported, he felt himfelf left to ftruggle with all the bitternefs of death; I fay, let us attend to thefe things, and perhaps we may have fome conception of that difmal ftate, in which our Saviour uttered this prayer; *Father, if it it be possible, let this cup depart from me: nevertheless, not as I will, but as thou wilt*; upon which, as Luke informs us, an interposition of providence became necessary, and an angel was sent from heaven to strengthen him. It is sufficient to mention, for it would be superfluous to prove, that by the first expression, *Father, if it be possible*, is meant, not if the request I now make is within the verge of Omnipotence, but if it is consistent with the plan of the divine government, and the great design of my mission into the world. That severe depression of mind which he presently felt, and the sufferings he was so soon to undergo, are evidently what he meant by that cup which he prays to be removed from him. The lot of human life in general may be figuratively expressed by a cup; and the figure is so frequent in scripture, and so apposite indeed of itself, that it must be readily apprehended. Thus the psalmist, to denote the felicity of his situation, uses the expression, *My cup runneth over* [B]. And our Saviour, when he rebukes the sons of Zebedee for their intemperate request, does it in these terms, *Are ye able to drink of the cup which I shall drink of* [C]? That is, to partake of the sufferings which I must endure.

Having said thus much in explication of the passage now under consideration, I proceed to my principal design in this discourse, to wit, to consider those virtues in the character of Christ which are here exhibited to us, and to illustrate them

---

[B] PSALM XXIII. 5.   [C] MATTHEW XX. 22.

SERMON XVI.

from the corresponding passages of his life. That I may not engage in too wild a field, I shall confine myself to the consideration of those features of our Saviour's character which appear in this passage in the most conspicuous light; I mean his piety, his resignation, and his fortitude: And of these I shall discourse in the order I have now mentioned them.

FIRST, The piety of our Saviour's heart is here discovered in the strongest light. The immediate recourse he has to prayer in this distressful situation, the humble prostration he used, the fervour of his address, and the tenor of it, all conspire to shew that he was actuated by the truest sense of the divine perfections, and the veneration that is due to them. And indeed, if we can be said to perceive the principal qualities of a person's character, who gave a perfect pattern of so many virtues, we may pronounce them to be, a perpetual impression of the divine perfections and government, and a humane and generous feeling for the distresses of mankind. The first discovers itself by all the expressions of veneration and zeal which the different circumstances of his life gave occasion to, and in the frequent acts of a rational and elevated devotion. All the answers which he gave at that time, when he was led up into the wilderness to be tempted of the devil, are plainly characteristical of this disposition. When the tempter desired a proof of his being the Son of God, by commanding the stones to become bread, he replies; *It is written, man shall not live by bread alone, but by every word that proceedeth out of the mouth*

mouth of God[D]. Upon a second effort to seduce him, by a quotation from scripture, he both shews his own piety, and insinuates a reprehension of the malicious employment of this wicked spirit. *It is written, Thou shalt not tempt the Lord thy God*[E]. The last answer he gives discovers entirely the same temper. *Thou shalt worship*, says he, *the Lord thy God, and him only shalt thou serve*[F]. In his sermon on the mount, which contains the sum of christian morals, there is this remarkable difference from every other system, that the duty of piety is not only recommended as an essential branch of morality, but that every other duty is insisted upon as flowing from or dependent upon it; and that in the performance of every one of them, we are called to consider ourselves as creatures related to the supreme Being, answerable to him for our conduct, and under the strictest obligation to promote his glory. The divine prayer which he taught his disciples is a perfect model of devout expression. It is impossible to read it with attention without perceiving that it breaths the sentiments of a heart under this particular impression, that the happiness of human creatures arises principally from the advancement and completion of the divine counsels. When his disciples had taken some offence at seeing him converse with the Samaritan woman; from a small incident which soon followed, he lays hold of an opportunity both of rectifying their mistakes, and of informing them of the great object he had in view.

[D] MATT. iv. 4. [E] MATT. iv. 10. [F] MATT. iv. 7.

When

When they *prayed him*, saying, *Mafter, eat. I have meat*, says he, *to eat that ye know not of. For my meat is to do the will of him that sent me, and to finish his work* [G]. As by the appointment of providence, food is necessary for invigorating our bodies, and for enabling us to perform the duties of ordinary life; so the exertions of piety, and the spreading its interests, seemed essential not only to the felicity, but also to the existence of the Son of God.

There is another very affecting passage in the life of Christ, which evinces in a striking manner the reality, the extent and the force of this principle of piety. While he was talking to the people, his mother and his brethren stood without, desiring to speak with him. Being informed of this, he answered, and said to him that told him, *Who is my mother, and who are my brethren? And he stretched forth his hands to his disciples, and said, Behold my mother and my brethren. For whosoever doth the will of my heavenly Father, the same is my brother and sister and mother* [H]. And to the same purpose, when a certain woman, struck with the divinity of his discourses, cried out, *Blessed is the womb that bare ye, and the paps that gave thee suck*, he answers, *Yea rather blessed are they that hear the word of God and do it* [I]. Even those relations which generally form the closest union, and which as appears from several incidents in our Saviour's

[G] JOHN iv. 27—35. [H] MATTHEW xxii. 46.
[I] LUKE xi. 27, 28.

life, he was far from overlooking, were ftill inferior to the connection formed by the prevalence of virtuous and devout difpofitions. It is remarkable too, that when any emotion of his heart is excited, it naturally mingles and affociates with that prevailing fpirit of piety, which feems ftill to have been predominant.

UPON one occafion, when he faw the multitudes, we are told, *he was moved with compaffion towards them, becaufe they fainted, and were fcattered abroad as fheep having no fhepherd. Then faith he to his difciples, the harveft truly is plenteous, but the labourers are few. Pray ye therefore the Lord of the harveft that he will fend forth labourers into his harveft*[k]. The afperity with which he rebukes the fcribes and pharifees, appears to have proceeded from the fame principle. They were not only guilty of grofs immoralities, but they practifed them under the cloak of religion; and it was this circumftance, which a pious mind muft regard with indignation, that gave rife to all that feverity of cenfure, which exceeds the ufual bounds of his mildnefs and moderation.

I MIGHT confirm the fame truth, and fhew the prevalence of the principle of piety in our Saviour's mind, from the ftrain of feveral of his parables, which are evidently intended to give men juft ideas of the divine nature and government, to inculcate the importance of thefe truths, and to

[k] MATTHEW ix. 36, 37, 38.

point

point out the eftimation which the belief of them beftows on human characters. Our Saviour makes this application of the parable of the loft fheep, and the loft piece of filver. It is equally obvious in that of the prodigal fon: and it is plain, that the principal circumftance which rendered the prayer of the publican more acceptable than that of the pharifee, arofe from the juft conceptions he entertained of the purity and perfection of the fupreme Being.

I shall now confider, as an illuftration of this fubject, fome of the particular acts of devotion which are recorded of our Saviour in the hiftory of the gofpel. It is to be remembered, that there are but a few of our Saviour's fayings and actions committed to writing: for if they fhould all be mentioned, as the apoftle John expreffes himfelf, *I fuppofe that even the world itfelf could not contain the books that fhould be written* [L]. But there is a fufficient number of facts for determining precifely his character; and the acts of devotion that are tranfmitted to us fully prove the fpirit by which he was actuated. The firft prayer recorded by the evangelift Matthew, is that which he offers up after having lamented the inattention and hardheartednefs of thofe cities, in which he had performed fo many mighty works. *I thank thee, O Father, Lord of heaven and earth, becaufe thou haft hid thefe things from the wife and prudent, and haft revealed them unto babes. Even fo, Father,*

[L] JOHN xxi. 25.

for so it seemed good in thy sight [M]. Can words express more strongly a deep impression of the divine government, and an acquiescence accompanied with gratitude in all its determinations.

WHEN our Saviour came to the tomb of Lazarus, we perceive by the answer which he gave Martha, that the glory of God was the principal object of his consideration, from the miracle he was about to perform. *Said I not to thee, that if thou wouldst believe, thou shouldst see the glory of God?* And when the stone was removed, he lift up his eyes and said, *Father, I thank thee, that thou hast heard me, and I know that thou hearest me always; but for their sakes I said it, who stand by, that they may believe that thou hast sent me* [N]. The exultation here expressed in the consciousness of the divine favour is evident; and when we consider, that a particular event which, in itself, could to our Saviour be nothing extraordinary, but which was so well adapted for impressing the spectators with a belief of his divine mission, the great mean of promoting the glory of God among mankind; when we consider, I say, that this event was the immediate object in view, we shall readily discern the propriety of the latter part of this prayer. The longest act of devotion that the scripture records of him, is that contained in the seventeenth chapter of John's gospel. If there were no other, surely this would fully evince the warmth of his devotional feelings, his ardent zeal

[M] MATT. xi. 25, 26.   [N] JOHN xi. 40, 41, 42.

for his father's glory, and his supreme veneration of his perfections. The prayer contained in the passage which I have taken for the foundation of this discourse, was repeated no less than three times; and it is put up with that earnestness, which touches the heart in such a manner as the longest comment upon it could not accomplish. The line betwixt agonizing sorrow and despondency of mind, is precisely marked; and the reiteration of the same petition, though his Father did not see proper to grant his request, proves beyond contradiction, that no disappointment could shake the strength of that piety which had grown from his earliest years, and which all the adversities of life had tended but to confirm. When we consider, in conjunction with all these, the regular and stated benedictions he used, when he was receiving the gifts of providence, or communicating them to others; the unwearied activity he employed in fixing in the minds of human creatures a sense of the importance of religious principles; those frequent retirements from the world for purposes of devotion, after one might have supposed that he was exhausted by the public ministrations of his office; his spending whole nights in prayer, and his rising often before day-break to the same employment: when we consider, I say, all these, they will certainly afford such proofs of the piety and the devotional spirit of the Son of God, as must tend strongly to affect the heart.

SECONDLY, Let us attend to that resignation of mind which is exemplified in this passage of holy writ, and marked in many other incidents of our
Saviour's

Saviour's life. Resignation arises so naturally from a spirit of piety, and is so inseparably connected with it, that we may view it as the offspring of this respectable parent; or perhaps we may rather consider them as kindred virtues, mutually borrowing from, and lending lustre to one another. Resignation supposes a state of life, in which there are various calamities and afflictions: and the greater mixture there is of these, the greater scope is given for the exercise of this virtue, which implies a calm and chearful submission to the will of God under the most adverse dispensations of his providence. As our Saviour was *a man of sorrows, and acquainted with grief*, and was exposed to a scene of suffering, that can in no respect be paralleled, there was the amplest scope for the exertion of this virtue: and accordingly no feature of his character is more plainly or distinctly discovered.

It is to be remarked that virtue in general is by no means ostentatious, and the more sincere and exalted the virtue is, the less it will affect to display itself to the best advantage. The pedant is always in quest of an opportunity to shine by a multiplicity of words without knowledge, while the man of real abilities never discovers them in an improper manner. You all know that the shallow stream murmurs along, while the motion of the deep river is unheard and unobserved. A formal exhibition of any class of virtues in our Saviour's life, though more obvious, must have been less natural, less striking, and less effectual for all the purposes of human reformation. We are

are in general therefore left to collect them as they occurred in thofe various incidents which gave proper opportunities for exemplifying them. The firſt proof of his refignation arifes from that filent and compofed manner with which he bears the various ills of human life, equally remote from the infenfibility of the ſtoic, and the pride of the cynic. When he had faſted ſo long, that the powers of nature muſt have been greatly depreſſed, and was afterwards expofed to a fevere temptation, he utters no repining expreſſion. It is incidentally and without the leaſt complaint, when juſtice ſeemed to require it, that he paints ſo ſtrongly the poverty and diſtreſs of his external circumſtances. *The foxes have holes, and the birds of the air have neſts, but the Son of man hath not where to lay his head.* While he travels through Judea working the will of his Father, we hear no complaint of the ſultry ſun by day, nor the unwholefome fogs by night, of the rough roads, or ſteep mountains, the rapid rivers, or dangerous lakes. In the execution of his office, though it was plain he was not infenfible of thoſe hardſhips he was called to undergo, yet we perceive no indication of peeviſhneſs or difcontent, He ufes no unbecoming ſhifts to avoid adverfity, nor any unworthy means to court profperity. On the other hand, he ſeems to confider all attention to every human accommodation beneath his notice, in as far as it would have taken up ſo much of that precious time which was folely devoted to the eternal intereſts of mankind. I appeal to thoſe who know the world, whether this general manner of life, joined to that perpetual

T - fenfe

sense of divine things that was upon his mind, does not prove a general resignation of temper with more force, and with less suspicion than a thousand declarations could have done. But the occurrences of our Saviour's life were so various, and some of them of such a particular nature, that in these the declarations of his resignation became perfectly natural and unsuspicious, and the exemplification of it altogether proper and conspicuous. There cannot be a more apposite instance to our present purpose than that which is exhibited in the text. Under the deepest agony of mind, and while he suffers a species of distress which he had never before felt in so great a degree, the powers of nature are ready to fail: he almost recoils from the hour for which he had come into the world: he falls on his face, and prays that the cup might pass from him: but though the conflict was terrible, and the prospect overwhelming, he immediately adds, *Nevertheless, not as I will, but as thou wilt, if this cup may not pass away except I drink it, thy will be done.* My request is fervent, because my suffering is extreme; but my sense of resignation is still more powerful than my aversion to pain. Can language express what he felt, or describe the submission of his soul? Let humanity here drop a tear, and the heart formed for the admiration of suffering virtue revere his resignation,

A VERY short time after he exhibits another striking instance of the same temper. When the zeal of Peter induced him to draw his sword in his master's defence, and to smite the servant of
the

SERMON XVI.

the high-prieſt; he deſires him to put his ſword up again into its place, and in the ſtrongeſt terms expreſſes his entire acquieſcence in the ſufferings deſtined for him by the counſels of the Almighty. *The cup*, ſays he, *that my father has given me to drink, ſhall I not drink it?* The evangeliſt Matthew likewiſe records another ſaying of his upon this occaſion, which equally proves the calm reſignation of his ſoul. *Thinkeſt thou that I cannot now pray to my Father, and he ſhall preſently give me more than twelve legions of angels? But then how ſhall the ſcriptures be fulfilled, that thus it muſt be*°? The ſame ſpirit is alſo ſhewn in that ſevere reproof which our Saviour gave to Peter upon a former occaſion. For when he foretold his ſufferings, this diſciple ſaid to him, *Be it far from thee, Lord; this ſhall not be unto thee.* But inſtead of approving an anſwer that in ſome meaſure diſcovered affection, he turned to him and ſaid, *Get thee behind me, ſatan, thou art an offence unto me, for thou favoureſt not the things that be of God, but thoſe that be of men* ᴾ. And to mention only one other particular inſtance which accompanied the laſt ſcene of his life: A little after having borne with incredible patience the tortures of his body and the anguiſh of his mind, he ſtill preſerved the union betwixt ſoul and body: and it was not till he perceived all the counſels of God accompliſhed that he cried out, *It is finiſhed,* and then bowed his head and reſigned his ſoul into

° MATTH. xxvii. 53, 54.   ᴾ MATTH. xvi. 22, 23.

the hands of that God to whom he had commended it.

THIRDLY, Let us confider the fortitude which our Saviour always difcovered under the preffure of the fevereft afflictions. Fortitude is fo much allied to refignation, that though perhaps we fometimes obferve the latter in people of a foft and tender caft, who cannot properly be faid to poffefs the former; yet the triumph and perfection of refignation always fuppofes an unfhaken fortitude and intrepidity of mind. Accordingly all the illuftrations I have ufed upon the former topic of difcourfe might with propriety be produced as proofs of the fortitude of our Saviour's mind. The coincidence of the fentiments of fortitude and refignation, with refpect to his character, appears the more unqueftionable from this confideration, that he was able to have avoided the fufferings he endured by an exertion of that intrinfic power which was permanent in him; and that the fole caufe of his fuffering the greateft load of calamities which ever fell to the lot of one man, arofe from his own native fuperiority of mind, and his unlimited fubmiffion to his Father's will. Thus he tells us himfelf. *No man taketh my life from me; I have power to lay it down, and I have power to take it again* [q]: and he who could have obtained *more than twelve legions of angels from his father*, was able to have ftruck dead with a word that armed, lawlefs multitude which came out of Je-

[q] JOHN X. 18.

SERMON XVI. 277

rufalem to apprehend him. The endurance therefore of calamities proves a degree of fortitude in our Saviour's mind, in fome meafure diffimilar, and in every refpect fuperior to that which was ever exhibited by any other perfon. And from what has now been remarked, it will appear how plain an example of this virtue is difcovered to us in the hiftory now before us. Fortitude by no means implies an infenfibility to the evils which befal us: on the other hand, wherever this infenfibility takes place, the exercife of fortitude muft be entirely excluded. It is no lefs indifputable that the greater fhare of fenfibility we poffefs, the greater merit arifes from a conduct decent and proper under diftrefs and affliction. Now it appears to me, that this paffage equally fhews the fenfibility of our Saviour's mind, the height of his diftrefs, and his refolution of enduring the utmoft extremity, rather than counteract the ends, or diminifh the dignity of his obedience.

I SHALL but juft mention two or three other inftances which fhew in a ftriking lignt the virtue now under our confideration. Fortitude not only difcovers itfelf in the actual bearing of afflictions, but in the general turn of our behaviour to thofe who poffefs power and fuperior influence, and in whofe hands are the means of inflicting punifhments, and taking vengeance for fuppofed injuries. In this view the manner of our Saviour's behaviour to the fcribes and pharifees, who were the moft powerful and popular leaders of their time, and whofe principal object was evidently the prefervation of their power, ftrongly indicates this
difpofition,

disposition. Instead of soliciting their favour by direct praises, or even by dubious silence; there is no set of men, against whom he uses the severity of censure with equal keenness. Every reader tolerably acquainted with the history of the gospel will perceive the justice of this remark. I shall only appeal to the twelfth and twenty-third chapters of Matthew's gospel, and the corresponding places in the other evangelists. In the same light we must consider that severe reply which our Saviour gives to the pharisees, when certain of them came to him, and said, *Get thee out, and depart hence, for Herod will kill thee.* Instead of a soothing or an evasive answer, which considering the power and disposition of Herod, could not perhaps have been censured, *Go ye*, says he, *and tell that fox, behold I cast out devils to-day and to-morrow, and the third day I shall be perfected* [R].

But there is nothing can set this virtue of our Saviour in a stronger point of view than his behaviour when the multitude, led on by Judas, came out armed with swords and staves, and at a time of darkness too, which, as it is most suited to the purposes of malice and cruelty, is also most apt to raise timidity, for they had brought with them, as the evangelist John expresly mentions, lanterns and torches. His conduct upon this occasion is throughout so noble and magnanimous, that I am sensible all words are unequal to my conception of its greatness. When Judas approached and

[R] LUKE xiii. 31, 32.

SERMON XVI.

said, *Hail, master, and kissed him,* he calmly replies, *Friend, wherefore art thou come?* It was no wonder that all the effrontery of guilt was silenced by the sedate majesty and meekness of divine virtue. Accordingly we read of no answer made by his revolted disciple at that period, tho' as his beloved disciple tells us, *he knew all things that should come upon him, yet he stepped forth to the multitude, and said, Whom seek ye?* When they replied, *Jesus of Nazareth.* He answers, *I am he. As soon as he had said, I am he,* says John, *the multitude went backward, and fell to the ground.* The intrepidity of his reply appeared so astonishing, that the hearts of the cruel and merciless were almost changed: and had he been anxious to save his life, no miracle would have been necessary to have diverted their purpose. Then he asks them again, *Whom seek ye?* And when they said, *Jesus of Nazareth,* he answered, *I have told you that I am he; if therefore you seek me, let these go their way* [a]. The brave are ever merciful and compassionate. And while Jesus himself meets suffering with a daring and unshaken mind, he discovers the most amiable attention to his followers, and that too in circumstances in which even a great mind might have been properly engrossed with its own concerns. It truly appears to me, that the mere superiority and intrepidity of our Saviour's conduct would have naturally produced such an effect upon the multitude, as to have sent them away without accomplishing their purpose,

[a] JOHN xviii. 4—6.

had

had it not been for the zealous interpofition of Peter, which gave them time to recover from their furprize, perhaps inflamed them anew, and beftowed fufficient courage to lead the unrefifting Jefus away. This difcourfe would admit of much practical improvement, if I had time to enlarge upon it. But I fhall contract what I have to fay into as narrow a compafs as poffible.

In the firft place, my brethren, *what think ye of Chrift?* Do not the exalted virtues which he practifed, fhew that he is the Son of the living God? Behold the admired wifh of the heathen fulfilled: Virtue itfelf affuming a human fhape, and dwelling among men. This is the divinity fet up in our temples. To him bow your knees, and to him offer your hearts.

Secondly, From this particular delineation of fome of the virtues which were fo confpicuous in the life of Chrift, let us learn not only a general admiration of thefe virtues, but let us afpire after the practice of them in the fimilar inftances of life and conduct in which the providence of God may place us. The refpect we pay to the qualities of the divine life, is by far of too general a nature. We too rarely defcend to particulars. Who is the man that profits moft by this difcourfe? He who goes away applauding a devout temper? Or he who forms the refolution of becoming more devout, and puts his refolutions into practice? The latter alone is the profitable hearer.

SER-

SERMON XVII.

John xix. 30.

When Jesus therefore had received the vinegar, he said, It is finished: and he bowed his head, and gave up the ghost.

AMONG the infinitely various characters of men, there are a few who are attentive to whatever seems to be serious and important; there are many to whose reason we speak in vain, if we cannot interest their hearts; there are some of so soft a mold, that whatever has the least degree of tenderness melts and affects them, while others can see and hear what is quite overpowering to such, and still remain unmoved. When we view men in a particular light, the variety of their characters, propensities, inclinations, and capacities is amazing. When we survey them in a different point of view, their resemblance is as evident and striking. Their resemblance consists in their original powers and principles; their difference arises from situation, education, improvement, and a great number both of known and latent causes.

causes. From their variety it happens, that different objects affect different men; from their resemblance it happens that some things affect almost all men, though in different degrees.

The general propensity of mankind to observe and regard the last words even of those who have been no way remarkable in life, cannot fail to be acknowledged; but this propensity particularly appears with regard to those who have acted a conspicuous part, or who are considered by us as our friends and benefactors. The last words of such impress the minds of most men in the strongest manner, and there is scarcely one on whom they do not produce some effect. The words themselves, the occasion on which they are spoken, the circumstances with which they are attended, the consequences which follow, naturally excite such a variety of emotions, that supposing a person to remain untouched by some of them, yet he feels the force of others. The verse now read, which contains the last words of our Saviour, affords a variety of reflections, which must prove interesting to every hearer. In treating of them I propose, in the first place, to consider the meaning and import of this expression, *It is finished*, which our Saviour used before he bowed his head, and gave up the ghost. 2dly, I shall consider the peculiar light in which this expression, with the consequence which immediately followed, discovers our Saviour's character to us.

In the first place: By this expression, *It is finished*, we may understand our Saviour as declaring

ring that the great plan of divine providence, for which he was fent into the world, was accomplifhed.

THOSE who live in the world propofe to themfelves various ends; and we unavoidably confider thofe ends, as objects either of praife, or of difapprobation. One aims at the gratification of his appetites, and the enjoyment of his pleafures. Another purfues riches, or makes ambition, and the love of power, the guide of his life. We cannot view thefe men in the fame light with thofe, who are fired with the love of virtue, of their country, of mankind. We term fome ends, mean and unworthy, unworthy of a rational creature like man; others laudable and becoming; and fome truly great and heroic. It is farther to be obferved, that we not only applaud the profecution of an end that is good, but if it be profecuted with a peculiar degree of fteadinefs, the more juftly and highly it obtains our approbation. It can fcarcely be faid of the worft, that they never purfued a good end; but how finifhed is that character, which never ftooped to any end that was mean and unworthy! The eye of the generality of men is captivated by every glaring object. Objects of this kind fometimes even attract the heart, and divert the aim of the well-intentioned. We can eafily apply to human life the fable which reprefents one as obftructed in the profecution of a race, by meeting with golden apples which were induftrioufly thrown in the way. But amidft all the variety of poffible purfuits, it will be acknowledged, that none can be accounted fo truly great and

and heroic, or so deserving of our utmost steadiness, as promoting the glory of God, and fulfilling all the designs of his providence. That this was the end which our Saviour ever had in view; and that he pursued it with the most unwearied steadiness and attention, is evident to every one who reads the gospel.

A LITTLE after his entrance upon his public ministry, when his disciples asked him to take some meat, to support him under the fatigues which he had endured, he takes occasion to inform them, that *his meat was to do the will of him that sent him, and to finish his work* [A]; and to the same purpose he declares in another place, *I came down from heaven not to do my own will, but the will of him that sent me* [B]. Anxious to fulfill the great plan of providence, he always discovers that it was uppermost in his thoughts. *I must work the work of him that sent me, while it is day; the night cometh when no man can work* [C]. In that long prayer which he offers to his Father a little before his crucifixion, recollecting what was already done, and conscious of his fortitude to endure the last trial, he declares, *I have glorified thee on earth, I have finished the work which thou gavest me to do* [D]. When the zeal of one of his disciples would have led him to oppose the unjust violence that was offered to his Master, he admonishes him not to resist the will of his Father. *The cup which my Fa-*

[A] JOHN iv. 34.   [B] JOHN vi. 38.   [C] JOHN ix. 4.
[D] JOHN xvii. 4.

ther, says he, *hath given me, shall I not drink it*[e]*?* If we attend to the actions of Jesus, we must allow that they were calculated for promoting the ends of divine providence, as far as we can conceive any course of life to be so.

WHEN we consider things in a very general view, it is true that every thing which happens may be said to constitute a part of the plan of divine providence. In this sense it is, *that the wrath of man praiseth God*, and *that he hath made all things for himself; yea, even the wicked for the day of evil.* The natural course of things is nothing but certain dispositions of his appointment; and under the plan of his administration is comprehended both the conduct of the virtuous, and the behaviour of the vicious. This we may call the natural plan of his providence.

BUT when we attend to the moral perfections of the Almighty, the declarations he hath given in the constitution of man, that he is the friend and patron of virtue and of virtuous men, the evidences he affords of his desire to promote the kingdom of righteousness among men, we recognize another plan of a more particular nature, in which he seems to be more immediately interested. This we may call the moral plan of his providence. It is in this latter sense that the words now under consideration are to be understood. The most exalted piety, the most extensive bene-

[e] JOHN xviii. 11.

volence, the greatest humility, the utmost meekness, patience, and resignation; Lo! these, and every other virtue shone forth with the greatest lustre through the whole character of Jesus. The uniform piety and purity of his conduct give an irrefragable evidence to every declaration that he made; and force us, if we will not believe himself, at least to believe him for his works' sake. It is proper to be remarked, that the scheme, or plan of providence, and the view of accomplishing it, were objects to the enlarged and comprehensive mind of the Son of God, in a degree and manner different from that in which they can be supposed to be objects to the wisest and most enlightened of his followers. The whole scheme was at once in his eye; the beginning, the progress, and the result of it were sensibly present to him. He discerned the connections and dependencies, and that infinite series of events which it comprehends. He saw the particular end, which every action of his life, and every instance of his suffering promoted as precisely as one skilled in works of human art, can discern the particular tendency and purpose of every part of any piece of workmanship that is presented to him. Ever intent upon fulfilling that part which was allotted to him, just before he resigned his spirit, he cried out, *It is finished*. As it appears therefore, both from the conduct and declarations of our Saviour, that the promoting the glory of God, and the fulfilling the plan appointed by his providence, was his constant and invariable aim while he dwelt with mankind; it is extremely reasonable to conclude, that by the last words he uttered he intended

SERMON XVII.

ed to fignify to the world, that this plan was now accomplifhed; that the intentions of divine providence, as far as they regarded his miffion, his life, his fufferings, his death, had their completion. The general ftrain and tenor of the paffage confirms what has now been advanced. *After this, Jefus knowing that all things were now accomplifhed, that the fcriptures might be fulfilled, faith, I thirft. Now there was fet a veffel full of vinegar, and they filled a fpunge with vinegar, and put it upon hyffop, and put it to his mouth. When Jefus therefore had received the vinegar, he faid, It is finifhed: and he bowed his head, and gave up the ghoft* [F]. But though this is the moft general fenfe in which we are to underftand thefe words, and though we cannot affign any other that is not comprehended in the explication now given, yet they very rationally admit of a more particular and confined interpretation. Let us therefore confider the more particular parts of this great and extenfive plan, which our Saviour might have had in view when he expreffed himfelf in this manner.

I would obferve then, in the fecond place, that we may confider thefe words as a declaration from our Saviour, that his fufferings were now ended. As endued with the feelings of human nature, fuch a long and continued courfe of fufferings, fuch an uninterrupted feries of the fevereft affliction, could not fail to affect his fpirit in the moft fenfible manner. And the confciouf-

[F] JOHN xix. 28, 29, 30.

ness that now the measure of his sorrows was full, joined to the foresight of his speedy deliverance from them, made him cry out in these memorable words, *It is finished.* Those consolations, which even the indulgent Father of mercy had by an extraordinary dispensation of providence withdrawn from his own blameless Son, were now in some measure restored. He commends his spirit into his hands. He saw the concluding scene of that wretchedness to which he had voluntarily submitted, the bitter and the baleful cup of grief he had drained to the very dregs. Still his unshaken soul with astonishing patience bore every shock, and encountered every foe; and not all the extremity of pain and ignominy engaged him to quit the body till he had experienced the last indignity which it was decreed for him to endure. But when he received the vinegar, he declared that all his sorrows were now accomplished, and by one voluntary effort he resigned that sacred spirit which had exhibited such miraculous instances of every human and divine virtue.

In the third place: We may consider these words as a declaration that the offences of men were now expiated, and that the justice of God was fully satisfied. This explication is perfectly agreeable to what has been advanced in the preceding part of this discourse; and in this light they have commonly been considered.

There is nothing more plainly asserted in scripture, than that Christ Jesus suffered in our room and stead, *the just for the unjust*; that he gave *his life*

life a ranfom for many; that *we receive atonement by him*. Men who have confidered the divine perfections in a particular view, have raifed many objections againft this doctrine: but I know of no method by which we can become acquainted with the nature and attributes of the Supreme Being but by a ferious and humble attention to the works of God, to the ufual method of adminiftration, as it is difcovered in the government of the world, and to the revelation which in his mercy he hath vouchfafed to difpenfe to mankind. If we attend to the method of God's government of the world, we meet with many inftances where fome are involved in punifhment for the faults and crimes of others. The deliverance from calamities that were deferved, and ready to be executed, is often procured by the aid of others who bear a fhare of thefe calamities though they had no hand in the guilt that occafioned them. Inftances of thefe, and fuch like difpenfations of providence, render the doctrines of the atonement and fatisfaction of Jefus, as they are revealed in fcripture, very credible to men of an attentive and humble difpofition of mind. We can never, my brethren, think with too much reverence, and judge with too much caution upon fubjects of this nature; and nothing can be more abfurd than that a creature like man, inftead of attending to facts and obfervations in order to form his opinions, fhould rely upon the combinations of his own imagination, and adopt thefe as the dictates of reafon and of truth. I have no intention of entering upon a full difcuffion of thefe fubjects. To the obfervations now made, and the texts of scripture already produced, I shall only add the following.

The apostles declare in their epistles, *that while we were yet sinners, Christ died for us* [G], and that *we are reconciled to God by the death of his Son* [H]; *Christ is the propitiation, not for our sins only, but for the sins of the whole world* [I]. Can it be expressed more clearly that the great purpose of the death of Christ was to expiate our offences, and to reconcile the Almighty to us his offending creatures? Whenever we attempt to explain things of this kind too particularly, we are in very great danger of running into error, by reckoning the objects, the manner, the ends, and the means of the divine government, too much alike to those of human governments, though there certainly is an infinite difference. By assisting the imagination to form distinct conceptions of the counsels and designs of Omnipotence, we are apt to confound the conceptions that are suitable to the Supreme Being, with those which man may be supposed to entertain in similar circumstances. Unguarded expressions have been used, as if the Divinity could be capable of revenge, implacability, weakness; all which are certainly far removed from him, and which it never was the design of those very men, who used the expressions, to ascribe to him. But to all my ideas of goodness, of justice, of mercy, it appears nowise contradictory to say, that in that great and extensive scheme of divine

[G] ROM. v. 8.   [H] ROM. v. 10.   [I] JOHN ii. 2.

providence

SERMON XVII.

providence which is carrying on in the world, and of which the wifeft of the fons of men fees but a very fmall part, it became fit and neceffary, perhaps unavoidable, that an extraordinary degree of fuffering fhould befall an innocent perfon, who, by his voluntary fubmiffion to it, fhould rectify a number of thofe diforders which were introduced into the world, and by conciliating the Supreme Being fhould thus prevent its final deftruction.

As therefore, my brethren, the expiation of fin, and the reconciliation of men to an offended God, were the principal parts of that plan which our Saviour was to execute upon earth; and as the affurance of the completion of it could not fail to afford the higheft comfort and joy to his followers; he, agreeably to the general benevolence of his nature, and the attention he ever paid to the great ends of his miffion, regardlefs of the pain and anguifh he endured, and folely intent upon what was great and becoming, juft before he refigned his foul, proclaimed aloud, *It is finifhed.*

HAVING thus taken notice of the different explications of which thefe laft words of our Saviour are capable, let us confider the peculiar light in which this difcovers his character to us.

WHAT has been now faid, may ferve to give us a view of the death of Chrift fomewhat different from that in which it is commonly confidered, but not lefs interefting. According to the general conftitution of the human frame, and the connection between the foul and the body, it is impoffible,

ble, by any mere effort of our own, and without some violence, to separate the one from the other. There is also a certain degree of pain and suffering which unavoidably produces this diffolution, and which no inclination nor defire of the individual can prevent. Thefe are eftablifhed laws, to which in general all the fons of Adam muft bow. But with refpect to our Saviour, it does not appear that they took place. He had that power over the connection which fubfifted between his foul and his body, that at any period he could have diffolved it, without the intervention of any ordinary means. On the other hand, he could have prevented any of the ordinary means which take away life from being ufed againft him; or when they were ufed, he could have been above their efficacy. The magnanimity then of our Saviour's life and death appears in this, that as long as the purpofes of divine providence required it, he endured the moft excruciating and intolerable pains, though it was in his power to quit that veil of humanity which fubjected him to them; and that as foon as the moment was come, when the will of heaven was fulfilled, he at once diffolved that connection which, according to the counfels of that will, and on account of a moft generous love for a perifhing world, he had fo long preferved. Thus he fpeaks always of laying down his own life; and exprefly fays, *No man taketh my life from me, but I lay it down, and I have power to take it again* [R].

[R] JOHN X. 18.

THE

SERMON XVII.

THE Jews sent out an armed force against him, and assaulted him as a common malefactor. He could have rescued himself by his own power, or called for legions of angels, who at his command would have immediately delivered him. But *as a lamb is led to the slaughter, and as a sheep before her shearers is dumb, so opened he not his mouth* [L]. Patiently did he bear every contumely, indignity, and torment, till the whole will of God, and all the designs of his miraculous dispensation were accomplished. Then by a like voluntary act which had occasioned his assumption of the human frame, he greatly resigned it. It has been justly observed, that the words which we translate *he gave up the ghost*, would be more properly and literally translated, *he resigned*, or *he dismissed his spirit*. And it is remarkable, that when the centurion heard him cry out with a loud voice before this happened, and observed that the force of his natural vigour was not abased, he immediately concluded that there was something miraculous in the manner of his death. For, (saith the evangelist Mark) *when the centurion which stood over against him, saw that he so cried out, and gave up the ghost, he said, Truly this man was the Son of God* [M].

IT is impossible to discover the conduct and character of Christ in a more interesting point of view, than that in which this exhibits him to us. In how faint a light does the virtue of patriots and heroes, of all the just, and good, and great ap-

[L] IS. liii. 7.   [M] MARK XV. 39.

pear, when contrasted with the virtue and magnanimity of Jesus! By an election properly his own, he submitted to misery. Though sensible of all its severity, and able to avoid its stroke, yet he never shrunk from the combat, or rejected the bitterest draught that was presented to him. The Jews went out against him with swords and staves, as against a murderer: the apparatus of his death, and the circumstances which attended his execution, were dispiriting and shocking; such as would have disarmed mere humanity of its fortitude. The extension of his body, the piercing of his hands and feet, the cruel and unrelenting malice of his enemies, doubtless produced a degree of pain that was excruciating. But with what meekness, composure and resignation does he not bear it, though we cannot doubt but he might have avoided it! Could not he have quitted that mansion in which his spotless soul was lodged, and would not heaven have immediately opened to receive its pristine, immaculate inhabitant? If he required it, would not the earth have heard the voice of its former Master, and swallowed up his merciless tormentors? The sage of antient Greece would not violate the law of his country, nor desert the prison where he was confined: a striking, but unequal representation of the magnanimity of our Saviour. He knew that the operation of poison would soon terminate a life that had been devoted to the service of his fellow-citizens; and rather than transgress the laws, under whose influence he had acted such a distinguished part, he submitted to death; and with true intrepidity met his fate. But our Saviour, unrestrained by any

any law, unsubjected to any necessity, suffered a thousand pangs, and though despised and insulted by a whole nation, deserted by his own disciples, deprived of every thing, to all human appearance, that can disarm death of its terrors, yet still refused to quit the prison in which his celestial spirit was lodged, 'till the whole purposes of heaven were fulfilled. "Yes," says a writer whose faith is not stable, but whose heart is open to the sentiments of greatness, of worth, and of humanity, when he considers merely the external circumstances which attended the death of the Athenian, and of our Saviour, " if the life and death of So-
" crates are those of a sage, the life and death of
" Jesus are those of a God.

" No person," says the antient maxim, can be
" called great or happy before his death." It is this which crowns the most illustrious life, and sets the seal upon the fairest character. Estimate our Saviour's character by this rule. To depart out of life with protestations of injured innocence, gives no unfavourable impression; but to suffer the life and actions to speak for themselves, and to remain unshaken under a load of infamy and injustice, as conscious of superior dignity, affords sensations far more pleasing and powerful. To forgive one's accusers, to pardon the most undeserved ill-treatment, is truly great; but to return condescension for malice, to shew the most generous piety, and to pour forth the most fervent prayers for one's bitterest foes, is a pitch of glory that is transcendent. To be solicitous about one's future state, and to support one's mind under unjust

just sufferings with the prospect of after-felicity, is becoming and manly: but to be solely intent at the hour of death, upon the execution of a plan undertaken to promote the welfare and happiness of others, is truly divine. That the soul upon the immediate prospect of its separation from the body, should hesitate and flutter, and leave its ancient receptacle with some reluctance, is natural to humanity; but to discover the precise moment, when the purposes of heaven are accomplished, to make a voluntary resignation of the soul to quit the body by a proper exertion of inherent power, are actions becoming a Deity.

SERMON XVIII.

Isaiah liii. 3.

He is defpifed and rejected of men, a man of forrows, and acquainted with grief.

YOU all know that thefe words are a part of a moſt remarkable and precife prediction of the character of our Saviour, whoſe death many among you defign to commemorate this day, by partaking of that facrament which he inſtituted for that very purpofe.

I need not tell you that you ought to be inflamed with the higheſt love and gratitude to your Maſter, and affected with the deepeſt forrow for your fins, on fo folemn an occafion. Not to raife in you thefe difpofitions, for I am perfuaded you feel them already, but to cheriſh, to improve, and to exalt them, I ſhall at this time relate fome of the chief fufferings our Saviour endured, which plainly point him out *as a man of forrows, and acquainted with grief.* And, O bleffed Jefus, I humbly implore thy affiſtance to enable me to

ſpeak

speak on this affecting subject, with that fervour which is becoming thy votary, and that divine energy which may touch the hearts of thy disciples.

Before we introduce the sufferings of our Saviour, let us just take notice of the primeval, and fallen state of the human race.

Man came out of the hands of his powerful and beneficent Creator, an innocent and upright being, feeling no disquiets within, and exposed to no tempests without, enjoying full means of immediately gratifying every desire, and entirely happy in the sensible friendship of the universal Parent of heaven and earth. With the most unbounded scope to satisfy every want, and liberty to range in a paradise of delights, there was imposed but one single prohibition, as the mark of his dependance, and the test of his obedience. This prohibition, however, man disregarded, and desiring to be equal to God, fell below the true dignity of a man, lost the favour of his Maker, his inward peace and tranquility, and introduced into the world sin, and diseases, and pain, and death. The race indeed increased; but ignorance, violence, oppression, and every kind of iniquity increased with them; and the calamities which were at first confined to two, extended to millions, and involved the numberless posterity of the apostate pair. To this deplorable condition, consisting in the loss of innocence, the consciousness of guilt, the dread of misery, and the train of

SERMON XVIII.

of tormenting thoughts, which muſt accompany
theſe, was man ſunk.

A HUMAN eye might have pitied his fellow-
mortals : but no human hand could have helped
them. This taſk was even too arduous for any of
thoſe exalted orders of beings which continually
ſurround the throne of God, and ſing his praiſes.
But it was reſerved for one who was fully able to
execute it: and while angels ſaw and compaſſion-
ated fallen man, in the aſſembly of heaven the
Son of God declares his merciful intention of ſub-
jecting himſelf to their ſtate, in order to be the
author of their ſalvation. His father approves,
and to preparing the way for his appearance, the
miniſtry of angels, and the ſchemes of man are
made ſubſervient.

AT length the appointed period for that wonderful event which prophets foretold, and for
which martyrs bled, arrives. The eternal Son of
God, *the brightneſs of his Father's glory, and the
expreſs image of his perſon*, by whom the heavens
and the earth were made, condeſcended to appear
among mankind. He put off the effulgence of
divine glory, and was cloathed with the robe of
humanity. Where ſhall I look for this divine perſon? Is he born in a palace? or does he make his
appearance with the pomp and ſplendour which
the misjudging world reckon the companions of
greatneſs? Behold he comes, the Saviour comes :
but it is in a mean and humble condition. He
left the joys of heaven, the boſom of his Father,
that ſeat of ſerene and unmixed happineſs, the
veneration

veneration of angels, and for thee, O man, he enters into the state of wretchedness. A stable is his birth-place, and a manger is his cradle. How extraordinary was this change? From living with cherubs and with seraphs, yea, from being their superior, he becomes an inhabitant of the same mansion, with the beasts of the field. O Jesus, in this humble condition, when tender and innocent upon the knees of thy mother, she beheld thee with divine complacence, who could discern the Son of the Almighty, and the Saviour of the world? None but heaven-directed minds. And they discern him. Lo angels acknowledge thee, and at thy birth proclaim *peace on earth, and good-will to men* [A]. Some of the wise and worthy confess thee as *the salvation of the Lord, the glory and the king of Israel* [B].

But this very confession becomes to Jesus a source of sorrow, and draws upon him the hatred and resentment of a powerful tyrant. To escape the fatal effects of these, it is necessary to convey him into a foreign land, and in those tender years which seldom raise envy, my Redeemer is forced into exile, and exposed to all the hardships that attend it. He is again brought into his own country, lives in subjection to his parents, enduring hard labour, and all the inconveniencies of a mean condition.

But now the scene opens. He prepares to execute the work for which he appeared among men.

[A] LUKE ii. 14.   [B] VERSES 30. 32.

The world confiders him as nothing elfe than the carpenter's fon: but his forerunner, that powerful preacher of righteoufnefs, declares his dignity. Yea, the declaration of heaven itfelf is given in his favour. That awful voice which the dead fhall hear and obey, the voice of the Almighty, pronounces him his *beloved Son in whom* he is *well pleafed*. Could he have been ufhered into the world in a way more ready to conciliate the love and approbation of mankind, to make the good to revere him, and the wicked to dread him? Thus one would judge. But attend to the hiftory.

The apoftate angel, the king of darknefs, the patron and head of the wicked, always watchful againft the firft appearance of any thing that is good, and ever defirous to feduce from righteoufnefs, has power allowed him to tempt him. He ufes his moft prevailing arts. But neither hunger the moft extreme, nor the offer of any earthly power and fplendour, could draw him from the direct path of integrity. Secure on every fide, a fuit urged with a religious appearance could not deceive him. At laft baffled, as when he fell from heaven, he leaves the Son of God, and angels receive him,

Our Saviour now enters upon his public miniftry: and what aftonifhing facts are we prefented with! Behold and wonder, the moft fingular predictions of the prophets are fulfilled! The eyes of the blind are opened, and the ears of the deaf unftopped, the lame leap like the hart, the dumb fing for joy, and the inhabitant of the filent tomb

tomb is restored to life. Surely these wonderful acts of love and kindness procured him such approbation, that he could want neither the necessaries, nor the conveniencies of life. Whose door would not have been open for the reception of so honourable a guest? Who that had two garments would not have bestowed one upon him? Or who would not have shared with him the very last morsel? But the case was far otherwise. I am covered with shame, when I reflect upon the ingratitude and inhumanity of the Jews, and hear my Saviour thus speaking of his own condition. *The foxes have holes, the birds of the air have nests, but the Son of man hath not where to lay his head* [c]. The rains did not sooner descend, the winds did not sooner blow, and the tempests did not sooner roar, than he, without aid, without shelter, felt all their force. Shrinkest thou, O christian, at the relation of those hardships? Let thy tears flow in admiration of that patience and fortitude which never shrunk from the feeling of them.

But I come to tell you of sorrows which pierced thy Redeemer much deeper. Those I am to mention, tho' to him unspeakably great, yet unless thy soul feel something of that benevolence which actuated him, will not perhaps strike thee much. Yet hear and consider them. I mean then the sorrows and grief which Jesus felt in being despised, *rejected*, hated by such numbers of his

[c] MATTHEW viii. 20.

SERMON XVIII.

countrymen. O the diftorted eye of malice, what will it not fee? Does our Saviour keep company with *finners*, in order to reform them? Then is he called their *friend.* Does he wear no forbidding or auftere appearance, but partake innocently and chearfully of the gifts of providence? Then he is *a glutton and a wine-bibber* [D]. Does he perform miraculous cures, in order to beftow health, in order to fpread happinefs and joy; and does his defire to be the author of thefe prevent him from obferving rights that were merely ceremonial, inftitutions that were merely pofitive, and never defigned to preclude fuch beneficient works? Then is he a difrefpector of their laws, a contemner of their law-giver. Yea, do the devils obey his word, and leave thofe who were poffeffed by them? He effects this by a combination with their prince; and works of piety, juftice, and charity, are the foundation on which the kingdom of Satan is reared [E]. Do you fay, were undeferved hatred and reproaches, which many men have borne bravely, fo difficult to be fupported by Jefus, when he had the inward teftimony that there was no guilt in him, and when unfpotted innocence and integrity were his robe, and his diadem? Miftake me not. The pain and forrow which Jefus felt, did not proceed from the reproaches which were thrown upon him: but from this caufe they proceeded, from knowing the difpofitions which prevailed in thofe who reproached him. How are we fhocked, and what pain do we feel when we

[D] MATTH. xi. 19.   [E] MATTH. ix. 34.

fee

see our fellow-creature in the last stage of a loathsome distemper? But could mental diseases, the diseases of malice, of hatred, of envy, of obstinacy be exhibited to our senses, how much greater anguish would a generous mind feel for the miserable sufferer? By looking forward, and considering the end, how would the anguish be increased? Now to the penetrating eye of Jesus, those diseases appeared in their blackest deformity: and the unhappy wretches who were infested with them he beheld ignorant and blind, ready to fall into that miserable state, where is *weeping and wailing, and gnashing of teeth*, where *their worm dieth not, and their fire shall not be quenched.* Ye benevolent minds, figure to yourselves what the benevolent mind of Jesus endured, when to the inhabitants of Chorazin, Bethsaida, proud Capernaum, and Jerusalem itself, he, foreseeing the final day of retribution, pronounced woes, the very thought of which must chill the warmest blood, and to avoid which they will but in vain call upon the mountains and hills to cover them for ever. Behold him then despised and rejected of men, and overwhelmed with grief, not on his own account, but on account of the very sinners who despised him. *O Jerusalem, Jerusalem, how often would I have gathered thy children together, even as a hen gathereth her chickens under her wings, and ye would not!*

But the measure of his sorrows is not yet full. And before I could relate all that even man can declare, the shades of night would cover the earth; for from the cradle to the grave, his life was one
uninterrupted

SERMON XVIII.

uninterrupted scene of the deepest affliction. Let us only then, in order to raise the highest emotions of love and gratitude, view him in the last period of it.

ATTENDED by his favourite disciple and Peter and James, he withdraws into the garden. In this solitude, removed from his enemies, can so innocent a mind suffer distress? But what an astonishing spectacle? He is in agony. He sweats drops of blood: and his own words, who never uttered a complaint, but when the cause was insupportable, are, *My soul is exceeding sorrowful, even unto death* [F]. He asks the aid of his friends, and entreats them to watch with him till that hour of extremity should be over: but the wakeful eye of friendship is soon sealed at this time; and alone, unsupported and unpitied, he endures the dreadful anguish. The united force of the powers of darkness, combined with the malice of all mankind, could not have filled him with such anguish. It is an invisible, but an infinitely powerful hand that afflicts him. The cup of his Father's wrath is now presented to him, and that vengeance which would have crushed a guilty world, is now directed against this innocent and holy one. For the iniquities of man, from the eating of that fruit which introduced all our woe, till the consummation of the world, the punishment was now inflicting upon him. I adore, O adore with me, that infinite love of Jesus, that entire submis-

[F] MATTH. xxvi. 38.

sion to the divine will which makes him say, 'Tho' the potion be bitter, yet for man I can drink it; *not my will, O Father, but thine be done.* Yet, all ye sons of calamity, ye children of affliction, I appeal to you, if ever ye felt, or if there ever was sorrow, like unto that sorrow wherewith the Lord in his fierce anger afflicted the Saviour of the world.

This scene is not over when his unworthy disciple comes to betray him. Thy Master, Judas, thy loving Master, thou betrayest with a kiss. This token of love that traitor makes the signal for seizing upon his Lord. Unhappiest of mortals! In thy hearing the purest, the most sublime and elevated doctrines were taught, the most pathetic exhortations delivered, and the wisdom of divinity itself displayed: but all without effect upon a heart which was harder than the rock. Yet know, that vengeance pursues iniquity. And deliver us, O just heaven, from ever feeling any degree of that remorse which hastened the exit of this wretched man. The spotless Son of God now a lawless, armed multitude drag away, and pour on him all manner of indignities. How meekly is he led along, though legions of angels would have appeared at his word to rescue him? How tamely does he bear the reproaches which malice invents, and spite utters? Harmless and innocent, like a lamb to the slaughter, is he led, and his mouth is not opened against his most inveterate foes. *The Shepherd is now smitten, and the sheep are scattered* [g].

[g] ZECH. xiii. 7.

His disciples, whom he had treated as his most familiar friends, who had been the companions of many of his former woes, now desert him. In his sufferings he did not behold the alleviating tear of sympathy shed upon his account. One disciple indeed, more zealous than the rest, who had greatly resolved rather to die with his Master, than forsake or deny him, mingles among the croud. But how weak is human resolution! In the very presence of his Lord, thrice he denies him with oaths. Yet struck by his eye, which looks on me, on all, he repents, weeps bitterly; and He, who never knew what it was to refuse pardon, forgives him.

IN the mean time, to all the insults of a tumultuous rabble, to the derision of the very lowest of the people is Jesus exposed. They mock him: they smite him: they strike him on the face. *His visage was more marred than any man, and his form more than the sons of men*[h]. How was the priesthood degraded on that day, when Caiaphas joined with the people in such unjust, such barbarous treatment of the Lord of glory?

HE is now hurried before Pilate's tribunal. Pilate sees no fault in him; but his enemies cry, *Crucify him.* Let never a judge deliver an innocent person to appease a multitude, or to preserve his own power. Let the laws ever be, as they ought to be, the guardians and avengers of the

[h] ISAIAH lii. 14.

righteous cause; and let their punishment never fall but on the guilty head. How different was the case at this time? That integrity and impartiality, which ought to be dearer to a judge than his life, is laid aside by Pilate. But his conscience smites him: he calls for water[1]. Alas Pilate! water could not cleanse from the stain which this heinous crime infixed. The multitude, whose rage had pushed them not only to devote themselves, but as far as they could, their children to destruction, having now the sanction of the high-priest, and the licence of the governor, drag my Saviour, and my King, to execution.

THOSE hands which had wrought so many miraculous cures, are bound like the hands of a common malefactor. The head which deserved to wear a crown of glory, and which now wears it, as a mark of their contempt, they crown with thorns. Happy woman! thou, who pouredst a box of precious ointment on this sacred head, shalt ever be mentioned with honour, and this shall ever be recorded as a memorial of thy name; while the crucifiers of the Lord of life shall be considered from generation to generation, as objects of the highest abhorrence. They renew their former insults. Having cloathed him with the mock ensigns of royalty, they bend the knee before him, saying, *Hail King of the Jews*[k]. They spit upon him, and take the reed which they had put in his hand, and smite him on the head.

[1] MATTH. xxvii. 24. [k] MATTH. xxvii. 29.

SERMON XVIII.

Then *he gave his back to the smiters, and his cheek to them that pulled off the hair; he did not hide his face from shame and spitting* [l].

AT last with relentless hearts they bring him to Calvary. But who is able to relate what passed at Calvary? A cross is erected, a punishment for the most atrocious criminals, and criminals of the lowest rank, remarkable too for the exquisite pain it inflicted, and for its long continuance. Here they fix the innocent Jesus between two men who were to receive the due reward of their deeds. Now his *lovers and his friends stand aloof, his kinsmen stand afar off* [m], and there is none near to help. Is not the hatred of his enemies now satiated? Suspended between heaven and earth, ready to die, and yet patient under the calamity, is he yet an object of derision? When *the golden bowl* is breaking, and *the silver cord* is loosing, is this a season for insult? Cruelty, be thou ever my abhorrence, and with thy sons let my soul never partake! In this very extremity they mock and revile him. O all ye that pass by! here humanity calls for your pity. Here ye may shed the generous tear; and the world will applaud it. But passengers join with his crucifiers and deride him. He is thirsty, and the soldiers present him with vinegar. His side they pierce with a spear: the very parting of soul and body they endeavour to render more insupportable than it generally is. Yet what a benign and merciful look was that,

[l] Is. l. 6.   [m] Ps. xxxviii. 11.

and what an earnest petition to his Father? Surely a prayer for his deliverance. No. O inimitable love! O divine charity! It is a prayer for his crucifiers. And now his soul is so overcast; his prospect of the end of impenitent sinners so striking, his concern for them so great, his love of mankind so infinite, and his Father's wrath so totally overwhelming, that is impossible to express his condition. Can the Father of goodness withdraw his aid from his own immaculate Son? Can mercy shut its ear against the cry of innocence? To proclaim to the world his abhorrence of man's transgressions, he can; and the words of Jesus are, *My God, my God, why hast thou forsaken me* [N]? This total desertion he could not support; and now one dying prayer, and one last groan, and the fountain of life fails, and the Son of God expires. That expiring groan, hear it, O ye heavens! and be astonished, O earth! Lo all nature hears it, and bears testimony to thy dignity. The sun withdraws his light, terrified at what unrelenting man performed. The veil of the temple is rent, the earth quakes, the rocks are rent. His very enemies now declare him innocent. Behold our Saviour now with his head dependent, his eyes closed in darkness, and his body stiff and cold. Could you see your enemy, O christian, endure such affliction as this man of sorrows endured, and not weep for him? But consider that he was your firmest friend, your most bountiful benefactor, ever true to your interests, ever anxious

[N] MATTH. xxvii. 46.

SERMON XVIII.

for your falvation, and that in order to promote it even death was welcome to him. *O that my head were waters, and mine eyes a fountain of tears, that I might weep day and night!* Here admiration, gratitude, love and fympathy prompt our tears. Here the dauntlefs hero fhould weep and not be afhamed. This day Jefus looks from heaven, and and fees how we are affected. He approves of our forrow; but kind and beneficent as ever, he would alleviate our grief on his account, and defires us to turn it into a mean of our improvement. He feems to fay, Why mourn ye for the living as if he were dead? *Behold I am alive, and live for evermore.* But as he addreffed the daughters of Jerufalem of old, he adds, *Weep not for me*, chriftians, *but weep for yourfelves, for I was wounded for your tranfgreffions, I was bruifed for your iniquities,*

O MY brethren, confider then all your fins as the caufe of your Saviour's fufferings. He was the *propitiation for the fins of many.* He gave his life a ranfom for finners. Efteem him not ftricken and fmitten of God for his own fake, but becaufe he bore the griefs which we fhould have felt, and carried the forrows which we deferved. Confider the fins by which we deferved them, repent of them, and forfake them, that you may have *redemption through the blood of Chrift, even the forgivenefs of our fins.*

SER-

SERMON XIX.

1 CORINTHIANS xi. 26.

For as often as you eat this bread, and drink this cup, ye do shew forth the Lord's death till he come.

IT was the intention of the apostle in this chapter to point out to the Corinthians some of those abuses which they had introduced into the worship of God, and to bring them back to a purer and more perfect plan. Their manner of celebrating the Lord's supper, had been remarkably indecent. When they met together for this purpose, instead of behaving so that this institution might promote their piety, and confirm their integrity, they had shamefully converted it into a mean of fostering sensuality, riot, and even inhumanity. The apostle openly charges them with their vices, and boldly condemns them on account of them. His zeal however is the zeal of an honest man, sensible of the faults, but anxious for the reformation of those to whom he wrote.

WITH

With a view to their reformation, he gives them a simple, yet full and perspicuous account of the Lord's supper; which, he declares, sprung not from the tradition of men, or from the suggestions of his own reason or imagination, but from the immediate revelation of the Lord Jesus Christ: *For I have received of the Lord, that which also I deliver unto you, that the Lord Jesus, the same night in which he was betrayed, took bread: and when he had given thanks, he brake it and said, Take, eat; this is my body which is broken for you: this do in remembrance of me. After the same manner also he took the cup, when he had supped, saying, This cup is the new testament in my blood: this do ye, as oft as ye drink it, in remembrance of me* [a]. After this account of the institution of the Lord's supper, the apostle endeavours to turn the attention of the Corinthians to its principal end, and thus to insinuate an argument for the decent and orderly observance of it: *For as oft as ye eat this bread, and drink this cup, ye do shew forth the Lord's death till he come.*

This and the similar passages of the new testament clearly point out the intention and object of this institution, and give us a distinct and full view of them. Can any thing be more plain than it is from scripture, that the bread and wine which are made use of in the Lord's supper, are intended to be memorials of the body of Christ which was broken, and of his blood which was shed upon

[a] Ver. 23, 24, 25.

the cross; and that the eating of this bread, and the drinking of this wine, were enjoined his followers as solemn acts to be performed in remembrance of his death? Almost every christian understands this. And yet, making allowance for the manner of speaking common at that period, and supposing nothing intended contradictory to our reason, and our senses, the words of Christ appear to me to be as intelligible and perspicuous as the paraphrase now given. But tho' the design of the institution may be easily understood, being delivered with that plainness for which the gospel in general is remarkable; yet certainly it is not for that reason to be regarded with the less reverence, or observed with the less solemnity. All religious and well-disposed christians, nay many of very indifferent characters, have commonly considered it as an institution extremely sacred, the neglect or contempt of which betrayed a very corrupt heart, and a very impious temper.

I PROPOSE, in discoursing upon the words now read, to inquire what those causes are, which have engaged men to view it in this light, to regard it with this peculiar reverence. Before I enter upon this inquiry, let me premise an observation or two.

1st, WHEN I speak of the causes which engage men to consider the Lord's supper as an ordinance peculiarly sacred and solemn, I do not intend to insist upon those causes which, though they may have at particular periods, and with particular persons, or even with large bodies of men, greatly

con-

contributed to this, yet are not founded in the reason of things, or the nature of the institution. I am very sensible that for many ages of the church, the mystery which the priests affected, and the ignorance in which the people were involved, together with many absurd doctrines respecting this institution, occasioned much of that veneration which was paid to the Lord's supper. With many men, there is nothing which more promotes admiration, than a strong faith, and little knowledge. Curiosity excited, but not gratified, proves the surest foundation on which superstition enthusiasm and error can be built. I wish that even in our days the veil, which is sometimes industriously, sometimes undesignedly, and sometimes ignorantly thrown over the ordinances of religion, be not often the principal cause of our reverence for them. But the cause of God and virtue have so many real supports, that they need no false ones. Every fraud is detestable: but a pious fraud (the very appellation is an affront to heaven) is the worst of all frauds. I propose therefore to consider only those causes of reverence for this sacred ordinance which I regard as just and well-founded, and which I believe chiefly to have prevailed in the first and purest ages of the church, and to prevail still with wise and sober christians.

2dly, In mentioning the peculiar reverence with which the institution of the Lord's supper is to be regarded, I do not mean to insinuate a comparison between that degree of reverence which is due to this ordinance of religion, and that which is due
to

SERMON XIX. 317

to other ordinances of God's appointment. Comparisons of this kind are generally improper; sometimes impious. But there may be some duties of religion, a failure in which does not discover so great corruption of heart, nor is accompanied with so bitter remorse as a failure in others: and there may be some duties of such a complicated nature, as to touch many of the feelings, and work on many of the affections of the heart at once; so that an irreverent behaviour in the performance of them may shock us more, and indicate a more abandoned character, and a more corrupted heart than the same behaviour in the performance of other duties; tho' in these also it would be highly impious. For instance, in reading the word of God, if we willingly permit the cares, anxieties, and temptations of the world to intrude upon us, we are certainly guilty of a sin: but if we indulge the same wandering and worldly disposition in our immediate addresses to God, we are guilty of a greater sin. Again, every address to God demands the most serious and recollected temper. For a weak creature to stand in the presence of the all-perfect God, to raise his soul to the contemplation of his wonderful nature, and at the same time to think of him as his father and his friend, ought at once to elevate and compose, to sooth, and to expand the soul: and infensibility, at the very time we seem to be employed in devotion, is surely highly criminal. Yet infensibility or irreverence in the participation of the Lord's supper is more highly criminal. For this participation not only implies prayer, and that too animated by the most affecting considerations,

but

but alſo recalls to our mind a character and an event, which have the ſtrongeſt tendency to work upon all the nobleſt, and the moſt generous principles of our nature. In this ſituation, irreverence diſcovers a ſoul not only loſt to piety, but almoſt deprived of the common feelings of humanity.

Having premiſed theſe obſervations, I proceed to take notice of the cauſes which ſhould engage chriſtians to conſider the Lord's ſupper as an ordinance extremely ſacred, and to regard it with peculiar reverence.

In the firſt place: I would obſerve that it is a poſitive inſtitution of chriſtianity, appointed in very peculiar and affecting circumſtances.

The poſitive inſtitutions of the goſpel have frequently been conſidered merely as means to an end, not eſſentially neceſſary, but fit and proper to be obſerved. Perhaps this ſentiment, under proper limitations, may be free from error. But I do not ſee that the obſervation is very important. I can conceive a ſtate, in which the performance of the poſitive duties of chriſtianity would not be binding, becauſe in that ſtate it might be impoſſible to perform them. I can alſo conceive a ſtate in which ſeveral moral duties may be lawfully omitted, nay muſt unavoidably be omitted, becauſe there would be no ſcope for the practice of them. But I can conceive no ſtate in which a chriſtian can with a good conſcience omit either a moral, or a poſitive duty, if he has a proper opportunity for performing it. Men may differ concerning

SERMON XIX. 319

cerning the times and seasons proper for the observance of positive institutions, or they may differ in their opinion concerning the frequency of their repetition; but they may differ also concerning the extent and obligation of moral duties. We know that these depend in some measure upon particular characters, circumstances and opportunities.

THUS much appeared necessary for removing a prejudice against the reverence due to positive institution of religion, which an incautious manner of expression may have sometimes occasioned. Let us now consider the particular circumstances and solemnity with which the institution presently under consideration was appointed.

OUR Saviour had gone with his disciples to celebrate the high festival of the Jews. He had given strong intimations of his immediate departure from his friends and followers. He had plainly told them, that he would not again partake in a feast which they probably thought was to continue through all generations. He had particularly informed them that, by the treachery of one of those few whom he had selected from the world, he was to be delivered into the hands of sinners. This threw a general damp upon the company, and each anxious and sorrowful for himself, said, *Is it I?* His reply confirmed all their fears. It could not remove their concern for the loss of their master, their friend and their benefactor; nor was it so precise, as to remove from any of them all a suspicion that his own fidelity was called in question: *It is one of the twelve*

twelve that dippeth with me in the dish[B]. It is added, *The Son of man indeed goeth, as it is written of him, but wo to that man by whom the Son of man is betrayed! good were it for that man if he had never been born*[C]. It was at this time, when the disciples could not fail to be in a state of the utmost anxiety, agitation and despondency, that our Saviour *took the bread, and having given thanks, breaks it, and gave it to them, and said, This is my body*[D]; and afterwards *took the cup, and gave it to them* with these remarkable words, *This is my blood of the new testament, which is shed for many*[E]. I ask any man, if this was not a scene which must leave the deepest impression on the minds of the disciples? Could they have been men, especially considering what followed, if they had ever forgot it? Can any thing, which tended to raise a greater variety of emotions and affections, be described or conceived? Could there ever be a solemn meeting in which the apostles and first christians were together where the conversation would not turn upon this subject, and where every apostle would not expatiate upon the words, the looks, the manner of his master; upon the anxiety, uncertainty and terror which possessed his own mind, and upon the emotions which his companions discovered?

IF this very transaction were painted upon canvas by a skilful hand, and presented to a man of sensibility who had refused his belief to the

[B] MARK xiv. 20. [C] VER. 21. [D] VER. 22.
[E] VERSE 23, 24.

SERMON XIX.

evidence of religion, yet he would for a moment become a chriſtian, as it were by contagion; and ſympathy would be the predominant emotion of his heart. But how dead is all deſcription, compared to nature and living object! if Judas was preſent, ſurely his heart relented for a little: had not the very ſpirit of ſatan dwelt in him, it had relented for ever.

WHEN we attend to theſe circumſtances, we muſt be ſenſible that in the primitive days of chriſtianity, this inſtitution could not but excite the utmoſt reſpect and reverence in chriſtians; and that the being engaged in it could not but call up every pious, every affectionate feeling in the higheſt degree of fervour. I allow that it cannot be expected to operate ſo ſtrongly upon us : but is it poſſible for any believer, who is not deſtitute of ſenſibility, ſeriouſly to read the deſcription which Mark or the other evangeliſts give us of this ſcene, and not feel the powers of his ſoul rouſed, its worldly deſires rebuked, and its religious affections awakened? The circumſtances therefore, and the ſolemnity of the original inſtitution render the Lord's ſupper highly worthy of our reverence, and ſhew the want of this temper in obſerving it, to be extremely culpable and criminal.

SECONDLY, Another reaſon which may properly engage men to conſider this inſtitution in the moſt ſolemn light, and poſſeſs them with the higheſt reverence when they are employed in it, may be diſcerned by attending to its nature and deſign.

SERMON XIX.

This reason had probably more influence afterwards, than at the first appointment: for at that time it is likely that the apostles were far from entertaining clear and distinct conceptions on this subject. We know sufficiently, that the Lord's supper was intended for a commemoration of the death of our Saviour, and that this great event is the object which it, sensibly represents to us. Now there is something in the very idea of death which tends to make men serious and thoughtful. The recollection of the last end of mortals, even when we do not view it with a particular respect to ourselves, throws the soul into a solemn stillness, which is friendly to every pious and religious meditation. But it is not merely the view of death in general that this ordinance suggests: it recalls to our thoughts the death of a particular person who stands in a particular relation to us, and who by his death procures inestimable blessings for us; a death which is described with all those circumstances that can lay hold of the mind, and excite either admiration, or gratitude, or sympathy.

To consider this subject in its full extent would be more than sufficient for a whole discourse. Let us therefore view the death of Christ as briefly as we can in these two lights; as the death of a great man, and as a mean of purchasing our reconciliation to God, and our title to eternal life. The first is a general view, into which even a heathen might enter, and express his admiration on account of it. The second is particularly interesting to christians..

Is

SERMON XIX.

Is it then possible to contemplate the blameless life, and the heroic death of Jesus, and not feel the workings of admiration and love? If I met an ignorant and untaught Indian, and could inform him in his own language that at a certain period there lived a most extraordinary person, who before he was thirty-three years of age, had done more good, and suffered more evil than any man ever did in the longest life; that his whole employment was to promote happiness, and prevent misery; that no human creature ever applied for his aid in vain; that he had the wonderful power of healing all diseases, of making men wise, gentle, kind, merciful; that in pursuing these ends, he refused neither cold, nor hunger, nor watching, nor poverty, nor reproach; that notwithstanding all his beneficent actions, his cruel and wicked countrymen, after making him suffer every hardship, led him to a shameful execution; that being persuaded he could live no longer for the good of mankind, he chearfully died to give them a proof of his firmness and constancy and resignation to the will of the great God; that he shewed neither fear of death, nor resentment against his murderers; that on the contrary, he expressed the tenderest solicitude for their happiness, and prayed for them with his dying breath; and that he expired after having exhibited a perfect pattern of patience, meekness, forbearance, generosity, fortitude, of every thing great and good; would not nature work in the honest savage, and would not his countenance declare the feelings of sorrow, love, and admiration? Shall a savage then feel, and a christian be hardened?

BUT this view of the death of Christ, interesting as it is, is still very imperfect. When, as christians, we reflect that for our sakes *he was a man of sorrows, and acquainted with grief*[F]: When we attend to the nature of the blessings which he purchased, the favour of God, the means of sanctifying our natures, our access to glory and immortality; must not all the best and most devout feelings of the soul be raised to the highest pitch of fervour! If we attend to the unspeakable dignity of his character, to his condescension in becoming man, to the amazing fortitude of his death, must not the highest admiration rise? If we view our sins as the causes of his sufferings, what can we feel but humility, compunction and penitence? If we turn our observation to the severity of his pains, the anguish of his soul, and the torments of his body, must not sympathy melt the heart and fill the eye? If we survey all the blessings of his purchase, must not gratitude to so generous a benefactor, and so divine a friend, exert its influence? But these, my brethren, are all subjects immediately connected with the death of Christ, which we commemorate in the sacrament of his supper. To render our observance of this institution acceptable, it is necessary indeed, that every one of these considerations should actually occur to the mind. But when an ordinance has a tendency to operate upon so many of the most virtuous principles of our nature, does not this shew

[F] ISAIAH, liii. 3.

that

that it ought to be regarded with the greateſt reverence and veneration?

THIRDLY, The ſolemnity of this ordinance, and the reverence due to it, will further appear, if we conſider that the obſervance of it implies the exertion of many affections, which are all in their own nature of high importance and excellence. If each of theſe be ſacred, ſurely that which implies them all muſt be particularly ſo.

Now though the principal end of this inſtitution be extremely ſimple, namely a commemoration of the death of Chriſt, yet it involves ſeveral other views. This may be collected from what was ſaid on the laſt head. If a ſenſe of the primary intention of this ordinance has a tendency to excite ſo various feelings as have been pointed out, it is impoſſible but theſe muſt produce their natural and ordinary effects. Let the communicant's view be turned to the ſufferings of Chriſt, and to the conſideration of ſin as the cauſe of them; ſurely this is extremely natural. But can theſe be the objects of attention to a ſincere and honeſt mind, without introducing a reſolution againſt ſin, or a prayer for its forgiveneſs? Holy reſolutions then, and fervent prayer, have both their ſhare in the devout obſervance of this inſtitution. Yea, the latter, from the practice of all ages, and the example of our Saviour, is eſſentially neceſſary before the ordinance can be celebrated.

I KNOW it may be diſputed, whether the examination of our conduct, and reſolutions againſt all sin, be absolutely requisite for a proper participation in this sacrament. I doubt not but circumstances might be supposed, in which a good man would think himself obliged to commemorate the death of his Redeemer, without having time for a previous examination of his conduct, or in which, during the time of his participation, his mind might be so totally occupied with love or gratitude, that he might form no direct resolutions against sin. But this is nothing to those who would be most anxious to have it determined that such exercises are not necessary. But put the case, that at the time of participation, a man's conscience condemns him for his sins, and impells him to resolve against them, which yet the corruption of his heart, and his attachment to vice, engage him to neglect. In this situation, could he approve of his conduct? would not his heart condemn him; and if his heart condemn him, will God justify him? At the tribunal of divine justice, would one choose to trust to the refinements of an acute understanding, or to the simplicity of an upright heart? Thus resolutions against sin may often become an indispensable part of our duty, during the participation of the Lord's supper.

In like manner, if the inimitable love of Jesus Christ, and the inestimable blessings of his purchase, are the objects of our reflection while we are employed in this duty; does not the gratitude which these excite, naturally engage us to vow perpetual attachment to him, and stedfastness in his service? If the outward meanness, the poverty, ty, and low condition of Jesus Christ, induce us to reflect upon the insignificancy and small importance of the things of this world; and if at the same time conscience bring to our remembrance an instance in which they have had influence enough to make us forsake the road of integrity, and abandon ourselves to sin; does not this lay us under an obligation to enter into a resolution of repentance, and to begin immediately to carry it into execution?

THUS prayer, pious and virtuous resolutions, vows of attachment, obedience and repentance, if not essentially necessary to the participation of the Lord's supper, yet may become indispensable parts of our duty during this action. What therefore implies such serious and solemn duties must be an object of the greatest reverence.

FOURTHLY, My brethren, this institution, which is designed to commemorate the death of Christ, is also intended to carry our thoughts forward to his second coming. The New Testament connects it with this event; it is particularly connected with it in the words of the text; *For as oft as ye eat this bread, and drink this cup, ye do shew forth the Lord's death till he come.* If there is any event in nature that can excite the awe, reverence and respect of reasonable and accountable creatures, it is surely the future judgment. But this judgment is only to take place at the second appearance of Jesus. *For God has appointed a day in which he will judge the world in righteousness by that*

that Man whom he hath ordained [G], even the Lord Jefus Chrift the righteous. The apparatus, the procedure, the dignity of the Judge, the particular part we fhall all have in this grand tranfaction, render it particularly interefting and important. If the foul of man can be occupied with any object, this muft command its regard and attention. To this important event the Lord's fupper naturally directs our thoughts. It is a lively reprefentation of that *obedience* of Chrift *unto death, even the death of the crofs* [H], on account of which *God hath highly exalted him, and given him a name which is above every name* [I], and which, being the ground of his whole exaltation, is confequently the very reafon why God *hath given him authority to execute judgment alfo* [K]. It confirms our faith of the general judgment, it is a pledge given us, that he *who was once offered to bear the fins of many, fhall unto them that look for him, appear the fecond time, without fin unto falvation* [L]. Can it fix our thoughts on the future judgment, can it enliven our conception of its folemn procefs, without imprefling every ferious and confiderate mind with the deepeft awe?

I shall but make two reflections on what has been faid. 1ft, Since the Lord's fupper is an inftitution of fo great folemnity, we fhould by no means neglect to obferve it. Shall any chriftian treat that with neglect, which deferves the greateft

[G] ACTS xvii. 31. [H] PHIL. ii. 8. [I] VER. 9.
[K] JOHN v. 27. [L] HEB. x. 28.

reverence

reverence from every chriſtian? Not to obſerve it, is to treat it with total neglect. 'Twas in the night in which he was betrayed to death for you, and it was with all the agonies of his death full in his view that your Saviour ſaid, *Do this in remembrance of me:* can you hear his voice uttered in that night, uttered in that endearing ſituation, and yet diſregard it? Every tender, every affecting, every intereſting circumſtance of the ſcene, which that night exhibited, is a ſtrong argument for our *continuing* in that *breaking of bread* [m], which was purpoſely appointed for the commemoration of it. The dignity of him who died, and the end of his death, which was to expatiate ſin, add ſolemnity to this memorial of his death; and they no leſs powerfully plead for every chriſtian's joining in this memorial of it. This is the tribute which you are called to pay to the greateſt perſon that ever trod this earth; it is the acknowledgment demanded from you, to him who made his ſoul an offering for your ſins. All thoſe good affections which this inſtitution is fit for drawing forth into exerciſe, it is fit alſo for improving: to neglect it ſhews indifference about the improvement of our beſt affections. It is only Chriſt's coming again to judgment, that can extinguiſh the obligation of chriſtians, *to ſhew forth his death*; till he come let us take every opportunity of doing this in remembrance of him.

[m] ACTS ii. 46.

SECONDLY,

SECONDLY, Since the Lord's fupper is fo folemn, fo fit to command the fincereft reverence of our fouls, we fhould be always careful to prepare ourfelves for partaking in it with ferious and fervent devotion. Irreverence in any act of worfhip is a heinous fin: but irreverence in obferving this chriftian inftitution, is in fome refpects peculiarly atrocious: it is a mark of very great depravity: It fhews infenfibility to the moft moving objects, and obduracy which the moft alarming views cannot overcome. This inftitution may make fome impreffion on the moft unthinking, it may force reflection for a moment on the moft diffipated, it may excite fome emotions of piety, in thofe who are for ordinary the greateft ftrangers to them. The Corinthians obferved it in an irreverent manner; and the apoftle reproves this irreverence with great feverity, and warns them that it was of the moft dangerous confequence; *Whofoever fhall eat this bread and drink this cup of the Lord unworthily, fhall be guilty of the body and blood of the Lord: He that eateth and drinketh unworthily, eateth and drinketh judgment to himfelf, not difcerning the Lord's body* [N]. The religious affections all prevailing in their greateft vigour, and mingling their warmeft exertions, form the temper which becomes this commemoration. By ex-

[N] COR. xi. 27, 29.

amining

amining ourselves, by humble confession of our sins, by earnest prayer, by meditation on whatever can most effectually melt our hearts into contrition, or touch them with love, and gratitude, and joy in God's salvation, let us prepare ourselves, as often as we have opportunity, for the religious performance of this duty.

SERMON XX.

Acts xx. 35.

And to remember the words of the Lord Jesus, how he said, It is more blessed to give than to receive.

THE most interesting concern of human creatures is happiness; and no rule so unexceptionable can be fixed for estimating the value of any object, or the propriety and importance of any disposition, or action, or course of behaviour, as its tendency to promote happiness. But the rule, however universally acknowledged, is often very ill applied, and indeed with respect to many pursuits and dispositions is scarce ever thought of. Nature has provided us with a touchstone, but we neglect to try the most precious metals by it, and by the neglect suffer ourselves to be imposed upon by the basest counterfeits.

THE happiness which is derived from the exercise of a beneficent temper, is very rarely an object of consideration, especially in an age, when
the

the spirit of commerce, the love of lucre, and a contracted regard to the individual, give the strongest bias to all our opinions and judgments. They who inherit overgrown fortunes, they who have received liberal donations, they who have acquired wealth, are reckoned among the happy, though they employ them only in fulfilling the purposes of folly, vanity and vice. A splendid table, a fine house, a handsome equipage, even gaudy apparel, we are more apt to consider as characteristic of the happy man, than generous efforts to relieve the wretched, to support the unfortunate, to comfort the disconsolate, to patronize the deserving. These we still regard as marks of virtue, but we seldom consider them as symptoms of happiness. Even the motives which excite the generality to actions of a publick and beneficent nature, when they are not merely sordid and selfish, are so dependent upon the views suggested by our reasoning powers, that they have little connection with the heart; and the man who should urge the pleasure of a kind and beneficent action, and the sweet enjoyment which it brings along with it, as the motive to a person's performing it, would be deemed ignorant of what is reckoned the most essential branch of human knowledge, the knowledge of the world. But in reality, under this boasted knowledge, the blindest prejudice, and the grossest ignorance often lurk: and the world, not only in its purest and most virtuous, but even in its corrupted and depraved state, affords argument sufficent to confute the men who value themselves for knowing it best.

Ir

It was hinted already, that the moſt infallible teſt of the value of any difpoſition or behaviour, is its being conducive to the natural and real felicity of men: and to this teſt I might fafely fubmit all the laws, and all the maxims of the gofpel. If the temperate, the manly, the confcientious, not the effeminate, the weak, and the timid, were to be the judges, I ſhould not fear the deciſion even with refpect to its ſevereſt laws, the endurance of perfecution, lofs of goods, refignation of life.

But our preſent enquiry is more confined. It was the faying of the Lord Jefus, *It is more bleſſed to give than to receive.* In this faying, the felicity of a beneficent temper is afferted in the ſtrongeſt manner. The encomium feems to be given to the action; but it is obvious that human actions are praife-worthy, only fo far as they reſult from right difpofitions, and that it is only the agent that deſerves commendation or blame, reward or puniſhment.

The circumſtances of our Saviour's life gave him frequent occaſions for introducing this fentiment with propriety; and as it is addreffed to the tender and generous feelings of human nature, it muſt have made the deepeſt impreſſion on his followers. The application which the apoſtle Paul makes of this faying in my text, difcovers the effect which it produced on him, and ſhews that he regarded it as a practical truth of the greateſt moment. In this laſt difcourfe to the elders

ders of Ephesus, whom he had assembled at Miletus, he was able to make this noble appeal to them; *I have coveted no man's silver, or gold, or apparel. Yea, you yourselves know, that these hands have ministered unto my necessities, and to them that were with me. I have shewed you all things, how that so labouring ye ought to support the weak; and to remember the words of the Lord Jesus, how he said, It is more blessed to give, than to receive.* Though in these words there is a comparison between the happiness of bestowing, and that of receiving, yet it will be putting no violence on them to consider them simply as a declaration of the blessedness of a beneficent temper. That with which this temper is contrasted, and to which it is preferred, being an acknowledged mark of good fortune, and a source of enjoyment, the other must be still more so.

I propose, therefore in this discourse, to confirm and illustrate the happiness of a beneficent disposition; and to suggest a few of those reflections which naturally arise from the consideration of this subject.

By a beneficent disposition, I mean a disposition to do good to others from the principles of kindness, affection, or humanity, which includes not only acts of charity, generosity and liberality, for these must in a great measure be dependent upon our external circumstances, but also all the means we use, the pains we take, or the wishes we

SERMON XX.

we entertain for the comfort, enjoyment and happinefs of our fellow-creatures. That fuch a difpofition muft be of the utmoft confequence to our own fatisfaction and happinefs, I think will appear evident from feveral confiderations.

In the firft place, This will appear by confidering in general what it is that muft conftitute human felicity.

To write a treatife concerning human nature requires perhaps as much knowledge, attention and reflection, as the compofition of a performance on any other fubject whatever; but fuch a treatife is not neceffary, either for directing our conduct, or for determining the operation of our feelings. We are all men, and we all feel that the gratification of our natural defires, where the gratification is not forbidden by any other principle of our mind, is always a fource of enjoyment to us. But the nature, and the kinds of our enjoyments are as different and various as the powers and principles which give rife to them. Except a few of them, however, which regard felf-prefervation, they are almoft all connected with our focial natures, infomuch that the enjoyments of a human creature entirely feparated from his kind, tho' poffeffed of all the neceffaries for fatisfying his hunger and thirft, his love of labour, and defire of repofe, would be totally different from thofe of the man who is placed among his fellows. As the fun nourifhes, invigorates, animates objects external to himfelf, and was certainly created with

Z a refe-

a reference to them; as the planets by their mutual attraction promote and preserve the regularity of their several motions, so man was created for man; and his state, his wants, his desires, point out his connection with, and his dependence upon his fellow-men. Philosophers have sometimes talked of man's being a selfish, and a solitary being, having all his views centered in the happiness of the individual, without the least regard to others: but the hut of the Indian, the cottage of the peasant, the pipe of the shepherd, the tent of the wanderer, as well as the concourse of the city, the palace of the prince, the government of the state, contradict the assertion.

RELIGION which, notwithstanding the imperfection of its effects, has occupied a great deal of the joint care and attention of the human race, in every age, and every nation, as far as ever I have read or heard, shews that a social concern for others is the object of man's heart, and the principle of his conduct. Without this, I should just as readily believe, that political statesmen and cunning priests have built in ancient times cities without hands, made men of mere clay, and supported mountains upon their feeble shoulders, as that they could have introduced religion as a general occupation and employment of mankind.

SINCE then the whole of the human frame points to a state of society and connection with others, the very nature of desire renders it impossible that the gratification of those affections which respect

SERMON XX.

respect others should not be attended with enjoyment and happiness. But the benevolent affections of our nature, our desire to shed the tear of sympathy over the distressed, to take part in the injuries of the oppressed, and to befriend them, to partake the innocent pleasures of the happy, are the affections which most immediately respect others; and therefore we may conclude that the indulgence of them will be a source of particular pleasure and delight.

It further deserves to be remarked, that though the gratification of desires which respect the individual, and the gratification of those which respect others, have this in common, that they are attended with a certain pleasure, yet they differ in a very material article: the pleasure which attends such desires as terminate in the individual, even when most intense, is confined to the moment of indulgence; to none but the groveling and the sensual, is it the object of agreeable reflection: but the social pleasures of our nature are not agreeable only in the mean time, but extend to distant periods, and are the objects of after-consideration, and the sources of permanent enjoyment. The flashes of heaven's lightning dazzle and overpower, but the resplendent and benign rays of the sun cheer, enliven, and afford a light constant, and invariable, and universal.

I add but one more general observation. Human creatures are made for action and exertion. Whenever these are employed, a separate and additional

ditional pleasure attends the gratification of all our desires. To do good, to bestow, to give, requires an exercise of our active powers. In that state when every impulse is felt, when every power of the mind is awake, we enter with the highest relish into every pleasure that nature warrants, and religion sanctifies. The mind that groaned under the load of suffering, is calm and serene when that load is removed, but the soul that removed it is elevated. The composed countenance of relieved distress, the affectionate look of gratitude combine with the pleasing efforts of liberality and kindness to increase the joy and felicity of the benefactor.

In the second place, the happiness of a beneficent disposition may be proved from fact and experience.

We are ignorant of our true happiness, only because we pay so little attention to what passes in our own minds, and suffer ourselves to be imposed upon by external appearances, from which we draw inferences often not in the least connected with them. But an impartial consideration of the sentiments and feelings of our hearts, of those suggestions which proceed from the constitution of our souls, or the immediate motions of that divine Spirit which pervades the universe, would free us from numberless mistakes, and lead us to expect our enjoyments from such objects as can really bestow them. Now can any man, when he attends to himself, doubt wherein his pleasure and enjoyment chiefly consist? Deep researches and
intricate

intricate difquifitions are not neceffary for determining it. An ordinary degree of attention only is requifite, and fortitude enough to take the anfwer implicitly from none, but to truft to the natural feelings of one's own heart. Can any perfon who has the foul of a man hefitate to pronounce that among the pureft and beft pleafures of which he is fufceptible are thofe which arife from the opportunities he has laid hold of, to be ufeful to his fellow creatures, to fupply their wants, to eafe the load of their fufferings, to add to the number of their enjoyments? When the rich have fpared of their fuperfluities to minifter to the neceffities of the poor, let the luxurious tell if what they referved had not a higher relifh. When the poor, out of real pity to thofe who were ftill poorer, have beftowed a fmall pittance to feed the hungry, or to clothe the naked, was it not natural for them rather to regret that they had not more to give, than that there was too little left behind? Did the widow, think you, who threw in two mites into the treafury with the beft intention, depart with a heavy heart, becaufe fhe had kept nothing to herfelf? If ever your prefence, your attention, your converfation, your look of filent fenfibility, your falling tears (for thefe I count more facred gifts than your gold, or your filver) have adminiftered confolation to a widowed mother, or difconfolate children, did not your hearts in that moment feel the bleffednefs of giving? and when you came away, would you have exchanged the melancholy pleafure for all the vain illufions of folly and vice? When the gratulations of the

blind

blind and the lame, and the benedictions of the perishing soul came upon Job, would he have compared the joy with what arose from the possession of his oxen, his asses, his camels, and his fields? It was the character of the Lord Jesus, that he went about continually doing good, soothing the penitent, comforting those that mourned, raising up the bowed down, and healing the diseased; and as he felt like a man, we may conjecture the inward joy which this continued course of beneficence gave him. I verily believe it to be the chief natural mean that rendered him so intrepid, so patient, so forgiving, so resigned. How similar to him should we become, if we yielded to the best impulses of our hearts! If the Ephesians had divided their possessions to enrich the apostle Paul; how small must his pleasure in receiving it all have been in comparison with what he felt from reflecting, that he had been the minister of God for good unto them, without prospect, or possession of human reward?

WERE the apostles in general, who watched with such vigilance, and laboured with such vigour to promote the salvation of mankind, strangers to the most heart-felt pleasure, because they were not loaded with gifts, secured in possessions, or surrounded with affluence? No. They had imbibed the maxim of their Master, *It is more blessed to give than to receive*; and while they suffered hunger, and poverty, and persecution, and death, they rejoiced, and were happy, because they were doing good. Abraham might reject
even

SERMON XX.

even royal gifts, and refuse a sepulchre for his family without paying an adequate value for it: his conduct neither proves that the patriarch was ignorant of the means of happiness, nor lessens him in our esteem. But no man ever yet omitted an opportunity of performing a kind, a generous, or a beneficent action, who did not in that instance abandon the happiness of his own soul, and render himself less worthy of the approbation of all mankind.

IT is needless to multiply instances. I appeal to yourselves. Happiness is within the mind. It is not of our own making, but flows from constitutions that are established by the same power that ordains the revolution of the sun, the course of the rivers, the ascent of the vapours. To suppose happiness entirely or chiefly placed in externals, is as ridiculous as to suppose that you are as much connected with the dust on which you tread, as with that portion of it which the Almighty operation has formed for your body. There is no disputing the point. If beneficence renders the soul calm, tranquil, and elevated, it it a source of felicity, If it assimilates the mind to God, and to Jesus Christ, it must render us partakers of their bliss. If the reflection upon it is agreeable, if it remains when *the lust of the flesh, the lust of the eye, and the pride of life* put on an appearance at best diminutive, often disgustful; if it casts an unfading ray on the latest hours of human life, and prepares for a participation of the life of angels,

tho

the reality, and the value of the enjoyment mufl be acknowledged.

In the third place; The felicity of a beneficent difpofition may be evinced from this confideration, that by this quality we are moft directly affimilated to God, and to Jefus Chrift, after whofe image we were at firft created.

As it is the nature of two drops of water, when placed near each other, mutually to be attracted, and coalefce; as it is the nature of heavy bodies to fall to the ground, and of light ones to be buoyed up; as it is the nature of worms to crawl upon the earth, of fifhes to fwim in the fea, and of birds to fly through the air; fo it is the nature of the human foul to afpire after a fimilitude to its divine original. The confequences of a fallen ftate, and of corrupted principles, are but too perceptible, and to thefe we juftly impute thofe miftakes, deceptions, difappointments, and difgufts with which we meet in our fearch after felicity. The piety, and the fall of David, the wifdom, and the weaknefs of Solomon, the zeal, and the infirmity of Peter, with a thoufand inftances that could be produced from facred and profane writers, of the virtue and the ambition of the fame princes, the allegiance and the turbulence of the fame people, might all be brought in proof of the fall of man, if any other proof were requifite, than merely to read the hiftory of this cataftrophe, and to look into our own hearts. But the inftances would fhew, that though man be
fallen,

SERMON XX.

fallen, he is not annihilated; that though his luftre be fullied, it is not extinguifhed. He ftill raifes his mind at times to the contemplation of uncreated excellence, and the inftincts of his heart indicate his relation to the divinity. In every approach that he makes to his primeval purity, he feels the gratulations of his own foul, and enjoys the triumphs of his confcience. But in no way can he become fo like his Maker, as when his heart is intent upon doing good. The beneficent hand of the Almighty formed, and his power fuftains the univerfe. *He maketh his fun to rife on the evil and on the good, and fendeth rain on the juft, and on the unjuft* [A]. *He is good unto all, and his tender mercies are over all his works* [B]. The divine perfon who was *the brightnefs of his glory, and the exprefs image of his perfon* [C], imitated him in his bounty and beneficence, and gave us an example that we fhould follow his fteps. If then the felicity of man confifts in his refemblance to his Maker, if the joy of the redeemed fhould bear a fimilitude to the delights of the Redeemer, if to participate in the blifs of the Supreme be the fupreme happinefs of us the emanations of his goodnefs; furely, *it is more bleffed to give than to receive*, and happy are all who have rightly learned the divine leffon.

The fubject I have been confidering would naturally give occafion for a variety of reflections

[A] MAT. V. 45. [B] PSAL. cxlv. 9. [C] HEB. i. 3.

concerning the regulation of our conduct. Let us select a few.

The general effect of what has been said ought to be, to inspire us with the love of a kind, humane, beneficent disposition, and to lead us to cultivate it in our hearts. It is the heart that is the source of good, or the source of evil. The streams will ever partake of the qualities of the fountain. If the love of goodness be not rooted in the heart, in vain will formal rules, or general, or particular precepts ever attempt to make a virtuous man. When the love of justice dwells in the heart, two neighbours of the most extensive property will easily agree together. But where this principle is wanting, all the statutes that were ever devised, all the complicated laws that were ever made, will only set the ingenuity of the mind at work to elude them. The design of the gospel is therefore to change the heart, to renew the mind where it is depraved: and the life of its Author, the manner, and the matter of his doctrine, and all his institutions are directed to these purposes. The language of the whole is, *My son, give me thy heart* [D].

If this general effect be in any measure produced upon them who profess themselves the disciples of Jesus, what has been said may suggest particular instruction to those of every rank. How

[D] Prov. xxiii. 26.

should it enlarge the sentiments, and dilate the benevolence of the opulent, making them consider riches as the gifts of heaven for the good of mankind, and the happiness of their own souls? With what wisdom is the advice given, to *make to yourselves friends of the mammon of unrighteousness, that when ye fail, they may receive you into everlasting habitations* [E] ? In every corner, upon every spot, the objects of misfortune present themselves to our view, if we will not shut our eyes from seeing them. I grant there is a selection and a caution necessary in dispensing our charity, or liberality. The avowed solicitors of it are neither perhaps the most meritorious, nor the most indigent. But blessed heaven! how generous is it, how delightful to prevent those whose hearts refuse to ask it, and to wipe away the tear that flows from secret sorrow, to befriend those that have known better days, and entertained happier prospects, to ease the anguish of a mother's heart, who suffers more for her orphans than for herself. What means of luxurious enjoyment does money thus employed afford! And know that, judiciously applied, even a small revenue may confer much power of doing good. Bestowed with sympathy, giving without ostentation, attended with the sincere look of honest kindness, a small thing to many is a great matter.

But farther, though the blessings of this world should not fall to our share, how much it is in the

[E] LUKE xvi. 9.

SERMON XX.

power of every man to bestow upon the wretched? The hard-hearted alone are ignorant, how far attention, compassion, seasonable advice, kind words can go to alleviate many of our sorrows, and our sufferings. The tear that mingles with mine as it falls, its value cannot be reckoned in gold, or silver. The affection I perceive in my friend when my heart is overwhelmed, if I could compare it with the idol of the interested, let my heart never perceive it again.

FINALLY, Let what has been said cherish in us a spirit superior to the little sordid views of being dependent upon others for the necessaries of life. The apostle wrought with his hands that he might be burdensome to none, and that he might have something to bestow. *It is more blessed to give than to receive.* All the duties of benevolence, of compassion and of kindness, to an honest heart must be granted, not solicited. The man that throws himself upon the charity of the world without absolute necessity, by that very action renders himself less worthy of it, and renders the best men less disposed to give it. The charity of a christian is an offering of his heart. The call to it is not the importunate cry of the mendicant, but the observation of human suffering and distress. As we are men, let us yield to this call where we discern it, and let us never try to raise the emotions of pity, or engage the hand of charity, when Providence calls us rather to give than to receive.

F I N I S.

www.ingramcontent.com/pod-product-compliance
Lightning Source LLC
Chambersburg PA
CBHW020244240426

43672CB00006B/628